GET A
REAL FOOD
LIFE

GET A
REAL
FOOD
LIFE

*Get a slimmer body, increased energy, a
better mood and good health for life*

Janine Whiteson M.Sc. *with Marion Rosenfeld*

Medical Adviser: Lisa Hark R.D., Ph.D.

This edition first published in the UK in 2003 by
Rodale Ltd
7–10 Chandos Street
London W1G 9AD
www.rodale.co.uk

Medical adviser Lisa Hark R.D., Ph.D. is director of the nutrition education and prevention programme at the University of Pennsylvania Medical Center in Philadelphia, USA.

Printed and bound in the UK by The Bath Press using acid-free paper from sustainable sources

A CIP record for this book is available from the British Library
ISBN 1–405–00665–X

This paperback edition distributed to the book trade by Pan Macmillan Ltd

Notice
This book is intended as a reference volume only, not as a medical manual. The information given here is designed to help you make informed decisions about your health. It is not intended as a substitute for any treatment that may have been prescribed by your doctor. If you suspect that you have a medical problem, we urge you to seek competent medical help.

Mention of specific companies, organisations or authorities in this book does not imply endorsement by the publisher, nor does mention of specific companies, organisations or authorities in the book imply that they endorse the book.

Internet addresses given in this book were accurate at the time the book went to press.

RODALE
WE **INSPIRE** AND **ENABLE** PEOPLE TO IMPROVE
THEIR LIVES AND THE WORLD AROUND THEM

This book is dedicated to my husband, Jonathan,

for without you there would be no book,

and to my son, Harris,

the source of my inspiration.

CONTENTS

PART 1

THE GOOD
FOOD LIFE

CHAPTER 1

LET'S GET REAL

Satisfaction. Pleasure. Comfort. Food can make us feel all of these things. But it can also make us feel guilty, gluttonous and overwhelmed.

OK, maybe food *itself* doesn't have the power to make us feel these things – but ever since we were children, we were fed values about food along with our daily breakfasts, lunches and dinners.

Maybe we were told it was a sin to waste food. Or perhaps we were scolded for eating certain foods we craved. Maybe our friends assigned positive or negative traits to a certain food based on what they thought it could do to their bodies and we blindly followed along. So we shunned chocolate because we were sure it would cause our faces to break out in spots. Or the athletes among us ate masses of protein because we thought it would make us bulk up.

And then, of course, there was all the food for special occasions. The birthday cake, chocolate Easter eggs, the Christmas lunch with its huge turkey and 10 different side dishes.

Even now that we're adults, food is entwined in our social and professional lives. On dates, we splurge on popcorn and cola at the cinema. A candlelit dinner for two usually ends with a decadent dessert. Many of us feed our ambition at our workplaces with a steady diet of coffee or caffeinated fizzy drinks and whatever crisps or chocolate bars are available in the company vending machines. And if we have jobs that allow us to travel and have our own expense accounts, we often find ourselves dining on rich meals that leave our clients impressed but our tummies bloated. Then there are all those other things that affect our relationships with food: children, worries about bills, stress.

Whether you're a man or a woman, a college student or a person nearing retirement age, a stay-at-home parent or a corporate executive, food affects you every day. And, no doubt, you spend an inordinate amount of time thinking about it.

What you need is a Real Food Life.

What Does It Mean to Have a Real Food Life?

Simply put, a Real Food Life is a life where you enjoy food and make conscious decisions about the best food to put in your body so that it works at an optimum level. It means not being obsessed by food and not feeling guilty when you eat something you crave. A Real Food Life means enjoying all the food you eat because you know it is nutritious, delicious and satisfying to your physical and emotional being.

It shouldn't be confused with having a 'perfect' food life. Indeed, I believe that the reason so many of us have a mixed-up relationship with food is because we've bought into the myth of a 'perfect' diet. We think that if we can just eat 'perfectly' – never splurging or giving in to cravings – all of our

problems will dissolve. But nothing and no one is perfect – not me, not you. Having a Real Food Life means eating when you are actually hungry, not because you are tired, stressed, lonely or angry. It means being in control of your food, not the other way around. When you're in control, even an 'indulgence' will be a conscious choice because you know where the treat fits into the rest of your food plan.

In this chapter, I'll explain how I came to develop an approach to food that eliminates the guilt and obsessiveness and gets back to using food for what it is – fuel to make our bodies and minds run efficiently and effectively. I'll also introduce you to some strategies you can start using *right now* to overcome everyday food obstacles.

In the chapters that follow, you'll get all the information you need to revamp your food life. You'll identify the obstacles that are hindering you and hone in on what you want out of your new food life. Perhaps you want to lose weight – and keep it off for good. Or maybe you're finding yourself in a 'food fog' after certain meals and want to learn how to use food for optimum performance. Perhaps you crash every afternoon and need to find some new, interesting lunches that will keep you humming along all afternoon and evening. Maybe, like many of us, your diet includes far too many food 'crutches' to get you through the day – caffeinated fizzy

Simple Steps to Boost Your Brainpower

With our fast-paced lifestyles, there's rarely a time when we don't need to be at our mental best. If you're having trouble focusing and staying mentally sharp, try out these all-natural strategies.

- Carbohydrates are the main source of brain fuel. So smarten up with a variety of vegetables and fruits. Also try wholegrain bread and crackers, with some protein, such as hummus, low-fat cheese or turkey breast.

- There's a reason why fish has a reputation for being brain food. It's rich in B vitamins, which fortify cognitive skills and memory. Plus, it's an excellent source of protein and omega-3 fatty acids. Be sure to serve up fish a few times a week.

- If you're getting too little of any of the B vitamins, you can become mildly depressed and have lowered mental functions. Eggs, brown rice, whole grains, seafood, dairy and nuts all have a good variety of B vitamins.

- Make sure you're eating a healthy breakfast. It really is the most important meal of the day and it keeps your brain ticking all day long.

- Exercise increases mental function and improves memory and concentration. Exercising several times a week is a good workout for your body and your mind.

drinks, coffee, sweets or junk food – and you've finally decided that you need to start feeding your body more nutritious fare. Whatever your motive, this book will give you the tools you need to get real with your food.

In order to understand how to best modify your diet, you'll need to learn a little bit about nutrition. In part 2 of this book, I'll introduce you to some basics. You'll learn the difference between simple and complex car-

bohydrates – and what each does for your body. Why certain kinds of fat are actually good for you. Why drinking lots of water – at least eight 225-ml (8-fl oz) glasses each day – will not only keep your body running smoothly but actually give you energy. Armed with information such as this, you'll be ready to start the 8-week Food Life Makeover Plan.

Through the 8-week makeover plan, I'll guide you every step of the way as you work towards getting a Real Food Life. No matter what your ultimate goal – having more energy, eating more healthily, losing weight – I'll help you to customise the plan to reach it. By keeping a journal of everything you eat, you'll be able to analyse your eating patterns and identify previously unrecognised road-blocks. You'll also gain insight into how your body uses and reacts to various types of food, such as proteins, carbohydrates and so on.

Together, we'll make over your kitchen so that you can't *help* but succeed. I'll also give you pointers so that when you go shopping you choose foods with a new awareness of what works best for your body. I'll even provide menu suggestions, tips for dining out, recipes, exercise hints and much, much more.

How do I know all this works? Personal experience.

How I Developed the Real Food Life Programme

I am Janine Whiteson and I'm a nutritionist. My clients call me their Food Life Coach, but I don't wear a whistle and I've never made anyone run a marathon. I have an MSc in nutrition and weight-loss programmes from King's College in London.

For more than 11 years, I've helped thousands of people to get a better food life. I've worked with TV personalities and shy college students, with busy executives and

new mothers, with the skinny, the obese, the healthy, the sick, the young and the old, the exercise fiends and the sedentary home-bodies. The one thing they all had in common was a need to get a better food life.

I'm not into fad diets. They're usually unhealthy and have no positive long-term effects. Plus, because we all have different needs and different lifestyles, the fact that these diets are one-size-fits-all means that they truly fit no one. I'm not into gimmicks. They don't work. What I am into is teaching and coaching people about good, sensible nutrition. I'll help you learn about eating wonderful foods that make you feel your best and help you develop positive habits that will last your whole lifetime.

I've had a lifelong fascination with food. When I was 12, I was diagnosed with severe hypertension or high blood pressure and spent three months in hospital. None of the many doctors who treated me could understand why someone so young had such a rare – and critical – illness. Their answer was to prescribe numerous types of medication, none of which worked.

Because the doctors guessed that the illness originated in my kidneys, I ended up undergoing a kidney operation. The doctors assured my parents and I that my blood pressure would return to normal after the surgery. It didn't. I had to continue on medication because that was the best treatment my doctors thought they could offer me.

Fortunately, my parents didn't settle for that. They asked the doctors, 'Doesn't diet play a role in high blood pressure? Don't Janine's emotions play a part in her high blood pressure? Isn't there anything we can do for our daughter other than give her medication?' Still, the doctors insisted that the only thing my parents could do for me was to make sure I took my medication.

My parents did a lot of research and changed our whole family's diet. They cut right down on processed foods and eliminated fast food. (I was devastated.) There were no more salty tinned foods (like soups and vegetables), no more pickles (my favourite), no more chips, no more frozen ready-meals, no more processed meats (I especially loved salami).

I had been a salt addict and especially loved crisps and other salty snacks much more than sweets. Before my illness, I used to buy very large bags of crisps and eat them in private or, sometimes, with a friend. I used to put salt on everything I ate, including burgers and chips. Because of this addiction, cutting salt out of my diet was a really hard adjustment for me to make.

My mother eliminated all salt from her cooking and started using a lot of garlic (she had read that it could help lower blood pressure) and other herbs and spices. We ate many more fresh fruits and vegetables. In addition to the vitamins my parents thought might help me, we started buying a lot more of our food from the health food shop, particularly bread (many supermarket brands can be surprisingly high in sodium), cereals (much cereal is high in salt as well as sugar) and low-sodium stock (to make fresh vegetable soups). Nowadays, healthy, low-sodium foods are increasingly available in supermarkets.

We ate a lot more fatty fish because my parents read that fish has a high water content and contains omega-3 fatty acids that may help to reduce blood pressure. We also ate much less red meat. This was pretty hard because my father is from Argentina, where they eat beef every day. Margarine was banned from the house completely and we had butter only on rare occasions. We used olive oil and canola (rapeseed) oil instead (again, because my parents read that it may help reduce blood pressure). When we went out to dinner at restaurants, my whole family would order food *without salt,* please!

My mother took me to weekly biofeedback sessions so I could learn how to relax and deal with my emotions. My parents suspected that emotions affected my blood pressure even though the doctors insisted that emotions had nothing to do with it (remember, this was 1980). I went to biofeedback sessions for a few years. What I learned proved helpful when I had to go to regularly scheduled doctor's appointments to get my blood pressure checked. Though I would initially get very upset, I was able to successfully use the biofeedback techniques to help calm myself down and lower my blood pressure.

The life changes my family and I undertook worked – and they're still working. My blood pressure finally became manageable through a changed diet and a new consciousness about food. The experience resulted in my whole family getting a better food life. We all became aware of how foods make us feel physically and emotionally; how important fresh fruit and vegetables are to feeling good; how more fibre and less meat gives us more energy; how cooking is a nurturing and nourishing family activity; how to speak up for our food needs when we're out to eat; and how to listen to our bodies. It also led me down the path to where I am today: helping people get Real Food Lives, with the understanding (and personal knowledge) that emotions play into people's eating habits and health.

After receiving my master's degree, I ran the nutrition department for the UK's largest sports club. It was there that I discovered that people want delicious, satisfying foods that are also good for them. And it was there that I realised the profound way in which people's food choices are wrapped up with their emotions. I began creating a down-to-earth philosophy towards food that really helps people to come to grips with out-of-control food lives. I even developed a wide range of recipes

that I share with anyone who wants them (I've included more than 70 in this book).

Every strategy in this book – from the shopping lists, to the coping mechanisms, to the 8-week Food Life Makeover Plan – is based on my 11 years of experience helping people just like you. My advice always takes into consideration the social, psychological and physical aspects of food, with the clear understanding that eating well is so much more than what should or should not be eaten. After all, food is an integral part of our lives and culture.

What I'll Do for You

For each client I work with, I create individual, daily food strategies. We are all unique and have our own sets of food issues: emotional, practical and so on. In my experience, I've found it is vital that each person gets his or her own distinct food plan that suits his or her particular lifestyle, eating habits, likes and dislikes, comfort foods and schedule. Likewise, I'll help you to create a personalised nutrition blueprint. This book will educate you on the right way to eat for your way of life. Whether you're a student away from home for the first time, a junior executive working your way up the ladder, a busy parent, a fiftysomething or a person looking forward to retirement, this book will help you shape a sane food programme suitable for your own lifestyle.

I like to tell my clients that by working with me for 8 weeks, they will become empowered about their food choices and, in effect, become their own personal nutritionists. So will you. Even if you can barely boil a pan of water or don't know the first thing about food shopping, this book will guide you towards the most fundamental and beneficial ways to eat in order to feel great.

Shedding Unhealthy Food Habits

Over the past two decades, too many gimmicky diets have been sold as life-changing panaceas. And while some short-term weight loss can be had from these 'diets du jour', people inevitably put the weight back on and then more (mainly because many fad diets slow the metabolism by at least 10 per cent).

Super Foods for Women

A lowered risk of breast cancer. Protection against anaemia. Sharper brain functioning. The following foods truly are superstars when it comes to their health benefits.

- Fatty fish, including salmon, sardines, tuna, herring, mackerel and trout, are great sources of omega-3 fatty acids and high-quality protein. Omega-3s have been linked to lowered blood pressure and reduced risk of stroke and heart attack.

- Eggs contain choline, which is important for brain functioning and development. They're also an excellent source of protein and nutrients. Enjoy up to seven eggs a week. (Limit yourself to no more than four eggs a week if you have diabetes or high cholesterol or are overweight.)

- Beef is loaded with haem iron, which is crucial in protecting against anaemia. Eating lean beef such as fillet or sirloin steak with iron-rich vegetables (such as spinach and Swiss chard) will help increase the absorption of the vegetables' iron.

- Soyabeans are high in protein, fibre, B vitamins and iron. They also contain phyto-oestrogens, which the body converts into hormonelike substances that act like a weak form of oestrogen. For premenopausal women, this can mean a lowered risk of breast cancer and possibly heart disease. In older women, phyto-oestrogens can ease menopausal symptoms such as hot flushes. Soya is delicious, versatile and available in many forms – from tofu to tempeh.

- Dark green, leafy vegetables are a great source of calcium, fibre, B vitamins, phytochemicals and antioxidants such as beta-carotene.

Not only do these fad diets have no positive long-lasting effects, but most people who follow them don't even realise that they are nutritionally unsound. Where three square meals, the four basic food groups and family dinners once reigned, many people today have never learnt how to eat properly in the first place, either at home or at school.

The modern world is filled with shortcuts, quick fixes and immediate gratification. In a world with so many high-tech conveniences, people want their food instantly, too. Add to this the media hype promoting what often turn out to be unhealthy diets, irresponsible and often incorrect reporting on nutrition topics, and not learning how to eat properly as children and no one knows what's good for them any more.

By using this book, you'll learn to shed old, unhealthy food habits and adopt healthy new ones. You will learn to listen to your body – not some celebrity with a quick-fix weight-loss programme – to find out what it needs from you. Many of us have become so used to punishing our bodies through restrictive diets, overeating, bingeing or regularly eating foods filled with saturated fats, sodium and chemicals – such as fast food – that we don't even know how our bodies should feel.

Your first step towards your Real Food Life will be to keep a food journal. This will be your companion for at least 8 weeks. By keeping an honest account of everything you put in your mouth and how you feel before, during and after eating, you'll learn to listen to your body. And by listening to your body, you'll hear if it's thirsty, tired or hungry. When you listen to your body, you'll start to understand which foods suit your body and make you feel alive, energetic and satisfied. You'll also discover which foods make you feel bloated, lethargic and mentally fuzzy.

Towards the Good Food Life

In the chapters that follow, I'll help you customise your strategy for getting a Real Food Life. To get you started, though, here are some broad tactics to employ on your journey.

Create Food Sanity

If you want a Real Food Life, you'll have to rid yourself of your food obsessions. Constantly thinking about anything – including food – will consume you and drag you down. Food is there to nourish your body and satisfy your soul. If you are obsessing about food, you aren't enjoying a necessary and pleasurable aspect of your life.

What brings on food obsessions? In my experience, they're often a result of people depriving themselves by over-restricting their diets and trying to 'control' their food. At other times people simply don't eat enough; they try to be 'good' with their food (they're usually trying to lose weight), so they eat too little of it. But eating too little promotes obsessive food thoughts, interferes with your brain chemicals and can lead to binges and eating disorders. When you eat too little, your levels of cholecystokinin (CCK) – a neurotransmitter whose function is to send signals to stop eating, switch off the appetite and activate feelings of fullness – become unbalanced. Conversely, when you eat a healthy, balanced diet, your CCK levels are balanced and your body will naturally tell you when it has had enough food.

Here are some tips to help you get started on eliminating food obsessions and working towards getting a Real Food Life.

Listen to your body. When you start listening to your body and hearing what it really needs, food will become less of an issue. Begin by simply noticing how you feel after eating. Are you tired or do you feel energised? Do you feel bloated and a bit queasy? Or ready to take on the world? Tune in to the connections between what you feed your body and how your body feels afterwards.

Keep busy. Do whatever it takes to have an active and full day, both physically and mentally. It may sound simplistic, but when you're busy and involved with other activities, you're not going to be thinking about food all the time.

Shop and cook. Going shopping for food and cooking for yourself – rather than simply picking up a meal at the local fast-

food restaurant or heating up a frozen ready-meal – are proactive ways to stop food obsessions. Not only do they make you more conscious of your food choices, but they also give you a sense of accomplishment since they help you to connect with what you're putting in your body. The simple act of preparing a meal also helps you to take time to nourish and provide for your soul.

Create an action plan. An action plan is a food life schedule where you write down what you will probably eat for the whole day. If you plan your 'food intentions', you can move on with the rest of your daily life. Don't worry if the plan doesn't work out exactly; just the act of creating a plan will help you think less about food.

Eat deliciously. All the food you eat, whether it's a snack or a meal, should be very tasty and gratifying. If you choose delicious foods every time you eat, rather than trying to choke down foods you don't like but you think are good for you, you'll be much more satisfied. And if you're always satisfied with your food choices, you are much less likely to obsess about food. Fortunately, there are literally hundreds of delicious and nutritious food choices out there, including many varieties of fruits and vegetables that you've probably never even tried.

Undo damaging thoughts. You have to put an end to negative thoughts about yourself. If you keep telling yourself things like,

(continued on page 14)

LIVING A REAL FOOD LIFE

Chelsea Dropped the Diets – and Became More Confident in Return

Name: Chelsea
Real Food Life Issues: PMS, diet mentality, family food pressures

Chelsea is a 30-year-old single solicitor who often works until midnight. On her evenings and weekends off, she's usually on dates or out with friends, eating and drinking into the small hours. When we met, she suffered from acute PMS, which contributed to her anxiety and chronic low energy. She was 'addicted' to caffeinated drinks and sweet foods and used them as energy- and mood-boosters. Here's where I found her:

> *2 December*
>
> *I'm drowning in holiday spirit. Things are getting a little out of hand on the social front. I'm expected to work about 200 hours in the next 3 weeks and I have no clue how this will be achieved at the peak of the party season. Will have to rely heavily on the talents of my good man Johnny Walker.*
>
> *Dreading the trip home. My (s)mother is gearing up to lay it on thick. I can feel it. She's been coming out with some classics lately. A current favourite: 'Have you got a flattering dress for the party this time?'*
>
> *Vicious cramps today. Face broken out into a dot-to-dot puzzle. Am seriously considering seeking solace in some chocolate cake washed down with a tub of toffee ice cream.*

Ever since she was a teenager, Chelsea felt 'too heavy'. Throughout her life, she had tried every new diet available – but eventually 'gave up' all of them. Chelsea would always feel guilty about everything she ate and despite her professional and personal successes, she felt like a failure with food and out of control with her food life.

First, we worked on getting rid of her diet mentality. I explained that restrictive diets don't work and will only drive her mad. She couldn't even remember how many diets she had tried. When I asked how many of them worked, she replied, 'None'. I think that was the turning point: after that, she started thinking that maybe the information I was giving her was right.

Next, we weaned her off caffeine. Instead of three cups of coffee and four daily fizzy drinks, she started drinking water, green tea and a single cup of decaffeinated coffee each day. Within 2 weeks, her anxiety was evaporating. When she recognised that caffeine made her feel more anxious than she actually was, she was relieved. To deal with the PMS, we upped her calcium intake. She started taking a calcium supplement and ate a few servings of low-fat dairy foods every day. She also started eating fatty fish three times a week, which was an easy change because she loved tuna and salmon. In addition, she incorporated some other foods that are high in essential fatty acids into her diet: she dressed her salads with olive oil and ate nuts and seeds for snacks. She also started taking vitamin B_6 supplements daily.

She became aware that the sweets and chocolates she ate simply because they were available at work just made her feel sleepy. I suggested she try more wholesome snacks, so instead of miniature chocolate bars and biscuits, she began to eat more whole grains and fruit. I also encouraged her to keep healthy snacks in her desk so she'd be prepared when hunger did strike.

Chelsea and I talked extensively about how her emotions were wrapped up with her food. Her mother, a demanding, opinionated and very slender woman, had always been critical of Chelsea's weight. We came up with specific ways to cope with the emotions and the calories of the big upcoming Christmas meal. One strategy she particularly liked was to eat small portions of the foods she loved so she wouldn't feel deprived, along with larger portions of vegetables and salads.

We also worked on her food intentions with all the other meals. She knew she would have a whole grain with a little protein for her breakfast, such as porridge oats with a few walnuts, cinnamon, a drizzle of honey and skimmed milk. The basis of her lunches and dinners would be lots of vegetables, with some good protein and grains. She could eat leftovers, but instead of leftover pudding, she ate the Brussels sprouts, the green beans, a small serving of cranberry sauce and some turkey, surprising herself with how satisfied she felt.

When her mother made comments, Chelsea asked her to respect her food choices and leave her alone. And much to Chelsea's surprise, her mother made an effort to stop. Afterwards, she was amazed how much calmer she felt around her family and food.

After 8 weeks, Chelsea's PMS symptoms improved. She was thrilled to finally get over the 'need' to go on a diet. Mostly, though, she felt more secure with herself and her ability to confront her negative emotional issues with food.

'I'm always going to be large', 'I'll always have problems with food', or 'I have no self-control', you'll sabotage your own efforts to achieve a Real Food Life. It's imperative to find a way to eliminate these types of phrases from your mind. The next time you catch yourself saying something negative, consciously replace the thought with a positive one. For example, visualise yourself eating in a more wholesome and healthy way, imagine yourself cooking a nutritious meal that makes you feel great or picture yourself full of energy and able to conquer anything.

Ditch the 'Good' Food/ 'Bad' Food Syndrome

In a Real Food Life, there is no such thing as 'good' and 'bad' foods. Instead, no foods are forbidden. I've found that labelling foods as 'good' or 'bad' leads to feelings of guilt. The interesting thing about guilt, though, is that it's a self-imposed emotion; you are the only one who can make yourself 'feel guilty'.

Did someone ever say to you that the chocolate you were eating 'will make you get spots' or 'will go straight to your hips' or that those crisps 'will make you fat and crave more'? These types of comments make people afraid of their food. In fact, many of us take to heart the criticism inherent in comments like these. But, once again, realise that only you can make yourself feel guilty about the food you eat. It is no one else's business

what you choose to eat and no one has the right to say anything about what you're eating – unless, of course, they want a bite.

To start on the path to overcoming the 'good' food/'bad' food syndrome, keep these general points in mind.

Realise that no food is off-limits. When you set limits, you'll break them – it's human nature. If you tell a child not to touch a certain lamp, he'll make a beeline for that lamp. By the same token, if you tell yourself you can't eat something, that something will be the only thing you want to eat. Permit yourself to eat any food – after all, savouring delicious, mouth-watering foods is one of the greatest joys in life.

Erect food boundaries. Just because no food is forbidden doesn't mean that there shouldn't be boundaries. Obviously, you do your body no good when you feed it a steady diet of fizzy drinks, crisps, ice cream and hamburgers. Know that you can have any food, but have a controlled, contained amount. For example, if you love chocolate, have a few squares rather than the whole bar. No doubt you'll come to realise that a taste of the chocolate satisfies you and is really all you want. Boundaries don't limit food; they put it into perspective.

Fortify your food boundaries. To keep from overindulging, write down the food you most crave and the amount you will eat (a small portion should do it). Then buy the food and eat just that amount. It's a good idea to buy a small, single-serving portion of the food you crave. If you can get it only in large sizes, though, throw the rest away after you've eaten the amount you specified; don't bring it home or keep it near you. After a few attempts, you may be able to keep the remainder of that food around, but if not, that's OK.

Accept Your Body

There's a lot of self-hate out there and it's usually about body size. While many men have low self-image issues, this seems to be a problem that most affects women. Remember this: there is no such thing as a perfect body. The perfect body is a fantasy created and perpetuated by the media. The average woman is 1.63 m (5 ft 4 in) tall, wears a size 14 and weighs in the 68 kg (10½ st) range. One-third of all women wear a size 16 or larger. The average model, on the other hand, is 1.7 m (5 ft 9 in) tall and weighs 50 kg (8 st), and usually wears a size 8.

To be female means to have curves, a rounded bottom and larger hips and thighs. Women have more body fat than men do and there's nothing you can do to change that biological fact. More curves – and fat – are how women were created and have evolved; they need their curvy bodies for their hormones to work properly, to be able to get pregnant, to hold on to a pregnancy and to give birth.

Male or female, if you spend your life at the gym, you will become fitter and more toned, but you'll probably never achieve the body of somebody you see in a magazine. Most models are very tall and very lean due to their genes; some eat, some don't. Their bodies are the exception to the rule; they are genetic eccentrics. The majority of people in the world don't look the way models do and never will. Ever.

Work with your body. The key to getting over your idea of a 'perfect body' is to accept what you have. If you hate your body, it won't work with you. Your poisonous thoughts about your body will always sabotage your efforts to have a great food life. If you accept your body – and even learn to like it – you can achieve peace with your food life. When you accept your body, you will realise that having a good food life leads to the body that is perfect for *you*.

Step Away from the Scales

You are not a number on a scale. What is important is how you feel – not what you weigh. If you place all your importance on what the scales say, you risk becoming controlled by it.

Your body is constantly changing and you'll weigh something different every day. If, for example, you ate a salty dinner last night, your body may be retaining anything from 1.3 to 2.2 extra kg (3 to 5 lb) of water weight. With variations like these, why live and die by what a mechanical numbers machine tells you?

It simply isn't fair to your body to choose an 'ideal' weight and then struggle to reach it. Any number you pick will be arbitrary and there are many factors, not the least of which is genetics, that will or won't let you reach that number. Instead, your 'ideal' weight should be what makes you feel most comfortable in your skin. It's the weight at which you feel the healthiest, the most energetic, the most *alive*.

Let your clothes be your guide. The most accurate indication of whether you've 'gained' or 'lost' weight is how your clothes fit. If you've noticed that all your clothes are becoming tight and you've considered buying clothes in a larger size than usual, it's probably a sign that you need to re-evaluate what you've been eating and exercise a bit more often.

Calculate your BMI. If you absolutely must have some form of size measurement, I

Your Body Mass Index (BMI) – metric

Height (m)	Weight (kg)													
1.50	43	45	47	50	52	54	56	59	61	63	65	68	70	72
1.52	44	46	49	51	53	56	58	60	62	65	67	69	72	74
1.54	45	47	50	52	55	57	59	62	64	66	69	71	74	76
1.56	46	49	51	54	56	58	61	63	66	68	71	73	75	78
1.58	47	50	52	55	57	60	62	65	67	70	72	75	77	80
1.60	49	51	54	56	59	61	64	67	69	72	74	77	79	82
1.62	50	53	55	58	60	63	66	68	71	74	77	80	82	85
1.64	51	54	57	60	62	65	67	70	73	75	78	81	83	86
1.66	52	55	58	61	63	66	69	72	74	77	80	83	85	88
1.68	54	56	59	62	65	68	71	73	76	79	82	85	88	90
1.70	55	58	61	64	67	69	72	75	78	81	84	87	90	93
1.72	56	59	62	65	68	71	74	77	80	83	86	89	92	95
1.74	58	61	64	67	70	73	76	79	82	85	88	91	94	97
1.76	59	62	65	68	71	73	77	80	84	87	90	93	96	99
1.78	60	63	67	70	73	76	79	82	86	89	92	95	98	101
1.80	62	65	68	71	75	78	81	84	88	91	94	97	100	104
1.82	63	66	70	73	76	80	83	86	89	93	96	100	103	106
BMI	19	20	21	22	23	24	25	26	27	28	29	30	31	32

recommend using the Body Mass Index (BMI) instead of scale weight. Doctors, nutritionists and other health professionals use the BMI to gauge an adult's weight-related health risk. The BMI is a ratio of height to weight and it's a fairly accurate standard for determining if someone is at a healthy weight or is overweight and at risk of weight-related problems such as high blood pressure, high cholesterol and diabetes.

Take a look at either the metric or imperial verison of the chart to calculate your BMI. Find your height in the left-hand column, then move across that row to find the number closest to your weight. Now follow that column to the bottom of the chart, where you'll find your BMI.

A BMI between 18.5 and 24.9 is considered healthy. If your BMI is between 25 and 29.9, you are overweight and may be at risk of health problems. (Bear in mind, however, that some women with BMIs of 25 to 27 are perfectly healthy. Take into account other risk factors, including your age, level of physical

Your Body Mass Index (BMI) – imperial

Height (ft/in)	Weight (lb)													
4'10'	91	96	100	105	110	115	119	124	129	134	139	143	148	153
4'11'	94	99	104	109	114	119	124	128	133	138	143	148	153	158
5'0'	97	102	107	112	118	123	128	133	138	143	148	153	158	163
5'1'	100	106	111	116	122	127	132	137	143	148	153	158	164	169
5'2'	104	109	115	120	126	131	136	142	147	153	158	164	169	174
5'3'	107	113	118	124	130	135	141	146	152	158	163	169	175	180
5'4'	110	116	122	128	134	140	145	151	157	163	169	174	180	186
5'5'	114	120	126	132	138	144	150	156	162	168	174	180	186	192
5'6'	118	124	130	136	142	148	155	161	167	173	179	186	192	198
5'7'	121	127	134	140	146	153	159	166	172	178	185	191	197	204
5'8'	125	131	138	144	151	158	164	171	177	184	190	197	203	210
5'9'	128	135	142	149	155	162	169	176	182	189	196	203	209	216
5'10'	132	139	146	153	160	167	174	181	188	195	202	207	215	222
5'11'	136	142	150	157	165	172	179	186	193	200	208	215	222	229
6'0'	140	147	154	162	169	177	184	191	199	206	213	221	228	235
BMI	19	20	21	22	23	24	25	26	27	28	29	30	31	32

activity, family history and eating habits, before becoming alarmed.) If your BMI is 30 or above, you are obese and have a substantially increased risk of developing weight-related disease. In one study, for example, scientists found that women with a BMI higher than 29 had a 230 per cent greater risk of heart disease.

Spin a Social Web

I believe that social isolation is an epidemic and a major reason why so many people are generally unhealthy and out of balance with their food. Humans are inherently social beings; we have been created to be with people, to live in close communities, to interact with each other, to belong.

In our hectic lives, we work long hours, get too little sleep and don't have enough time to look after ourselves and create and nurture friendships. In addition, many of us now spend countless hours surfing the Web or writing e-mails rather than having face-to-face contact with others.

For some people, the problem is shyness. Others have crippling insecurity and are afraid of being judged, so they avoid interacting with others.

When we don't have meaningful contact with other people on a daily basis, we begin to feel isolated. We lose our support systems and feel we are alone in this world. The side effect for many people who feel lonely and isolated is overeating. They eat for company, they eat to feel less alone and they eat to cope with the pain of their loneliness.

For your own good health, work on developing bonds with other people. Not only will these relationships help to strengthen your resolve as you work to get a Real Food Life, but they'll also enrich you emotionally.

Find fun. A great way to meet people is to join your local gym or take a class at a college or community centre. Do you have a hobby? Find a club and explore it further. At these types of venues there are people who share your interests, so building a friendship is easier since you have a basis of similarity. Once you get involved, keep going regularly; that way people get to know you and you get to know them.

Get yourself a buddy. Ask someone who seems approachable and friendly – perhaps a family member or someone at work, school or your place of worship – to go through the 8-week Food Life Makeover Plan with you. Working with someone who is helpful and not judgemental can make the whole process easier, more fun and more social.

Give away your time. Find an organisation that you admire and ask how you can help. Doing voluntary work is a great way to meet people, plus you're doing something for the community at the same time. Giving your time and talent is the best way in the world to fill yourself up without eating a thing.

CHAPTER 2

THE 24 MOST COMMON FOOD ISSUES

For me, being a personal nutritionist is, in some ways, like being a detective. Of course, it would be simple enough to just give my clients a diet, tell them to follow it and send them on their way. But not only do I think that's professionally irresponsible, it's not how I work. Instead, I investigate my clients' eating habits and try to uncover their hidden food issues, because these issues directly relate to what they put in their mouths. I'll do the same for you, my newest client.

Everyone has food issues. Most stem from childhood experiences with food – when eating patterns are etched, when we're indirectly taught to ignore natural hunger cues, when we start using food as something other than a way to nourish our bodies.

In order to have a healthy food life, it's important that you honestly assess your eating patterns and come to understand your food issues and their source. When you know what your food issues are, you will be able to implement strategies to make permanent changes.

In this chapter, I've identified the 24 most prevalent food issues. I've also included proven strategies that will enable you to overcome these food issues and help you to take greater steps towards getting a Real Food Life.

This chapter is quite lengthy, so feel free to glance ahead at the titles of each of the 24 issues. Carefully read the descriptions and strategies for those issues that affect you. You might also want to skim through the others, though, since there could be subtle issues that affect your eating patterns without your even being aware of them.

1. I Am Always on a Diet but Can Never Stick with It

▶ Do you obsess about your body?

▶ Do you think that if you become thin, your life will be perfect?

▶ Do you find it difficult, if not impossible, to stick to diets?

▶ Do you feel that you lack the willpower to stay on diets?

▶ Are you 'good' for the first half of the day but then usually end up 'cheating' later in the day?

Restrictive diets are the bane of our existence. Lots of people spend the better part of their lives on them. Even before adolescence, many girls start obsessing about their bodies and comparing themselves unfavourably to the very thin actresses, models and celebrities they see on TV. Lots of women think that being a size 8 is an obtainable goal – if only they just keep dieting.

Low-calorie or restrictive diets are difficult, if not impossible, to stick with. It's hard work to be constantly counting calories, reading diet books and limiting yourself to a highly regimented daily food intake. Plus, dieters often are left with a feeling of failure when they 'go off' the diet. They may binge in private or become consumed with the 'If I just lose (fill in the blank) pounds, my life will be fabulous' mentality. When you spend your life on a diet, there is no way you can get a Real Food Life.

Strategy: If you're constantly following low-calorie diets, the first thing you need to do is stop. Restricting your diet is the worst thing you can do to your body and mind. If you diet, you're depriving yourself – physically and emotionally. Deprivations lead to obsessions and having obsessions leads to binges and 'failed' diets.

Simply put, the diet industry wants you to fail. The more times you attempt various diets, the more money the industry makes. Because they're too restrictive in both food choices and calorie intake, most low-calorie diets set you up to fail. Also, most diets are not for the long term – they're for the quick fix and don't teach you how to eat for the rest of your life.

Restrictive dieting typically means severe calorie deprivation: consuming fewer than 1,200 calories a day. Regardless of what diet you're on, low-calorie diets have the potential to slow down your metabolism and reduce the amount of lean muscle tissue you have. This means that the calories you consume burn more slowly. Very restrictive dieting slows down your heart rate, lowers your body temperature (making you feel cold all the time), reduces your intake of vital nutrients your body needs to function properly and ultimately promotes an increase in body fat. This type of dieting causes moodiness, lack of energy, food cravings and food obsessions. It also disrupts your body's chemical balance and wreaks havoc on nerve chemicals, which could cause you to binge – especially on fat and sweets, which, of course, leads to weight gain.

Diets with fewer than 1,200 calories per day put your body into starvation mode. The body will naturally try to take care of itself, so if it thinks it's starving, it will slow down all functions and hold on to its fat stores to carry out essential body functions. If you normally consume 2,000 calories a day but then begin consuming only 1,200, your body will stop burning calories just to keep itself functioning. If your metabolism slows down, you will need only 1,200 calories to maintain your 'starting weight' and will need much less to lose any weight. Basically, your body needs fewer and fewer calories to keep itself running and permanent weight loss becomes almost impossible. If you go back to consuming 2,000 calories, those extra 800 calories will be stored as fat. It can take up to a year for your body to readjust itself and raise its metabolism back to where it used to be.

Now you see why low-calorie restrictive diets don't work. In order to begin your new food life, you have to start listening to your body. The first step to doing this is to start keeping a food journal. In it, you'll write down everything you eat and drink in the course of a day – as soon as you eat or drink it. You'll include the amount of food or drink you consumed and how you felt before, during and after eating. From these details, you'll learn about your food preferences, your cravings, your eating triggers and your hunger levels. When you pay attention to your hunger levels – and this is key – you usually don't eat when you aren't hungry. You'll learn all the specifics of journal-keeping and get started on one in the first week of the 8-week Food Life Makeover Plan (see page 142).

By using this book, you will learn how to have a great food life that suits you as an individual. In the chapters to come, I will help you create a food programme that takes care of your personal food needs. It's time to start taking care of yourself, stop looking for the shortcut and stop the dieting syndrome.

2. I'm Always Bingeing

▶ Do you try to have 'perfect' food days and when that doesn't happen, you stuff yourself until you feel sick (then feel out of control with your food)?

▶ Does bingeing make you feel 'good' in the moment, but as soon as it's over, you're disgusted with yourself?

▶ Are you so used to bingeing that you

never know when you're actually hungry?

▶ Is bingeing like a drug – whenever you feel you can't deal with life, you eat to relieve the pain?

▶ Do you starve yourself all day and then overeat wildly at night?

Many people who watch their weight wake up every morning saying, 'This will be the start of my new diet programme'. By the end of the day, though, they're so hungry they binge – often in a big way. Bingers don't have to be dieters, however; bingeing is just some people's unhealthy and out-of-control way of eating. They may even binge twice a day, consuming a few thousand calories at a time. For many people, bingeing is like a drug: whenever they feel they can't deal with life, they overeat to relieve the pain and stress they're feeling. The food binge becomes their coping mechanism.

If you're a binger, take heart in knowing you aren't alone. Twenty-two per cent of all dieters say they binge at least once a week. Clearly, bingeing is a common practice. But if binge eating has always been your coping mechanism, you know it doesn't make you feel any better, especially when the binge is over.

Bingeing is terrible for your body. Bingers tend to be less healthy than people who don't binge; their immune systems tend to be compromised because they binge on

junk food rather than on vegetables or healthier choices.

Strategy: In order to control your binge-ing, you must stop blaming yourself and feel-ing like a failure if you do binge. But you also need to start reprogramming your body and mind not to use food as a drug or coping mechanism. To help with this, start keeping a food journal. By writing down how your body – not just your mind – feels before, during and after eating, you can begin to reprogramme your eating and start getting back to eating when you're actually hungry, not when you're feeling other things. Bingers tend to get to the point of starving before they will eat anything – then they eat every-thing. When you get a Real Food Life, you'll stop starving yourself and start eating when you feel real hunger. (See 'Identify Your Hunger Level' on page 39.)

3. I Crave Sweets or Salt

▶ Do you feel that your sweet tooth is out of control?

▶ Do you love to snack on sweets, but usually feel dazed after the sugar binge is over?

▶ Do you put salt on your food before you even taste it?

▶ A week before your menstrual cycle, do you crave salt so much you have occasionally wondered if you're sodium deficient?

Healthy Substitutes for Sugary Snacks

The next time a sugar craving hits, reach for one of these tasty snacks. Not only are they more healthy than biscuits, cake or sweets, they are also filling and will completely calm your craving. Unlike when you eat snacks filled with empty calories, you'll be so satisfied after you eat these foods that you won't find yourself foraging for more!

- 1 slice wholegrain toasted raisin bread with 1 tablespoon low-fat cream cheese (or 2 tablespoons low-fat cottage cheese with 1 tablespoon all-fruit spread, such as St Dalfour)
- 1 small pot low-fat vanilla yogurt mixed with one small box of raisins and 2 tablespoons low-fat cottage cheese (for a protein boost)
- 2 wholegrain crackers or 2 brown rice cakes with 1 tablespoon peanut butter and 1 tablespoon jam or all-fruit spread
- 2 wholegrain crackers or 2 brown rice cakes with 2 tablespoons low-fat cream cheese and 1 tablespoon jam
- 1 muffin from recipe on page 319 with 1 tablespoon jam or 1 teaspoon peanut butter or 2 tablespoons low-fat cream cheese
- 1 wholemeal muffin with 2 teaspoons cream cheese sprinkled with a dusting of cinnamon and 1 teaspoon sugar
- 1 medium biscotti with 225 ml (8 fl oz) low-fat hot chocolate or chocolate milk
- 10 g (½ oz) piece of best-quality dark chocolate (such as Valrhona, Lindt 85% or Green & Black's)
- 1 bowl (approx 40 g/1½ oz) Honey Puffed Kashi or other high-fibre, low-sugar, low-salt cereal with 110–225 ml (4–8 fl oz) skimmed milk or soya milk
- 1 small scoop low-fat frozen yogurt
- 1 baked apple (see recipe on page 321) with 2 tablespoons low-fat vanilla yogurt
- 2 Oatmeal Raisin Cookies (see recipe on page 317)

People who crave sweets are everywhere. They may crave sweet food only at night or all through the day with doughnuts for breakfast, chocolates for lunch, sweets as a 4 p.m. pick-me-up and pudding after dinner.

They're the ones who will go out in any weather for their chocolate fix. They are practically addicted to sweets, but usually feel dazed or nervous after their sugar binges.

Then there are the people who crave

salty foods, such as fast food, chips, crisps and salted peanuts. After consuming salt, though, they often feel bloated. Their eyes get puffy and their hands swell, making it difficult to put on or take off their rings.

Cravings for sweets usually stem from a desire for fat. It's actually sweetened fats – rather than plain sugar – that people crave. Cakes, ice cream and biscuits have almost as much (and sometimes more) fat as they do sugar. It's the combination of fat and sugar (creamy and sweet) that ignites sweet cravings. Fat on its own has very little flavour, but when combined with sugar, its taste is qualitatively better. Fats make food flavoursome and contribute to wonderful aromas and tantalising 'mouth feel'. Think of the butter in biscuits: it makes them smell great, become crunchy and, of course, taste delicious. Studies have shown that people are less likely to crave low-fat sugary foods such as fruit gums and boiled sweets than high-fat sugary foods such as brownies, ice cream and chocolate.

The body needs fat – it's long-term fuel. Your appetite for fat (in the form of creamy, textured foods) is controlled by the brain chemical galanin. Galanin levels rise progressively throughout the day (which may explain the craving for creamy salad dressings at lunchtime or a creamy sweet snack, like a chocolate bar, in the late afternoon). Galanin levels also rise when oestrogen levels are high, which may explain why women often crave high-fat sweet foods during their premenstrual cycles.

Strategy: Eat smaller but more frequent meals throughout the day, which will make your blood sugar levels more stable and that may keep sweet cravings at bay. Also, eat a variety of complex carbohydrates all day long, but combine them with a protein whenever possible. The carbs keep serotonin (a brain chemical that regulates sleep, mood, food intake and pain) levels normal, so you crave sugar less. The protein helps you to feel fuller longer. Good snacks to try include a slice of wholemeal toast with some peanut butter and a glass of skimmed milk, or baby carrots dipped in hummus and a low-fat yogurt. Also try increasing the amount of water you drink, since sugar cravings can be a sign that your body is dehydrated.

Putting on your trainers and getting some exercise may also help you to avoid sugar cravings. Exercise releases the same 'feel-good' endorphins that sugar does. Studies show that people who exercise regularly binge less and have fewer food cravings because they're getting their endorphin rush through exercise.

Finally, if you really crave a sweet, indulge yourself – if you try to ignore the craving, you'll eventually binge. But eat what you crave; don't opt for a diet product made with sugar substitute. Simply have a small

Healthy Substitutes for Salty Snacks

Try one of the following snacks the next time you get a craving for a salty treat. Not only will you appease the craving, but you'll also be giving your body a more healthy alternative to other salty foods like full-fat crisps and fast-food French fries.

- 1 small bag low-fat, low-salt, oven-baked crisps
- A handful of snack sized pretzels
- 25 to 30 Twiglets (a small bowlful)
- 15 to 20 pistachios
- 6 to 8 walnuts
- 40 g (1½ oz) sunflower or pumpkin seeds
- A handful of low-fat oven chips
- Unlimited Roasted Vegetables with 1 to 2 teaspoons grated Parmesan cheese (see recipe on page 267)
- 1 medium bowl (350 ml/12 fl oz) Chunky Mixed Vegetable Soup (see recipe on page 281) sprinkled with 1 to 2 teaspoons grated Parmesan cheese
- 4 slices (50–75 g/2–3 oz) smoked tofu on wholegrain crackers with mustard
- 2 tofu sausages in a small wholemeal pitta bread with mustard
- 3 tablespoons hummus in a small wholemeal pitta with lettuce and tomato
- Prawn salad (5 cooked prawns chopped with 1 celery stick, chives or red onion and 1 tablespoon low-fat mayonnaise) on 2 wholegrain crackers or in a wholemeal pitta
- Egg salad (1 hard-boiled egg and 2 cooked egg whites mixed with 1 tablespoon low-fat mayonnaise and chopped spring onions) on 2 wholegrain crackers or in a wholemeal pitta
- 300 g (10½ oz) cherry tomatoes dipped in 1 tablespoon Blue Cheese Dressing (see recipe on page 263)
- 1 small tin water-packed tuna mixed with 1 chopped celery stick, 1 tablespoon raisins, ¼ teaspoon curry powder and 1 tablespoon low-fat mayonnaise on 2 rice cakes

portion of what you crave and then end it. You do not have to have the whole packet of biscuits to enjoy one.

While sugar cravings may be physiological, salt cravings are usually a learned response, a habit. The more salt you eat, the more you want it. Sodium is necessary for survival, but we need fewer than 500 milligrams of sodium a day to supply all vital functions and maintain normal fluid levels, healthy muscle function and proper acidity (pH) of the blood. Getting too little sodium is rarely a problem, but too much can lead to high blood pressure (hypertension) and fluid retention. It can also aggravate medical disorders such as congestive cardiac failure, kidney disease and PMS.

If you are used to a high-salt diet and want to cut back, do so gradually. If you take salt out of your diet too quickly, it may trigger even fiercer cravings.

Salt cravings may also be due to a craving for food with stronger, fuller flavours. Lemon is a great salt substitute. Try adding a squirt of lemon to low-salt soups and meat and chicken dishes – you might not even miss the salt. You might also try dried herb mixtures, cayenne pepper, vinegars, fruit juices, mustards, garlic, basil, oregano or curry powder. Of course, stop adding additional salt to food after it has been cooked.

Finally, read the 'Nutrition Information' label on packaged foods to discover how much sodium they contain (see 'Anatomy of a Label' on page 48). You'll probably be surprised to learn how much hidden sodium is in a lot of the foods you love.

4. I Sometimes Crash Diet

▶ Are you so desperate to lose weight that you'll go for days living on diet cola and cottage cheese?

▶ Do you buy clothes that are too small and hope you'll be able to fit into them in time for that big date?

▶ Do you try crash diets to be thin, thinking you'll be able to attract more men (or women)?

▶ Do you starve for a day or two and then binge wildly on the third day?

▶ Do you deny yourself most foods when you 'feel fat' or have overeaten?

When I hear the phrase 'crash diet', I get upset. It means that someone in a country of abundance is willing to forego food in the hope that it will cause immediate weight loss. Starving yourself – and the binge that inevitably follows – is no way to have a Real Food Life. People have all sorts of reasons for wanting to lose weight really quickly; these reasons often have to do with dating or a big event or the misconception that a crash diet will jump-start a good food life.

Crash diets are one of the most unhealthy weight-loss options around. These diets drastically cut out most foods when, in fact, the body needs a variety of food. They dehydrate you (which causes lethargy and dizziness); they break down lean muscle mass (and that slows down the metabolism and heart rate); they can make you feel cold and irritable; and they can cause illness (because they impair the immune system). Since these diets advocate eating nearly nothing or only one type of food, they lead to food obsessions, then cravings, then binges. That, in turn, leads to depression, guilt and even feelings of hopelessness. While people might lose weight on crash diets, they're not losing fat; they're losing water and muscle weight.

People who crash diet can end up with compromised immune systems and tend to be low in vitamin C (which comes only from eating foods rich in vitamin C or taking vitamin C supplements). Being deficient in vitamin C can lead to gum disease and gum bleeding, joint pains, low energy, poor digestion, slow wound healing, bruises, water retention and an increased susceptibility to infection, such as colds and bronchitis.

In addition to all this, starving yourself will only cause you to overeat eventually. It doesn't work as a weight-loss programme and never will.

Strategy: You need to develop and maintain an eating programme that's specifically tailored to you. This programme must allow you to eat nutritious foods consistently and throughout the day. Only then will you be able to end the cycle of starving and bingeing and develop a Real Food Life. You'll learn how to create an eating programme that will suit your lifestyle when you begin the 8-week Food Life Makeover Plan, starting on page 131.

5. I'm Addicted to Junk Food

▶ Are you obsessed with junk food? Do you sometimes wake up in the middle of the night just to grab some?

▶ When you drive past a fast-food restaurant, are you compelled to stop off and order something even when you're not hungry?

▶ When you're at the supermarket with your children, do they beg for junk food and you give in to them – and end up eating it, too?

Junk food is a hot issue in our culture. It's available almost everywhere, advertised almost everywhere and consumed practically everywhere. But, ironically, everybody knows it's 'no good for you' – that's why it's called junk food.

Because of its accessibility, junk food is an easy way to eat, which leads many people to indulge in it even if they don't intend to. But other people crave it. They love the taste (which is better: a cheeseburger or carrot sticks?) and they never seem able to say no. Having children makes the junk food situation especially tricky, since most children love the stuff and it's hard to deny them because it's always on hand. One thing about junk food: once you've had a taste, it's difficult to stop eating it, try as you might.

Strategy: Junk food is practically a constitutional right. You can't avoid junk food and if you love it and completely ban it from your diet, you will probably crave and obsess over it. Having something small (and decadently satisfying) may help you get through the initial cravings if you're trying to cut back. Not everyone can live with the discipline, but if you can limit yourself to just a taste, then end it, you can move on from your craving.

Many people simply don't eat enough during the day, so by 4 p.m. their blood sugar levels are as low as the South Pole. This is a prime time for cravings to hit. Not surprisingly, chocolate is a very common afternoon treat – especially for women – because chocolate satisfies many of the body's natural cravings: sugar and a little caffeine for an

The Cleanse and Flush Plan

If you have severely overindulged and want to reduce that bloated, lethargic feeling, you can use the following plan. You will lose a pound or two, but be aware that the loss is temporary – because it's only water you're losing, the weight will come back. You can safely stay on this programme for 3 days, but you should resume your new eating programme as soon as you feel better. The plan is loaded with fresh fruits and vegetables and fish because they all have a high water content, which means they'll fill you up and flush you out. And, yes, you do eat the same things every day.

First thing in the morning:
2 glasses warm water with lemon

Breakfast:
1 cup green tea
Fruit salad made with half a cantaloupe melon, 75 g (3 oz) raspberries and 75 g (3 oz)
    blackberries
1 small pot of fat-free natural yogurt with a sprinkle of cinnamon
1 whole hard-boiled egg

Midmorning snack:
2 glasses warm water with lemon
1 pear
5 walnut halves

Lunch:
2 glasses warm water with lemon
Large mixed vegetable salad (try to include all or some of the following vegetables:

afternoon pick-me-up and creamy fat, because the body naturally craves fat later in the day. Eating small meals throughout the day can help to curb cravings because it stabilises your blood sugar and insulin levels, so you'll feel less hungry and less likely to crave junk.

Junk food is a habit that you can learn to break. There are many foods that you can prepare at home in nearly the same amount of time it takes to stop at a fast-food restaurant, but that are cheaper and much more wholesome than fast food. For nearly instant at-home meals and snacks, consider veggie burgers or veggie hot dogs (both cook in minutes), dried fruit or a handful of nuts

cucumbers, spinach, broccoli, tomatoes, cos lettuce, peppers, watercress, shredded carrots, cooked beetroot, cooked asparagus) with 2 teaspoons olive oil

¼ avocado

110 g (4 oz) cooked (grilled or baked) fresh fish, such as salmon, tuna, herring, sardines, mackerel, trout; or any tinned fish (but make sure it's packed in spring water or olive oil and then drain it well)

Lemon (as much as you want on the fish and the salad)

110 g (4 oz) fresh or tinned beans (any type, rinsed very well)

Afternoon snack (spread throughout the afternoon):

2 glasses warm water with lemon

75 g (3 oz) mixed berries

110 g (4 oz) low-fat cottage cheese mixed with 75 g (3 oz) salsa and (unlimited) baby carrots to dip

1 steamed artichoke with lemon

Dinner:

2 glasses warm water with lemon

Large mixed vegetable salad (same as lunch) with 2 teaspoons olive oil and as much lemon as you want

¼ avocado

2 servings Roasted Vegetables (see recipe on page 267)

110 g (4 oz) fish (same as lunch) or 110 g (4 oz) grilled or baked chicken breast (see recipe on page 311)

1 small baked potato 75 g (3 oz)

½ melon (any type)

Great 'Junk' Food

Not all junk food is created equal. Check out the following items – they will probably satisfy your cravings, but they're kinder to your body than many other types of junk food. Pay attention to the serving size: when they're available, individual-serving-size containers can mean the difference between a snack and an out-of-control feast.

Crunchy and Salty

1 small bag low-fat, low-salt, oven-baked crisps (check out supermarket-own brands)
1 small bag tortilla chips (low-fat if available)
40 g (1½ oz) roasted, salted mixed nuts
2 large handfuls of unsalted or unsugared popcorn

Crunchy and Sweet

2 fig rolls
2 digestive biscuits
1 bowl (40–50 g/1½–2 oz) Frosties with 110 ml (4 fl oz) skimmed milk
5 lollipops
2 pretzel sticks with 1 tablespoon honey to dip
1 waffle drizzled with 1 teaspoon chocolate syrup

Creamy and Sweet (and/or Chocolatey)

1 Milky Way Light bar
1 small bar (20 g) of Green & Black's organic chocolate
3 After Eight mints
2 Jaffa cakes
20 chocolate-covered raisins
1 small pot low-fat chocolate yogurt
1 small pot Provamel Chocolate Soya Dessert

(instant) or lower-sodium tinned soup or vegetarian chilli (merely heat and eat). You might also want to try a piece (or two) of fruit before you reach for the junk food. If you have some fruit first, about half the time it will squash your craving for junk food.

A good strategy is to make exchanges. For example, try peanut butter and jam on crackers instead of having biscuits. If you wake up in the middle of the night craving something, have a small snack of crackers and cheese, or a small bowl of cereal, or a low-fat hot chocolate. If you fight the craving, you'll probably end up bingeing. But if you try eating a small amount of a more healthy food, the cravings may eventually stop. In my experience, stress is often the culprit in cravings, so make sure you note how you are feeling when your cravings hit.

Don't keep your favourite junk food in the house. If it's not around, you can't eat it. I've found that the occasional bag of crisps always calls me into the kitchen, where I usually can't shut it up until I've finished the bag. So, to keep my Real Food Life in check, I don't keep crisps in the house. Or, if I do buy them, I purchase the small bags that can be easily managed.

Finally, set limits on your children when they accompany you food shopping – this also sets limits on yourself. Before you go food shopping, tell the children that they can pick out only one 'junk' item. Then stick to the plan when you're in the shop, even if they start to complain and beg for other items.

6. 'I'll Start Tomorrow'

▶ Have you ever tried to be 'good' with your food day, but when you overate at lunch, you gave up for the day, figuring you'll 'do better' tomorrow?

▶ Do you constantly 'diet' but then get bored and spend the day eating all sorts of junk food, knowing you can always 'make it up' tomorrow?

▶ Did you have an extra-busy day and end up eating whatever was easiest since you figured you could eat better starting tomorrow?

Many people put off healthy eating until 'tomorrow' (or later). They want a fresh start if they feel they 'messed up' – perhaps they ate a big, high-calorie meal or had a mini-binge. They feel they can't keep their food lives together if they indulged and psychologically they can't move on until they have a clean slate.

Typically, people who procrastinate about improving their food lives get caught up with the idea of perfection. This type of person believes that unless her food life is perfect, she can't have a good food life at all. Anything can trip up a so-called perfect day – it could be a busy day at work or college, a deadline, travelling, problems with the children or just life in general.

Strategy: The solution isn't 'starting tomorrow'. It's saying to yourself 'I binged', or 'circumstances got the better of me', and moving on. You need to start eating sanely at your next meal – not the next day. Getting a Real Food Life means losing the procrastination mentality. Every single day you'll encounter all sorts of obstacles at home, at work and with food. That's OK. Not only is it OK, it's life and it's normal. There's no such thing as a perfect food day.

The key is knowing how to manage your food day and not getting caught up with how you are 'supposed to eat' or what your friends or family are eating. Everyone is different and you need to find food strategies that work for you, that you can live with, work with and play with.

When you get a Real Food Life, you realise that you don't need to eat perfectly, so there's never a need to have a clean slate. If you binge or indulge or if circumstances get the better of you, don't beat yourself up about it or think that you need to delay eating well until tomorrow. A Real Food Life is forever.

7. I'm Always Hungry, Especially at Night

▶ Do you go through the day making sensible food choices, but as soon as it's dark outside – even if you had a good dinner – your good food sense seems to fly out the window?

▶ Are you worried that getting a Real Food Life means you'll never be satisfied and always be hungry?

▶ Do you feel that because you are hungry all the time, food is always on your mind and you're obsessed with food?

▶ Are you always dieting, but you don't find food satisfying and you're always hungry?

▶ Do you always feel hungry at work?

Many people never feel satisfied with their food, so they always eat because they feel

Don't Ignore the Signs of Extreme Hunger

Many people – especially those who have been on various fad diets – have become so out of touch with their bodies that they no longer recognise signs of extreme hunger. Others, desperate to lose weight, ignore the cues their bodies are sending them. The symptoms below are all signs of extreme hunger. Try never to allow yourself to get to this point before eating, because the chances are you'll be so famished that you'll make poor food choices. If you do have two or more of these symptoms, you're probably overdue for a meal.

- You feel faint.
- You're lightheaded.
- You have difficulty concentrating.
- You have a headache.
- You feel irritable.
- You have noises in your stomach.
- There's a gnawing feeling in the pit of your stomach.

Is It Hunger or Thirst?

If you think you're hungry but have the following symptoms of dehydration, you may simply be thirsty. Try drinking a glass of water before reaching for something to eat.

- You have recently eaten a reasonably sized meal but are still hungry.
- Your urine is dark (it should be almost clear).
- You have a dry mouth.
- You feel very tired – mentally and physically – and don't know why, since you had a decent night's sleep.
- You're constipated.
- You're excessively thirsty. (Keep in mind, though, that you can be dehydrated and not feel thirsty.)

hungry all the time. Maybe they're always hungry in the late afternoon or maybe, for women, they're especially hungry right before their periods. Maybe they're always hungry at night, even if they ate sensibly during the day. People who are chronically hungry inevitably have food on their minds and become obsessed with food. Often, it's the fear of hunger that prevents people from eating more healthily; they incorrectly equate a Real Food Life with dieting and deprivation.

Strategy: There are a few ways to cope with the 'I'm always hungry' syndrome. The first step is to learn to recognise whether you're actually hungry. You need to listen to your body and this takes some practice. Is it hunger pangs you are experiencing or is it really your mood that's making you turn towards food? Are you angry, stressed, depressed, nervous? Food is often used as a stress reliever and a balm to troubling emotions.

Another way to combat this syndrome is to eat small meals all day long. It's that easy. Eating smaller amounts of nutritious foods throughout the day (instead of just three larger meals) helps your metabolism stay active, gives you the sensation of fullness and produces less insulin after you eat. What that means is that the calories you eat are burned more efficiently and if they are burned more efficiently and don't exceed your energy needs, they're not stored as fat. Eating smaller meals more often gives the power of food back to you. It keeps your blood sugar levels balanced and keeps your mood in

'Free' Foods

The following foods are low in calories and high in nutrients. They're pretty much all-you-can-eat foods. They do have calories, however, so you might think twice if you plan on eating loads of each of these every day.

- All vegetables (except starchy ones such as sweetcorn, peas and potatoes), including artichokes, asparagus, beetroot, pak choi, broccoli, purple sprouting broccoli, Brussels sprouts, cabbage (any colour), carrots, cauliflower, celery, celeriac, cucumbers, mushrooms (any variety), parsnips, peppers, tomatoes and turnips
- Aubergine, courgettes and other squash such as acorn, butternut and spaghetti
- Endive, fennel, kale, mustard greens, radicchio, spinach, Swiss chard, cos and any other type of lettuce
- Grapefruit and watermelon

check. If you spread out your meals, you can learn to have small portions of food that you love (where a large portion might have too many calories for your eating plan).

If you're truly hungry, you should eat; but whether it's a snack or a meal, try to make everything you eat count. All the food you eat should be both delicious and nourishing. When you can, make sure you have a balance of protein, carbohydrates and good fats, such as those found in fish and peanut butter.

If you're always hungry, you can eat 'free' foods like vegetables all day long. I consider them 'free' because they have almost no cost when it comes to calories. Furthermore, they're filled with fibre, so they fill you up; they're also high in vitamins and minerals. Eat as much of these foods as you desire and

make soups and other veggie dishes from them to have in your refrigerator at all times. See '"Free" Foods' for the complete list.

When you develop an eating plan, it should include plenty of low-calorie, healthy snacks. (For some suggestions, see 'Healthy Substitutes for Sugary Snacks' on page 23 and 'Healthy Substitutes for Salty Snacks' on page 25.) If you're always hungry, be sure to create an eating plan with flexibility – build in some days that are 'foodier', where you eat more than other days. If you have some lighter food days, those will balance the heavier ones. By the same token, if you're always hungry at night, plan for that. Pick out some sensible snacks that fit into your eating plan. Determine what you really crave and what will really satisfy you. Sweet? Salty? Creamy? Crunchy? There are lots of low-calorie snacks available that will satisfy these cravings. Check out 'Great "Junk" Food' on page 30 for some ideas.

Finally, make sure you drink water – lots of it. In fact, it's a good idea to drink one or two glasses of water before each meal. You should strive for at least eight 225-ml (8-fl oz) glasses of water each day, but there's practically no such thing as drinking too much water. Water helps to fill you up and it also flushes you out.

8. I Eat When I'm Stressed Out

▶ Do you eat when you have a deadline to meet?

▶ When you're at a party and you're uncomfortable, do you hover around the snack table?

▶ Do you eat when you feel over-whelmed?

▶ Do you use food as a coping mecha-nism?

Stress comes in many forms: deadlines, demands, crises, children clamouring for attention or getting into trouble, the feeling that you have to please everyone, nervous-ness (social, financial, career or otherwise) and even worries about your food life. Whatever its origin, feeling stressed out often leads to eating. We use food to soothe our anxieties. For many of us, food is a coping mechanism, a comfort, a release.

The thing is, stress-eating is mostly unconscious eating. It's reaching for food without even thinking about it; it's eating whatever is placed in front of you or what-ever you can find – and often when you're not even hungry.

Strategy: The first way to cope with stress-eating is to not deny yourself some edible stress outlets. If you deny yourself, you'll start to obsess about food. Keeping a food journal is critical when you're learning to calm your stress-eating because it makes you accountable for what you eat – and when you're accountable, you can help keep your food life in check.

You won't always know when you're going to be under a lot of stress, but if you build in to your eating plan foods that help you get through the day (a small bar of your favourite chocolate or a small bag of lower-fat crisps, for example), these can be your goodies in times of stress.

In addition, exercise is an amazing stress reliever. When you work out, your body releases endorphins (feel-good brain chemi-cals) that make you feel better and calmer and also stimulate T lymphocytes (cells that play a crucial role in attacking pathogens within the body). Since stress can compro-mise your immune system and make you more prone to getting colds and infections, exercise is a great option. Even a moderate

How Stress Sabotages Your Health

Unless you live in a fantasy world, chances are you've felt the effects of stress in the form of a nagging headache or upset stomach. But did you know that stress can affect your body in many other ways as well? Here's a laundry list of the ways stress can affect your health. Use it as motivation to incorporate some stress-reducing activities, such as exercise, meditation or even yoga, into your day.

- Stress can cause fatigue, chronic headaches, irritability, changes in appetite, memory loss, cold hands and gastrointestinal problems, including irritable bowel syndrome.

- Stress slows down the healing of cuts and the recovery from colds.

- Researchers say stress causes at least 80 per cent of all major illnesses, including back problems, heart disease, infections and skin disorders.

- When a person is under stress, major body changes occur, including increased blood pressure and heart rate, increased cholesterol levels and decreased immune system functioning. In addition, digestion may slow, fats and sugars may be released from stores in the body and blood may tend to clot more easily.

- Stress can lead to nutritional deficiency caused by an increase in production of the adrenal hormones. These hormones cause the body to step up the metabolism of protein, fats and carbohydrates. What this means is that stress causes your body to burn the nutrients it needs more quickly, so your body can't absorb those nutrients as well as when you're not stressed.

- When you're stressed, your body excretes amino acids (building blocks of protein that are needed to build muscle), potassium (a mineral important for a healthy nervous system and regular heart beats) and phosphorus (a mineral important for bone and teeth formation, cell growth and heart and kidney functions). All this depletes magnesium and if magnesium is low, it will lower the amount of calcium in your body (because magnesium helps calcium uptake).

- Stress may cause a B-vitamin deficiency. Since the B vitamins are needed for the proper functioning of the nervous system and the nervous system kicks into overdrive during times of stress, the body has greater requirements for B vitamins during these times. In times of stress, people tend to overeat and overdrink – or, conversely, undereat – which will also compromise their B-vitamin stores. Symptoms of a B-vitamin deficiency include irritability, lethargy and depression.

- Stress can set off food cravings because the stress hormones norepinephrine and corticosterone raise levels of the brain chemical galanin and increased galanin levels lead to an increased appetite for fat, overeating and possible weight gain.

walk will help. And if you just can't find any time to get those endorphins flowing by exercising, a quick fix can be a glass of skimmed milk with a tablespoon of cocoa, since both lactose and fat may help release endorphins as well.

Foods That Soothe

When you're feeling particularly stressed, reach for one of the following foods. They're all known for their ability to soothe and calm you and each contains about 100 calories.

3 fresh apricots

75 g (3 oz) dried fruit (apricots, prunes, raisins)

1 medium banana

150 g (5 oz) fresh blueberries

1 small baked apple

2 medium fresh figs

150 g (5 oz) grapes

2 large slices (300 g/10½ oz) honeydew melon

2 medium kiwifruit

1 fresh mango

1 or 2 fresh papaya

1 large orange

1 pink grapefruit

1 large peach or nectarine

175 g (6 oz) fresh cherries

4 dried dates

1 small bowl (225 ml/8 fl oz) split pea or lentil soup (try organic brands including Simply Organic, Heinz Organic, Seeds of Change, Meridian)

1 small pot low-fat vanilla yogurt sprinkled with 1 tablespoon wheat germ

1 small pot low-fat cottage cheese

25 g (1 oz) Edam cheese on 1 wholegrain cracker

The Antioxidant All-stars

Antioxidants help to protect the body from attacks by free radicals, unstable oxygen molecules that play a role in the development of cancer, heart disease and ageing. Fortunately, there are numerous foods that are good sources of antioxidants.

Green tea, dark chocolate, soyabeans and tofu are antioxidant all-stars in that they contain high levels of many different antioxidants. Below are other members of the all-star team. These foods have made the cut because they contain particularly high levels of a certain antioxidant.

Beta-carotene: Asparagus, broccoli, Brussels sprouts, dark green, leafy vegetables (including cooking greens like spring greens, kale and spinach), orange and yellow vegetables (including apricots, carrots, nectarines, peaches, squashes and sweet potatoes)

Coenzyme Q_{10}: Beef, mackerel, peanuts, salmon, sardines, spinach

Selenium: Brazil nuts, broccoli, brown rice, chicken, dairy foods, garlic, salmon

Vitamin C: Asparagus, avocados, berries, broccoli, Brussels sprouts, cantaloupe melon, citrus fruits, green leafy vegetables, mangoes, papaya, potatoes, red and green peppers, spinach, tomatoes

Vitamin E: Avocados, brown rice, cereals and breads made with 100 per cent whole grain, eggs, extra-virgin olive oil, green leafy vegetables, legumes, milk, nuts, oatmeal, rapeseed oil, seeds, soyabeans, wheat germ

Zinc: Butterbeans, egg yolks, fish and shellfish, lamb and other meats, legumes, mushrooms, oysters, pecan nuts, poultry, pumpkin seeds, soyabeans, sunflower seeds, whole grains

There's no magic bullet, but some foods can actually help in the battle against stress. Fruits, vegetables and whole grains all contain carbohydrates, which release serotonin, a brain chemical that makes you feel more relaxed. (The corollary is that stress may actually stimulate the breakdown of serotonin.) If you have a breakfast that includes carbohydrates, it may help to set a mellower mood for the whole day.

In addition, try to eat foods that are high in antioxidants, such as vitamins C and E and the B vitamins. (See 'The Antioxidant All-stars' for a list of some of these foods.) Antioxidants are a group of vitamins, minerals and enzymes that protect the body from free radicals, atoms that attack the immune system and can cause cell damage, infections, heart disease, cancer and ageing.

There's no getting around it: our lives are filled with stress. But by eating right, exercising and having snacks on hand that you can turn to in difficult times, you no longer need to be its victim.

9. Food Cheers Me Up (and Is My Companion)

▶ Do you soothe your sadness, unhappiness or depression with food?

▶ When you've suffered a disappointment, do you eat?

▶ If you're upset about working too much or not working enough, do you eat?

▶ Do you use food to cope with loneliness?

▶ Do you eat more when you're alone – and you're alone a lot, so you eat a lot?

Sadness, depression and feeling alone often lead to overeating. Whether you're struggling with a professional disappointment, a failed exam, wintertime sadness (clinically referred to as Seasonal Affective Disorder or SAD), a personal frustration or social isolation, it's common to try to soothe yourself with food.

You might use food as a comfort, a diversion or a friend substitute. But using food in this way is a cycle that repeats and repeats with the same consequence: mindless overeating.

Identify Your Hunger Level

When you listen to your body, you'll learn how hungry you are (or aren't). By helping you to tune in to the feelings in your stomach before, during and after eating, the following scale can aid you in gauging your hunger level. You should start eating when you drop to level 3 and stop eating at level 7.

Level 1:	Empty stomach – can't function; in pain
Level 2:	Functioning barely; serious unease
Level 3:	Functioning, but very hungry; tolerable unease
Level 4:	Functioning, but can't wait to eat
Level 5:	Neutral
Level 6:	Still hungry, but aware of food in stomach
Level 7:	Still some room in stomach, but satisfied and comfortably full
Level 8:	Slight unease; somewhat overfull
Level 9:	Uneasy; much too full
Level 10:	Can't function; in pain

Strategy: Using food as comfort and company is a way of nurturing yourself. You probably learned early in life that eating makes you feel better, so you turn to this strategy even as an adult. Eating to deal with loneliness or sadness is rarely about being physically hungry. By learning the triggers of emotional eating, you can stop yourself before you pig out and ask, 'Am I truly hungry or emotionally hungry? Is it really depression, anger or loneliness that I'm feeling?'

Head hunger is the need for something else that is not food, but food is a comfortable stand-in. Head hunger is used to keep emotions that you think you can't cope with at bay. The problem, though, is that you're not facing the actual issues that made you feel upset in the first place. Food is used as self-medication – it's numbing and makes you feel good instantly.

This type of eating often occurs because people wrongly believe they're bad or weak. If this is true of you, ask yourself what you are hiding from. Facing issues such as loneliness or depression is painful, but it has to be done if you want to get out of the cycle of overeating. You have to get in touch with your feelings – not mask them by eating. For example, if you're bored or lonely, ring a friend and try to brainstorm things you could do together. Even if you end up just going for a walk around the block, the

change of scenery may be enough to keep you from reaching for food. If you're sad, know that it's OK to cry. And if you're lonely, make some positive step in interacting with people, such as doing voluntary work, joining a club or going to a lecture. If you're feeling really low and cripplingly shy and you can't find a way to help yourself, seeking professional counselling is probably the best thing you can do for yourself.

Interestingly, depression can be caused by your diet. Eating large quantities of simple carbohydrates like sugar and refined grains (such as white bread) causes your blood sugar level to rise and then fall very rapidly, creating a 'high' followed by a severe crash that induces feelings of depression. Cutting back on sugar, refined grains and caffeine, which also raises and drops your blood sugar level very quickly, can help to regulate your mood swings.

Another possible cause for depression is inadequate vitamin B_6, which is needed for proper functioning of the central nervous system. Low B_6 can be a result of too much exercise, constant dieting or too much alcohol. To increase your level of B_6, eat more bananas, carrots, chicken, eggs, nuts, fish, meat, cheese, spinach, sunflower seeds and wheat germ.

To deal with mild depression, try eating complex carbohydrates, which increase levels of tryptophan (mellowing brain chemicals) and serotonin (feel-good brain chemicals). These chemicals can help brighten moods and decrease irritability. Crackers, fruit and even potatoes can provide temporary relief for low moods. Niacin can also help fight depression, but you should get it only through food, not supplements. Particularly good sources of niacin are broccoli, carrots, cheese, dates, eggs, fish, milk, potatoes and wholewheat products.

A good way to learn about the causes and effects of head hunger is to keep and analyse a food journal. By jotting down what you eat, when you eat and what your mood is before, during and after eating, you can learn if it's your diet that's making you feel down or if you feel down regardless of your food intake. If you discover your depression isn't diet-related, discuss this with your doctor, who can identify other causes for your depression and refer you to a specialist as needed.

10. I Love to Snack

▶ If you could snack all day without gaining weight, would you?

▶ Do you think that snacking is bad?

▶ Do you munch on your children's left-over chicken nuggets, mini pizzas and maca-roni cheese?

Snacking is a Western obsession. Lots of people would opt to snack all day if they knew they wouldn't put on weight. Snacking has a bad reputation: people think that they should eat only three 'proper' meals a day with noth-ing in between. But when chosen wisely, snacks can be part of a healthy eating plan.

Of course, if you snack all day long, that's basically a binge. And if you snack only on junk food such as crisps and sweets, that's not good snacking. If you're emptying the vending machine, a regular at fast-food places or munching on your children's left-overs, that's not smart snacking either.

Strategy: Snacking can be healthy, but you have to be smart about it. Snacks need to fit in with your individual eating plan; they can't simply be mindless eating without hunger. If you love to snack, you should be snacking smart.

Smart snacking is a very efficient way of burning calories. You get the same benefits as you do when you eat small, frequent meals – less insulin is released and your metabolism is more active. Smart snacking keeps blood sugar levels balanced, it relieves that 'starv-ing' feeling so you don't overeat at your next meal and it helps you feel less obsessed with food because you know you can eat when you feel hungry.

Non-smart snacks tend to be foods high in simple or refined carbohydrates, such as crisps, popcorn, white bread and biscuits. These foods raise and lower your blood sugar levels very quickly and cause tiredness, hunger and cravings. They're also emptied from your stomach quickly, so they don't keep you satisfied for very long.

When you have a snack, try to have a protein combined with a carbohydrate. That way, the food stays in your stomach longer than if you ate a carbohydrate alone. Fat also delays emptying of the stomach and keeps you fuller longer. Having a snack of a small handful of nuts, which will provide protein and fat, with a low-fat yogurt or a slice of wholegrain bread with hummus (mashed chickpea spread) will probably keep you full and satisfied for a few hours.

It takes time to find the snacks that really suit you – both body and mind. Be aware that snacking is not for everybody. Some people find that snacking leaves them feeling out of control with food. If this is the case for you, larger meals spaced farther apart should help you feel satisfied and in control.

11. I Eat When I'm Bored

▶ Do you eat to pass time when you're bored?

▶ When you're working long, tedious hours, do you eat?

▶ When you're watching TV or working on the computer, do you finish a whole bag of crisps or biscuits without even realising it?

When you're bored, eating can be a (temporary) saviour. Food becomes the focus of entertainment and eating keeps you busy. And while the TV and computer can connect us to nearly anyone around the globe, they're also passive activities and mindlessly eating while watching or working on them is natural.

Strategy: Eating can be a coping mechanism to deal with boredom, whether you're at work, college or home. When there is no other emotional arousal, eating gives you something on which to focus.

Boredom-eating usually has nothing to do with hunger. It is mindless eating, eating whatever's there, eating without taking into account your actual hunger level. (Mindful eating, on the other hand, is eating consciously and only when you're hungry, with awareness that your food life is nourishing for your body and your emotions.)

An effective way to monitor mindless eating is to keep a food journal. When you write down everything you eat, when you eat, and how you feel as you're eating, you'll discover that you're not actually hungry every time you eat. (For specific information on how to start a food journal, see page 142.) After just a few days of keeping a food journal, you'll start to notice how often you engage in mindless eating. You'll soon be able to determine if you are actually hungry or if you are simply in the habit of eating to get through a situation (even if that situation is watching TV or working on the computer).

One of the best ways to keep yourself from turning to food when you're bored is to find what I've dubbed anti-boredom activities. For at least 10 minutes out of every hour you're on the computer or watching TV, move. Try dancing, jogging in place, doing jumping jacks or walking. Or, instead of just surfing the channels and not really watching any one programme, buy exercise tapes and use them. Once you've memorised some exercises, you can even work out while watching a favourite programme. You might want to keep a pair of weights next to the sofa and do lifts during the adverts. On days when you're feeling less ambitious, just getting up and getting a drink of water during the adverts is better than nothing – you'll increase your daily water consumption and get a bit of exercise, too.

Although incorporating some movement while you watch TV will help, also try to find activities that get you off the sofa and limit the amount of time you have available to watch TV. Instead of watching TV for hours each week, read, practise a hobby or try physical activities like walking, jogging, doing yoga or even cleaning the house. These will help to relieve boredom, get you away from food and get your body moving. As a bonus, physical activities help reduce depression and anxiety because they release endorphins that help you to feel more relaxed.

Even with these safeguards, all of us eat out of boredom occasionally. When this happens to you, simply choose your boredom-foods wisely. Try to have healthy snacks nearby and throw out food that leaves you feeling out of control, such as huge bags of crisps and supersize chocolate bars. Challenge your cooking skills by making nutritious and delicious snacks for yourself and your family. (Look at the recipes beginning on page 259.) Finally, stock up on a variety of vegetables, which are considered 'free' foods, in that you can eat as much as you want without consequence. (See '"Free" Foods' on page 34.)

12. I Make Deals with Myself to Eat What I Want

▶ If you're 'good' during the day, do you feel you deserve a tub of ice cream at night?

▶ Are you 'good' for the week and then pig out over the weekend?

▶ If you overindulge one night, do you rationalise that you'll work 'extra hard' at the gym the next day (but of course you're either too tired or too hung over to work 'extra hard' when the day comes)?

Bargaining with yourself about food is not a way to have a healthy food life. I see this fairly often: people have a deal-making mentality that if they are 'good' (which usually means eating too little), they 'deserve' a food reward (and then wonder why they're putting on weight). Or they rationalise that since they're working long, hard hours, they deserve to eat what they want today and they vow to eat better the next day (but that never happens and then they get depressed).

Strategy: Making deals never works. Negotiating your food intake with yourself only makes you feel angry and frustrated. Food isn't a business transaction. Making a 'deal' with your food continues the cycle of not trusting yourself and sets you up for failure.

Allow yourself to have some of the foods you crave. This helps to keep food from becoming an emotional issue. If you feel you need some chocolate or chips, have a small quantity and then move on. You don't have to binge to indulge a craving. You can allow yourself to splurge once in a while. So once a month, say, indulge in an extraordinary meal.

In the 8-week Food Life Makeover Plan beginning on page 131, I'll help you to create a programme that works with your lifestyle and makes you feel good. Then you'll be able to stop making deals with yourself and get a better grip on your food life.

13. I Can't Get Organised to Eat Regular Meals

▶ Do you feel so busy with work, college or your family responsibilities that you can't eat properly?

▶ Are you so busy that it's easiest to 'just grab something' on the road, from a vending machine, at a fast-food restaurant or from the cupboards?

▶ Do you find it too overwhelming to prepare three proper meals for the day, so you go to the other extreme and eat mindlessly throughout the day?

Many clients tell me the same thing: 'My life is so fast-paced that I can never "eat right" or sit down for a regular meal.' They're not even sure what a 'regular' meal is, since they're used to having 'irregular' meals. They spend their days picking at food (rather than having meals) or they feel so full after a 'regular' meal that they need to unbutton their trousers. They're tied up with work, college or the children and don't have the focus or time to have a balanced, nourishing meal, so they grab whatever they can find. And then they feel guilty for not sitting down to eat 'actual' meals.

Some people never learnt how to cook: how to prepare a simple omelette or baked potato or how to stock the refrigerator. They think the only way to get organised with their eating is to hire a nutritionist, a food shopper, a cook and a cleaner. (As if that's a practical solution!) They want a quick and effortless way to eat well.

Strategy: It's time to get back to food basics. It may take a little time, practice and

Caffeine Quotients

Caffeine is most often consumed in beverages, where it is either naturally occurring, as in tea and coffee, or added to the final product, as in fizzy drinks. To find out how much caffeine is in some popular drinks and foods, check out the following table.

Item	Amount of Caffeine (mg)
Fresh coffee (300 ml/½ pt)	120–270
Instant coffee (300 ml/½ pt)	60–240
Decaffeinated coffee (300 ml/½ pt)	2–10
Brewed tea (150 ml/¼ pt)	20–110
Iced tea (350 ml/12 fl oz)	65–80
Green tea (150 ml/¼ pt)	12–60
Instant tea (150 ml/¼ pt)	25–50
Hot chocolate (225 ml/8 fl oz)	2–20
Chocolate milk (225 ml/8 fl oz)	2–8
Coca Cola or Diet Coke (1 x 330-ml can)	47
Dr Pepper (1 x 330-ml can)	40
Pepsi Cola (1 x 330-ml can)	39
Diet Pepsi (1 x 330-ml can)	37
Milk chocolate (25 g/1 oz)	5–35

patience to get organised to eat in a smart way, but it can be done. This book is filled with ways for you to get organised with your food. In part 3, I'll take you step by step through my 8-week Food Life Makeover Plan. As part of that plan, I'll give you directions for doing a kitchen makeover (see page 176), a shopping list (see page 186) and many other strategies and new ideas for getting a Real Food Life. There's even a whole chapter full of simple and quick-to-make recipes (see page 255).

A regular 'meal' doesn't have to mean a three-course dinner. It can mean small but frequent 'meals' throughout the day, which is a healthy way to eat. When you 'graze' on small but frequent meals, less insulin (a hormone that helps regulate blood sugar) is released into your body, so your metabolism is more active.

Finally, grazing on healthy foods all day can actually make you feel more comfortable. Whereas a larger, 'regular' meal may leave you feeling too full, grazing makes you feel full but not stuffed. It also gives you greater control over your food, thereby making you less obsessed with food.

14. I Can't Live without Caffeine

▶ Do you find it hard to think straight until you've had a cup of strong coffee?

▶ Do you go through at least a litre (1¾ pt) of fizzy drinks a day?

For many people, coffee and fizzy drinks are an addiction. They can't get up in the morning unless they know they'll have their fix. Many have been doing it for years and are certifiable caffeine junkies, drinking up to 10 cups of caffeinated beverages each day. Some use caffeine only to get through the morning and over the afternoon hump. Some prefer cola and other caffeinated fizzy drinks. They'll start their day with a pop and don't stop until after dinner. They might believe that as long as they drink 'diet' pop, it's OK.

Strategy: Huge amounts of coffee, tea and fizzy drinks are consumed every day. Coffee bars are springing up all over the place and we're all drinking more and more of what they have on offer.

Caffeine is absorbed into your blood within half an hour of consumption and affects your brain, heart rate, respiration,

muscle coordination and central nervous system almost immediately thereafter. It stays in the body for up to 4 hours. Coffee drinkers take longer to fall asleep, they don't sleep as well and they wake up not feeling as refreshed as people who don't drink coffee.

Coffee (and the caffeine in it) is not 'bad' per se – it does help people to think faster, elevates the mood and improves motor skills and short-term memory. But too much has the opposite effect: it causes fatigue. Because caffeine is a diuretic, excessive consumption may cause dehydration and one of the results of dehydration is fatigue. In addition, dehydration can potentially lead to constipation. Furthermore, caffeine consumed in excess may decrease your body's iron stores, which in turn may compromise your immune system, making you more prone to colds and flu. Unfortunately, these symptoms often begin a vicious cycle: the coffee junkie ends up consuming more caffeine to fight fatigue and soon she needs to drink more and more to get the same results.

You don't have to stop drinking coffee altogether – just cut back on the amount you drink. The average mug of coffee has about 200 milligrams of caffeine. Try to limit yourself to one-and-a-half mugs or less in the morning. (Of course, you'd want to limit your intake even more if you are highly sensitive to caffeine, but in that case, you would probably know this already.) You can try decaf, but try to buy coffee that is 'Swiss water process' decaf – a safer decaffeination process than others.

It's not wise to try to replace your coffee with cola or tea. It's true that both have less caffeine than coffee, but ingesting more than 300 milligrams of caffeine per day – whether it's from coffee, tea or colas – isn't a good idea. Since many people use colas or tea as their replacement 'fix' from coffee, they'll typically just end up drinking more cola or tea to compensate.

You might try switching to decaffeinated green tea, which is filled with amazing amounts of antioxidants. In addition, you should drink plenty of water all day long to stay energised and hydrated (and to make up for caffeine's dehydrating effects).

If you want to try to kick the caffeine habit, reduce your intake slowly. Withdrawal symptoms from caffeine can include headaches and fatigue. You might try switching to a grain- or cereal-based drink such as Whole Earth No Caf, Barley Cup, Bambu or Yannoh Instant. None of these products have caffeine and they're low in calories.

Finally, beware hidden caffeine. It is found in coffee ice cream, chocolate and quite a few over-the-counter medications, including headache remedies, diet pills and sleep suppressants.

15. I Don't Have Time to Shop (and Its Evil Twin: I Don't Know *How* to Shop)

▶Are you so busy you can't possibly fit food shopping into your schedule?

▶ When you go shopping, do you get confused and overwhelmed by too many choices?

▶ Do you wonder what the labels on products mean?

▶ When you do find the time to go shopping, are you immediately overcome with the urge to eat everything in sight?

Food shopping can sometimes be a chore, but it doesn't have to be something you dread. Many people claim that they simply don't have the time to shop. And if you have children, taking them shopping adds a major challenge to the process. As soon as you enter the supermarket, inevitably the children are screaming or bored or they start tossing junk food into the trolley.

Strategy: A motto of mine is 'if you shop right, you'll eat right'. Finding the time to shop and getting over the dread of food shopping are big steps towards getting a Real Food Life. One way to start is to create a shopping list. Even a couple of days before you go to the shops, stick a list on the fridge and get the family to add to it whenever they finish something. On page 186, I've created a shopping list for you. It includes the best,

Anatomy of a Label

If you take the time to learn how to read the Nutrition Information labels found on nearly all packaged foods, you'll find that they can be treasure troves of valuable information. Here I've explained the most important elements.

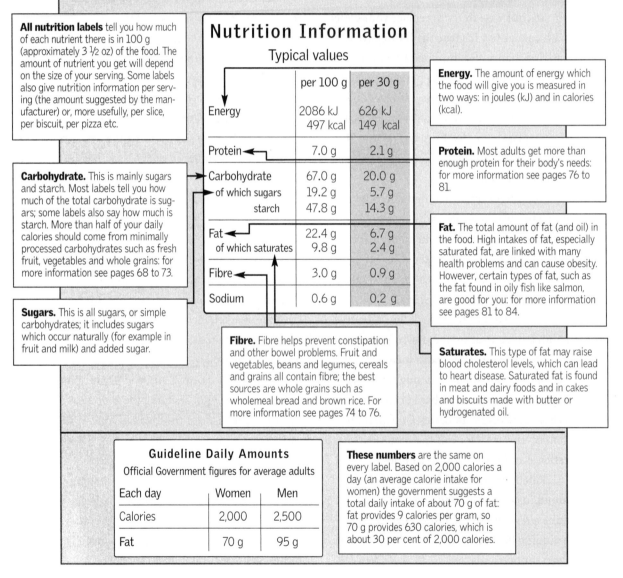

All nutrition labels tell you how much of each nutrient there is in 100 g (approximately 3 ½ oz) of the food. The amount of nutrient you get will depend on the size of your serving. Some labels also give nutrition information per serving (the amount suggested by the manufacturer) or, more usefully, per slice, per biscuit, per pizza etc.

Carbohydrate. This is mainly sugars and starch. Most labels tell you how much of the total carbohydrate is sugars; some labels also say how much is starch. More than half of your daily calories should come from minimally processed carbohydrates such as fresh fruit, vegetables and whole grains: for more information see pages 68 to 73.

Sugars. This is all sugars, or simple carbohydrates; it includes sugars which occur naturally (for example in fruit and milk) and added sugar.

Nutrition Information

Typical values

	per 100 g	per 30 g
Energy	2086 kJ	626 kJ
	497 kcal	149 kcal
Protein	7.0 g	2.1 g
Carbohydrate	67.0 g	20.0 g
of which sugars	19.2 g	5.7 g
starch	47.8 g	14.3 g
Fat	22.4 g	6.7 g
of which saturates	9.8 g	2.4 g
Fibre	3.0 g	0.9 g
Sodium	0.6 g	0.2 g

Energy. The amount of energy which the food will give you is measured in two ways: in joules (kJ) and in calories (kcal).

Protein. Most adults get more than enough protein for their body's needs: for more information see pages 76 to 81.

Fat. The total amount of fat (and oil) in the food. High intakes of fat, especially saturated fat, are linked with many health problems and can cause obesity. However, certain types of fat, such as the fat found in oily fish like salmon, are good for you: for more information see pages 81 to 84.

Fibre. Fibre helps prevent constipation and other bowel problems. Fruit and vegetables, beans and legumes, cereals and grains all contain fibre; the best sources are whole grains such as wholemeal bread and brown rice. For more information see pages 74 to 76.

Saturates. This type of fat may raise blood cholesterol levels, which can lead to heart disease. Saturated fat is found in meat and dairy foods and in cakes and biscuits made with butter or hydrogenated oil.

Guideline Daily Amounts

Official Government figures for average adults

Each day	Women	Men
Calories	2,000	2,500
Fat	70 g	95 g

These numbers are the same on every label. Based on 2,000 calories a day (an average calorie intake for women) the government suggests a total daily intake of about 70 g of fat: fat provides 9 calories per gram, so 70 g provides 630 calories, which is about 30 per cent of 2,000 calories.

tastiest and most nutritionally sound products I have found – and used – over the years.

You do need to set time aside for yourself to shop. While food shopping may not be glamorous, it can be fun. It doesn't have to take hours, especially if you have a list before you go that takes into consideration your meals and eating plan. One way of finding time is to employ a strategy many of my clients use: split up the shopping. For example, shop for a few essential items on Monday at a small local shop and go to the big supermarkets at the weekend. If you do a really big shop, you're OK for several days or even weeks. Take advantage of your freezer, your refrigerator and your cupboards. Fill them with healthy foods for all occasions, meals and snacks, and you'll have to go shopping less often.

The Internet can also be a boon. Several supermarkets offer online grocery shopping. Many have a wide variety of fresh fruits, vegetables, meats and fish, as well as wholegrain breads, cereals and pastas.

Food shopping may not seem like such a chore if you view it as an opportunity to start your food life off on the right foot each week. Take the time to read food labels. This way, you'll be sure that you're buying only those foods that fit into your eating plan. Nearly every packaged food now carries a 'Nutrition Information' label (see 'Anatomy of a Label'). This label tells you how much of certain nutrients a product contains; labels sometimes give additional information about vitamins and minerals.

A great way to get the children involved with the family's food life is to ask them to help you find new products that are good for them – and taste good. This is a great way to educate your children about nutrition. Take this opportunity to teach them about Nutrition Information labels.

Another way to make food shopping fun for children is to involve them directly. Before you go shopping, choose a recipe with your children, then shop for the ingredients together and get them to help you cook it. This helps to foster great eating habits early on. If we involve children in a good food life when they're young – by showing them how to shop and cook and eat – they will be healthier (and ultimately happier) children.

Finally, never go food shopping when you're hungry. This leads to overbuying and impulse buying (usually of the unhealthy foods that are at eye level, near the checkout). Have a small snack before you venture to the supermarket.

16. I Don't Know How to Cook (or I Don't Have Time to Cook)

▶ Are you too busy to cook?
▶ Are you scared of cooking?

▶ Do you think, 'Can I really cook myself a good meal late in the evening when I'm tired from work or a day running around with the children?'

▶ Do you read cooking magazines and watch cooking shows on TV and think, 'If I can't cook that way, I don't even want to try?'

A lot of people don't know how to cook. Or if they do, they can't find the time. Maybe they never had the opportunity to see home cooking in action or simply weren't interested in learning at the time. Whether you have a full-time job or course load or are a busy parent, carving out time to shop and cook can be a challenge.

Strategy: Cooking for yourself or your family doesn't have to feel like an overwhelming project. Even without much cooking experience, you can turn out quick, simple and delicious meals that are satisfying to your body and soul.

Cooking doesn't have to be hard. I've never taken a cooking lesson in my life, but I was able to learn how to cook by reading cookbooks (and making some mistakes). Once you try out a few simple recipes, you'll gain some confidence in your cooking skills – and a sense of empowerment over your food life. When you cook, you have control over the food you put on your plate and in your body. Cooking, like most things, takes a little preparation, patience and practice. But once you

start to confront your fears, you'll be amazed at what you can do. On page 186 you'll find a shopping list and strategies that will make your cooking life and food life easier.

If you lead a particularly fast-paced life, you might want to prepare food on the weekend that you can eat all week. Also, don't think that you need to prepare a three-course meal each night. I'm a big fan of simple, quick meals, such as Unfried Chicken Breasts (see recipe on page 311) with mixed sautéed vegetables. Or try a baked potato with tinned vegetarian chilli and a mixed salad. In chapter 15, there are many fast and tasty recipes to help get you started.

17. I Always Eat More When I'm with My Family

▶ Do holidays with your family make you eat more because you're served one calorie-packed meal after another?

▶ Does going out to eat with your family mean going to an all-you-can-eat buffet?

▶ Does your family say you're 'no fun' when you try to resist the family food traditions, so you always give in and eat?

▶ Do you take your family to fast-food restaurants since they're convenient and inexpensive and your children love them?

Families are great! We love them, need them and, for the most part, are lucky to be a part of them. But think about what brings us together most times – mealtime. We have so many traditions centred around food that it's hard and frustrating to have to think about what and how much you're putting into your mouth when you're just trying to have a good time with your family.

Strategy: There's no way around it: most family visits and meals are emotionally charged, so overeating at these times is common. But you can change your behaviour – especially if you're prepared. For example, if you're going to stay with the family, prepare ahead by writing down your meal plan before you leave – including what you'll eat for every meal and snack – and sticking to that plan.

A little less structured approach is to have a clear mental picture of your 'food intentions'. Know that the basis of your breakfasts, for example, will be whole grains, such as cereal or crackers and some low-fat protein, such as yogurt or low-fat cheese. Do this for all your meals: that way, you'll have a clearer plan for eating healthy foods at each meal, but you won't be tied down to a specific menu. Before the big family meal, exercise or go for a walk and visualise what you'll eat. Also, know that it's OK to change your food plan as you go along. If you're too rigid, you might inadvertently set yourself up for a downfall.

One good strategy is to eat what the family is eating – whether it's a celebration dinner, fast-food meal or all-you-can-eat buffet – but have half the portions. This isn't an easy task, but it really does work. When you have a fast-food meal order sanely: grilled chicken instead of a burger, a salad instead of chips.

If a meal will be served to you without your input, make sure you aren't starving when you sit down. This may mean that you eat before you go to your family meal. Try snacking on some 'free' foods (see the list on page 34) prior to the meal. These are foods you can eat mindlessly, since they're high in nutrition and low in calories. If you're reasonably full before you sit down, the food served to you isn't such a big deal. You can simply have a taste of it and not blow your eating plan. Also, try having just a small portion of meat or fish and fill the rest of your plate with lots of vegetables. That way, you're taking in fewer calories by bulking up on the veggies, but still satisfying your eating needs.

Finally: speak up. It may be difficult, but muster your courage to talk to whoever is preparing the feast. Tell that person that you'll bring foods that you can eat or ask to have less on your plate. And when you go out for a meal with your family, tell them you want to eat at a more healthy place with food that everyone can enjoy. Ask them to respect your food choices and amounts. It's your body, it's your food life.

18. I Eat When I'm Tired

❱ Do you eat to stay awake?

❱ When you're sleepy, do you overeat?

❱ Are you so tired you don't care what you eat?

Whether you're a student with deadlines, an overworked employee, an overextended parent of a teenager or a new parent of an infant, lack of sleep is an epidemic. On average we get only 6 hours of sleep a night, but adults actually need about 8 hours. Sleep deficiencies are bad enough, but they also lead to mindless overeating. Furthermore, recent studies suggest that people with poor sleeping habits are at a higher risk of developing diabetes.

Strategy: Though it might sound obvious, the key to dealing with this problem is to get enough sleep. (New mothers: I know from experience that this isn't always easy.) Everyone has his or her own sleep requirements, but generally, just trying to sleep more (and better) than you currently do is a good start. If you're one of those lucky people who can fit it in, try a 20-minute 'power nap'. A short nap will make you feel

Are You Sleep Deprived?

If you answer yes to four or more of the following questions, you're sleep deprived and need to get some shut-eye!

- Do you have problems waking up in the morning?
- Do you get really irritated with other people during the day?
- Do you get colds often (more than two in the past 6 months)?
- Do you fall asleep immediately after turning out the lights?
- Do you drink caffeine all day long to stay awake and have a cocktail at night to wind down from the day?
- Do you cancel social events or give up personal hobbies because you feel too tired for them?
- Do you have trouble focusing your eyes (or keeping them open) when you drive in the late afternoon or at night?
- Do you have trouble concentrating in the late afternoon and evening?
- When you go to the gym, do you feel too tired to have a good workout?
- At weekends, do you sleep in really late and/or take lots of naps?

Top 5 Drinks for Energy and Vitality

The next time your energy lags, reach for a cup of one of the following beverages. Consider it liquid energy!

- Water, water, water
- Green tea (hot or cold)
- Ginger tea (hot or cold)
- Sparkling mineral water with lemon or lime or a splash of orange or cranberry juice (make sure the water is low or no sodium)
- Chamomile tea (for certain individuals, chamomile tea can actually cause sleepiness, so test it out)

energised; a longer nap might make you groggy and grouchy.

Being low on B vitamins may be a cause for poor sleeping. B_6, in particular, is essential for the normal production of serotonin, a brain chemical that makes you feel calm and relaxed. Adequate amounts of folic acid and vitamin B_1 may also help you sleep better and increase your energy. If you're on a severely restrictive diet (less than 1,000 calories a day), you may be tired because you wake up hungry in the middle of the night (the most restful sleep tends to be continuous sleep). Making sure you consume enough calories for your body throughout the day may help you to sleep better.

Tiredness is also a symptom of both dehydration and iron deficiency. Make sure you're always well hydrated by drinking at least 8 glasses of water a day. Iron brings oxygen to your red blood cells and is important for growth, a healthy immune system and energy. Women, especially, are at risk of iron deficiency because iron is lost during menstruation. Try pumping up your eating plan with dark green, leafy vegetables, lean red meat and whole grains – all of which are excellent sources of iron – and see if that increases your energy levels.

If you're eating to stay awake, you might actually be eating because you're bored or stressed. If so, turn to Issue 8 and Issue 11 (see pages 35 and 42).

If you're exhausted in the evening, after you come back from college or work or after a day with the children, eat plenty of 'free' food (see the list on page 34). Also drink at least two glasses of water before you eat everything in sight. The water will help to fill you up and help prevent dehydration.

19. I'm a Fussy Eater

▶ Are the only vegetables you like sweetcorn, potatoes and peas?

▶ Do you think fish belong only in the sea (or an aquarium) and not on a plate?

▶ Do you always eat the same foods because they're 'safe' and you 'trust' them?

▶ Do you prefer 'plain' food without herbs or spices and live on meat, cheese and pasta?

Everyone has different tastes, preferences and food histories. While many people love all different types of food and all different types of cuisine, there are others who won't even look at certain dishes or food groups. They might have memories of being forced to eat something when they were children. They may have been fussy eaters all their lives. They might be able to tolerate certain foods only if they're drowned in sauce. Or they may avoid new foods because they're scared of how they taste or are sceptical that they can be prepared to taste delicious.

Strategy: Let's get back to basics: if you're in pursuit of a Real Food Life, you owe it to yourself to try to eat new things (assuming that you're not allergic to them, of course). You may be surprised by what you like. Eating a variety of foods is not only an amazing sensual pleasure, but a delicious and vital component of good health. If you have children, it also sets a good example for them to follow. Being fussy may not be a big issue now, but it could be in the long term. Are you always tired? Do you often get colds? Is your skin dry? Are you often moody? These conditions may be due to the food you eat – or, should I say, don't eat.

Learning to love vegetables, fish or whatever you don't currently eat may take some time if you've spent your life avoiding them, but start slowly and try something new every week or two. If you open your mind and palate, you can learn to love new foods and the benefits can be enormous. To get more comfortable with these foods order them in a restaurant to learn how a professional prepares them. Explore your local farmers' market or deli and ask the vendor for preparation tips. Also, refer to chapter 15 for lots of ideas for quick, easy and truly tasty dishes.

You might also consider taking a cooking class to become more comfortable preparing a wide variety of food. Cooking classes aren't available only at cooking schools; many colleges and community centres offer classes on vegetarian cooking or fish preparation, for example. And once you see an instructor effortlessly whip up a dish, you're sure to have the confidence to try it at home.

20. I Eat What My Children Eat (Yuck!)

▶ Do you always eat the same food as your children?

▶ Do you steal your children's food after they go to sleep?

▶ Do you 'snack' with your children and then eat with your adult partner?

New and veteran parents alike are often surrounded by more junk food than they could have imagined before they became parents. Children are growing machines and tend to eat all day long to keep up with their changing, hungry bodies. It's easy, then, for parents to become accustomed to eating with their children, which often means a round-the-clock schedule of snacks and meals.

Strategy: Did you know that eating a handful of your children's chips twice a week can lead to a 2 kg (4 lb) weight gain in a year? One way to crack the eating-your-children's-food dilemma is to limit the amount of junk food in your house. Also, find healthier foods that your children actually like and buy those foods. For example, instead of regular crisps, get baked crisps or, better yet, have low-fat cheese with crackers. Get sorbet instead of regular ice cream; buy chocolate-covered rice cakes instead of chocolate chip cookies.

Don't allow yourself to get in the habit of eating whatever your children left on their plates. Take the leftovers and save them for your children's next meal or simply throw them away. If you're cooking, make only enough food for that meal so there's no waste. (Or make extra and freeze the additional food for later.) Finally, eat when you feed your children instead of later – even if that's at 5 p.m.

21. I Eat More When I'm Out with Friends

▶ Whenever you get together with friends, does it seem to turn into an out-of-control eating festival?

▶ When you're with friends, do you succumb to peer pressure to eat?

▶ Do you devour the bread basket after you've had a few pre-dinner drinks?

▶ Do you and your friends order fried or other high-fat foods 'just to put something in your stomachs' while you're drinking?

▶ When you're at a party, do you find it hard to resist the nibbles?

▶ Have you ever lost control with your food after you've had a few drinks?

Food and friends go together. And when you add alcohol to the mix, things can get even more out of control. Just as alcohol lowers social inhibitions, it also lowers inhibitions with food. Eating at restaurants and going to dinner parties are inherently social activities. Whether you're a guest, a host or just one of the gang, when you're in a social situation, it's easy to overeat.

Strategy: Eating with friends is definitely hard. Most people tend to over-order or cook too much. In fact, researchers at Georgia State University found that when people eat with one companion, they eat 28 per cent more than if they were dining alone. When they eat with two companions, they consume 41 per cent more and when they eat with six or more companions, their consumption increases by a whopping 76 per cent. And you're at even greater risk of overeating when alcoholic beverages are part of the festivities, since alcohol stimulates your appetite and lowers your commitment to being smart about food.

Fortunately, smart eating doesn't mean you have to become a hermit. Before going out, verbalise or write down your food (and booze) intentions. If you're seeing friends who drink and you're prone to eating after you've had a couple, promise yourself that you'll have only one drink. Do drink plenty of water or soda water, though, since it will help fill you up and hydrate you.

The key to drinking is moderation; for women I'd recommend fewer than 1½ drinks daily and for men fewer than 2 drinks daily. The risks of drinking to excess – liver damage, high blood pressure, cancer and so on – aren't worth it.

Don't deny yourself food – this will cause you to feel deprived and you may very well binge when you get home. Before you go out with your friends, eat plenty of 'free' foods (see the list on page 34) or have a bowl of vegetable soup. If you do this, you won't be starving when you arrive, so you'll be less tempted to overeat. If you're sharing food, family-style, choose two or three dishes and serve yourself half-size portions (don't let anyone serve you); that way you will satisfy yourself physically and emotionally.

22. Love Wreaks Havoc with My Food

▶ When you first fall in love, do weight concerns seem to melt away?

▶ When you're in a new love relationship, do you lose your appetite?

▶ Do you and your partner shop for food, cook and eat together?

▶ Does your love life revolve around going out to eat?

▶ Do you show your affection by sharing sweets with your sweetie?

Ah, love. We look for it for years (sometimes decades) and when it finds us, we're elated. The side effects are great: we're energised, excited and busy and food no longer is a looming issue. The flip side of new-love weight loss, though, is the added pounds that often come with a long-term relationship, whether it be marriage, cohabitation or a committed partnership.

New love or old, lots of couples' lives together revolve around a shared love of food, including going out to restaurants and cooking and eating together. Sometimes women eat more because their partners eat larger portions. And often this leads to unwanted weight gains.

Strategy: Love works in mysterious ways and it can decrease your appetite temporarily. When you're in love, your brain releases feel-good endorphins that may help to decrease your appetite. Furthermore, being in love keeps your mind (and body) busy, so food becomes much less of an issue.

On the other hand, when things get comfortable between a couple, overeating often becomes a problem. We want to indulge, because food can make us feel special and, after all, food is an important part of our social lives. While overindulging on occasion is not a problem, when it becomes a daily habit, it can be detrimental physically and emotionally. Talk to your partner about your plans to have a better food life and ask for his or her help.

You need to create a plan of action for both of you every time you eat. Know your food intentions and visualise yourself eating healthily. If you two always go to a certain restaurant, continue to go, but have two starters instead of a starter and a full-size main course. Say no to pudding or share a pudding only once a week. Also, don't arrive at the restaurant starving; have a light snack before you leave so you can ignore the bread basket.

When you're cooking together, eat only half of the portion you would usually have (save the rest for the next day). This way, you've cooked together and can eat together, but you'll just eat less.

If your partner refuses to help you in your quest for a healthy food life, you must speak up and tell him or her that you need to take care of yourself and do what is best for you. If your partner still refuses to help even after you've asked for support, enlist a friend or other family member to be your Real Food Life support system.

23. Lunch Is My Downfall

▶ Is the only lunch option at your college or workplace a cafeteria filled with high-fat or unnourishing food choices?

▶ Do you use the vending machine as your lunch stop?

▶ Do you work out during lunch and skip eating?

▶ Do you get confused about what to eat when you're out to lunch?

Being a slave to college or work geography is

a drag. Perhaps your only lunch option is a cafeteria filled with greasy food or the only lunch place within miles is fast food or there's a variety of eating places nearby but you don't know what you should choose. Maybe your only lunch option is to order a takeaway and you wonder what your best choices are. Or maybe you are one of those people who think endless cups of coffee are all the lunch you ever need.

Strategy: Eating a good lunch is important – it keeps your blood sugar levels balanced, keeps your metabolism burning high, keeps you energised, helps you to focus your thoughts, cuts down on afternoon sweet cravings and keeps you from overeating at dinner.

An ideal lunch is heavier on protein such as fish, which is high in omega-3 fatty acids, the good kinds of fat or lean meat, such as chicken or lean beef. It also includes a small amount of grains and some vegetables. Eating a high-protein lunch can help increase your energy level because protein ups the level of the amino acid tyrosine, which has been found to increase alertness, vigilance and concentration.

A lunch high in carbohydrates has its pluses and minuses. Some people truly feel they have more energy after eating a meal with lots of carbohydrates such as bread, rice, pasta and starchy vegetables. While women are more prone to feeling tired after a carbo-hydrate-rich meal than men are, people of both genders feel more likely to want a nap after a bowl of pasta than after a roast beef sandwich. Recent studies show that eating a lot of carbohydrates may decrease alertness. Of course, this doesn't mean you should stop eating them – carbohydrates are important – but you shouldn't have a whole meal of them. Listen to your body and note how you feel after eating certain types of food for lunch.

Finally, avoid high-fat lunches such as a cheeseburger with French fries. They will just make you feel more tired because they increase the levels of tryptophan (mellow brain chemicals) in your blood.

For specific ideas on what to have for lunch, see page 206.

24. I'm a Vegetarian

▶ Have you adopted a vegetarian diet but aren't sure what you should eat?

▶ Are you concerned that if you don't eat meat, you won't get all the nutrients your body needs (especially if you're not yet an adult)?

▶ Are you a vegetarian but hate vege-tables?

▶ Is your meat-free diet causing you to be tired all the time?

▶ Are you worried that you won't be able to follow my eating plan if you're a vegetarian?

More and more people are becoming vegetarians. They may be sympathetic to the animal rights cause or to environmental concerns. Others simply don't like the taste of meat or they've read that being a vegetarian is good for them. But even people who adopt a vegetarian diet are sometimes confused about what they should eat.

Strategy: You can get a Real Food Life and be a vegetarian. There are loads of vegetarian options throughout this book.

Many people think vegetarian diets are great for weight loss, but this isn't necessarily true. A vegetarian diet can be high in fat and calories, particularly if you rely on full-fat

Vegetarian Sources of Protein

It shouldn't be hard to get the necessary protein your body needs each day when you have the following tasty vegetarian options.

- Fresh tofu, plain or flavoured (smoked, hot and spicy, and so on)
- Nuts and seeds (raw or roasted)
- Nut cutlets
- Quorn
- Soya mince
- Soya cheese
- Low-fat yogurt or low-fat soya yogurt
- Tofu sausages
- Tofu hot dogs
- Tofu slices
- Bean burgers
- Hummus
- Bean-based soups or dips
- Tinned beans, such as black-eyed beans, chickpeas and kidney beans
- Vegetarian baked beans
- Vegetarian chilli (Meridian Organic or supermarket-own brands)
- Quinoa (a high-protein grain)
- Mozzarella, Cheddar, ricotta or cottage cheese (low-fat preferably)
- Lentil Salad with Lemon and Feta (see recipe on page 284)
- Vegetarian Asian Tofu Sandwich (see recipe on page 299)

dairy products. By the same token, animal foods can be low in fat and calories and, when eaten moderately, can enhance your health. So don't become a vegetarian thinking it will help you to lose weight. Too many calories from *any* food will cause weight gain.

Getting enough protein is usually not a problem. The average person needs just 50 to 60 grams of protein a day – an amount that can easily be obtained even on a vegetarian diet. In recent years, increasingly more high-protein vegetarian foods have become available at supermarkets (see 'Vegetarian Sources of Protein' on page 59). If you're a 'vegetarian' who chooses to eat fish, know that fish is a great source of high-quality protein and is rich in good fatty acids (known as omega-3s) that are great for your hormonal system, your heart, your hair, and your skin and nails.

If you're tired all the time and you think it's due to your vegetarian diet, you may be anaemic and need more iron. Great vegetarian sources of iron include tofu; kidney, butter or black beans; Swiss chard; acorn squash; spinach; green peas; and strawberries. Eating foods high in vitamin C will help your body to absorb the iron in the foods you eat.

If you eat no animal products at all – no dairy, meat or fish – you will need to take a vitamin B_{12} supplement every day, because B_{12} is found only in animal sources. Lack of B_{12} causes fatigue, impaired mental function, a shorter attention span, moodiness, agitation and confusion. You should take a multivitamin as well. Personally, I believe everyone – vegetarian or not – should take a multivitamin daily.

PART 2

NUTRITION BASICS

CHAPTER 3

NUTRITIONAL BUILDING BLOCKS

Whenever I work with clients, I give them handouts on the basics of healthy eating and good nutrition. Consider this section to be those handouts, but with even greater detail. I think it's absolutely crucial to learn some basics about what makes up certain foods and drinks and why they're good for you or should be avoided.

I've always found that this information serves as a good background and reference tool when people begin developing Real Food Lives of their own. My clients have found that by becoming familiar with the information in this section and understanding how the human body uses the fuel it is given, they are better able to stick to their Real Food Life plans. As you work through

the 8-week Food Life Makeover Plan later in this book, you might want to refer back to this section occasionally in order to bolster your food knowledge and remind yourself of why you are making certain choices.

Water

Unlike the other items discussed in this chapter, water is not a food group per se, but it is essential for maintaining good health and well-being. Water is vital to us because it is involved in almost every function of our bodies, including transportation and absorption of nutrients, body temperature maintenance, circulation, digestion and waste excretion. Water is also necessary for lubricating joints and providing a protective cushion for the organs and tissues. While the human body can survive without food for 5 weeks, it cannot survive without water for more than 5 days.

Water is also vital because our bodies are made mostly of water. Men's bodies are composed of about 60 per cent water (that's about 50 litres or 11 gallons) and women's are about 53 per cent water. Women have less water than men because they have a higher percentage of body fat, and fat (about 23 per cent water) has less water than muscle tissue (about 73 per cent water).

Blood is made of about 90 per cent water. Blood transports nutrients to the muscles and carries away waste such as carbon dioxide and lactic acid. When you're not getting enough water, your blood volume drops, which keeps your body from functioning properly.

Perspiration accounts for much of the water your body uses. Sweat prevents the body from overheating. Muscles in motion produce heat and the body responds by sweating. The sweat then evaporates on the skin's surface and helps to cool the skin and muscles. Every day, the average person loses up to 455 ml (16 fl oz) of water through sweat (when not exercising); if you exercise, you can lose up to 2 litres (3½ pt) of water, depending on the intensity and duration of your workout.

Water also plays an important role in digestion and waste control. The water in saliva and gastric (stomach) fluids helps the body to digest food. And without enough water, the colon can't process fibre as well as it should. Fibre without enough water makes solid waste too bulky and concentrated to pass comfortably and is a primary cause of constipation. My clients know if they don't drink enough water, food becomes like cement in their digestive systems – a graphic image perhaps, but true.

Dehydration

Because our bodies are made mostly of water, even a little dehydration can be dangerous. If you lose just 1 per cent of your body's weight in water, it can impair bodily functions and can cause a variety of ailments, including kidney stones.

Thirst is not a good indication of your body's water needs; by the time you feel thirsty, you're already dehydrated. Strenuous exercise can interfere with your thirst mechanism, as can hunger, too much caffeine, taking laxatives or diuretics, and having a bout of diarrhoea. When you drink alcohol or excessive amounts of caffeinated drinks, both of which are diuretics, you may not realise how dehydrated you're becoming.

The best way to tell if you're well hydrated is to check the colour of your urine. If it is brightly coloured or deeply concentrated and is low in volume, you're probably

The Low-down on Water

Water, water, everywhere . . . but which kind should you drink? Tap water is the most convenient. But depending on where your water comes from, it could contain chemicals like chlorine and pesticides or impurities like bacteria and parasites. In some places fluoride is added to tap water to keep it clean, 'soften' it and protect against tooth decay. Some tap water is considered 'hard', which means it has a high concentration of calcium and magnesium, minerals that can affect the taste of the water.

Filtering can improve your tap water because the filter removes contaminants and makes the water cleaner and, ultimately, better tasting. I happen to like filtered water; it's a cheaper alternative to bottled water and is very convenient.

If you prefer drinking bottled water, here is a mini glossary to help you understand the differences among a variety of waters:

Natural mineral water contains several mineral compounds and comes from natural springs usually in the UK or Europe. Mineral water must flow freely from the source (that is, it can't be pumped or forced from the ground) and must be bottled at the source. If you drink mineral water exclusively and aren't mineral deficient, you might be taking in more minerals than your body needs or can use. However, many Europeans drink only mineral water and claim it helps aid digestion.

There is no legal definition for **spring water** and it may not actually come from a spring at all. But real spring water is unprocessed and originates in underground reservoirs that naturally rise to the earth's surface.

Sparkling water is water that is either naturally fizzy (generally from UK or other European mineral springs) or water to which carbon dioxide has been added to make it fizzy. Buy brands that have no or low sodium. Flavoured sparkling water may be made with sugars in addition to the flavouring agent, so always read the label. **Soda water** is filtered carbonated water that has added sodium in the form of bicarbonates, sodium citrates and/or sodium phosphates. If you're cutting down on salt, stick with sparkling water with no added sodium.

dehydrated. If it's almost clear and plentiful, you're probably well hydrated. (Bear in mind, however, that some vitamin supplements can make urine a darker yellow.)

How Much Water Do You Need?

I always tell my clients that water is instant energy. If you think of water this way, you'll want to drink it all day. If you're feeling tired or lethargic, a glass of water will often bring you back to life. That said, to keep your body functioning properly, you must drink at least eight 225-ml (8-fl oz) glasses or 2 litres (3½ pt) of water each day. If you are working out or feel bloated from eating a salty meal, go up to 12 to 14 glasses.

You don't have to drink only water to stay hydrated. Drinks that are equivalent to 100 per cent water are skimmed milk, fruit juice, hot chamomile or ginger tea, and decaffeinated hot coffee or tea. You can get 50 per cent water from caffeinated hot teas, such as black and green tea, as well as iced tea. Alcoholic drinks count against your water intake since they dehydrate you.

You can add to your daily water intake by eating foods that have a high water content. Check out 'High-water Foods' for a list of these foods.

Here are some strategies to help you get those 2 litres of water each day.

▶ Keep a large 600 ml (1 pt) glass of water by your bed. When you wake up, you can start drinking immediately.

▶ Carry a bottle of water around with you. This will make it easier to get your water while you're on the move and it's also a constant reminder to drink.

▶ Take bottled water with you in your car, especially if you're a commuter.

▶ Keep a bottle of water on your desk or near your work area and sip from it through-

High-water Foods

You can supplement your daily water intake by eating foods that have a high water content, but you still need to drink at least eight 225-ml (8-fl oz) glasses of water a day. Here are some of the most water-filled foods around. The number following each is the percentage of water that makes up each food.

Cucumbers: 96%	Honeydew melon: 91%
Lettuce: 95%	Cantaloupe melon: 90%
Summer squash (all varieties): 94%	Carrots: 88%
Tomatoes: 94%	Artichokes: 87%
Watermelon: 93%	Brussels sprouts: 87%
Asparagus: 92%	Oranges: 87%
Cauliflower: 92%	Peaches: 87%
Spring greens: 92%	Raspberries: 87%
Mushrooms: 92%	Apricots: 86%
Peppers: 92%	Blackberries: 86%
Strawberries: 92%	Blueberries: 85%
Broccoli: 91%	Porridge (made with half milk, half water): 81%
Grapefruit: 91%	Yogurt (natural, fat-free): 85%

out the day (and keep refilling the bottle all day long).

▶ Take a bottle of water to the gym – you'll drink more than you would if you relied on the water fountain.

▶ Log your water intake in your food journal. That way, you know how much you're drinking.

▶ Monitor your urine. You're looking for a heavy flow of light-coloured urine.

Carbohydrates

Carbohydrates should be an essential part of everyone's diet. Despite what gimmicky 'no-carb' diets proselytise, for the human body to function optimally, more than half of the foods you eat each day should be carbohydrates.

Carbohydrates are the major fuel source for human beings; they provide energy and help the body function properly. Carbohydrates are composed of carbon, hydrogen and oxygen and are found almost exclusively in plant foods like fruits, vegetables, beans and whole grains. They're even found in sugar cane. Milk and milk products are the only foods that come from animals that contain significant amounts of carbohydrates.

There are two main types of carbohydrates: simple and complex. Simple carbohydrates are sugars; complex carbohydrates are also referred to as starches and are found

in breads, grains, potatoes, peas, corn, rice, beans, pasta and cereals.

All carbohydrates are the primary source of blood glucose, also known as blood sugar, which is either used as energy immediately or stored in the liver or muscles for future use. Stored glucose is called glycogen. When the body needs more energy, glycogen is taken out of storage and converted back to glucose. It is a major source of fuel for the body's cells and is the preferred source of fuel for the brain and red blood cells.

Carbo-phobia?

The increasing popularity of high-protein/low-carbohydrate diets has given carbohydrates a bad reputation. People who have lost weight on these fad diets are afraid to eat any variety of carbohydrates because they fear they will 'get fat' from them.

High-protein/low-carb diets are usually extremely high in saturated fat, since the basis of this type of diet is meat and dairy. These high-protein diets overwork the liver and kidneys, dehydrate the body, leach calcium from the bones and may compromise the immune system.

These diets do often cause you to lose weight because calories are significantly reduced in the long term. The weight loss isn't particularly healthy, though, nor is it usually permanent. The glycogen stores of people on these diets diminish as their bodies

The Glycaemic Index

Every carbohydrate food has a different effect on blood sugar levels and that effect is measured by the glycaemic index (GI). The index measures how quickly a food is digested, turned into glucose and absorbed into the blood – basically how much a certain food causes blood glucose levels to rise. The higher the glycaemic index of a food, the faster the glucose is released into the bloodstream and the greater the outpouring of insulin. (Insulin is a hormone that controls the transport of glucose from the blood into cells.) Foods with a high glycaemic index quickly enter the bloodstream and are quickly converted to blood sugar (that is, they provide fast energy that fades fast); foods with a moderate or low glycaemic index enter the bloodstream more slowly and provide longer-lasting energy.

Most people don't have to be too concerned with the glycaemic index of foods. While many diet books are based on the premise that if the body produces too much insulin it causes the person to store fat, there is no scientific evidence to prove this. Studies have revealed, however, that a diet high in foods high on the glycaemic index may lower HDL (good) cholesterol and increase the risk of diabetes, especially if someone is predisposed to diabetes already.

The index values shouldn't be too much of a concern for most of us, however, because they're calculated for individual foods, eaten alone. For example, potatoes are high on the index when eaten alone. But when they're eaten with a meal, they'll have much less of an effect on blood sugar because the meal will necessarily contain fat and protein, and will affect the glycaemic index of the potatoes.

try to maintain the blood glucose levels needed for proper body functioning. During this process, a lot of water is lost through urine as the glycogen storage tanks become depleted. This process happens fast and dieters love what they see on the scales. However, since the weight loss is mostly water weight, especially in the beginning of the diet, it is always regained when the dieter begins to eat carbohydrates again.

Another reason people lose weight on these diets is because they're required to eat the same high-protein (and generally high-fat) foods all the time, so they literally become uninterested in eating. As a result, they will consume less than usual. Also, the body is more satiated with high-fat foods, but a high-fat diet can lead to high cholesterol and blood pressure levels. I am against any type of diet that requires people to forego an entire category of food and that has the serious health implications of high-protein/low-carb diets.

What Kind of Carbohydrates Should You Eat?

Over half of your daily calories should come from a variety of unrefined, or minimally processed, carbohydrates. Good choices include any carbohydrate that's as close to nature as possible, such as whole grains and fresh fruits and vegetables. Oranges, strawberries, peaches and sweet potatoes are particularly high in carbs. A diet rich in these foods has lots of B vitamins, minerals, fibre, antioxidants and phytochemicals. Even if you take a vitamin supplement, it can't compete with the benefits of eating these wholesome foods.

Refined carbohydrates, such as those found in biscuits, sweets, processed cereals, white bread and white rice, on the other hand, often lack the nutrients crucial to good health. Refined carbohydrates can also be high in saturated fats and trans fats. Eating too many refined carbohydrates can ultimately increase your risk of diet-related diseases including diabetes, hypoglycaemia, cancers, heart disease and obesity.

Complex Carbohydrates

Complex carbohydrates are elementally different from simple carbohydrates. An easy way to think about it is that complex carbohydrates are made of three or more sugars and simple carbohydrates contain two or less. In addition, complex carbs tend to be lower in fat than simple carbs. Beans, legumes, potatoes, rice and whole grains are all rich in complex carbohydrates. Here's a quick rundown of two of the biggest sources.

Grains. Whole grains are a great energy-providing carbohydrate because they're instant fuel for the muscles. Grains are the seeds or 'fruits' of cereal grasses and, in their unrefined form, contain fibre, unsaturated fat, protein, iron, niacin, thiamin and riboflavin. Refined grains (like those in white bread) have the bran removed. If you want the health benefits of bran, especially the fibre, you need to eat whole grain products. Studies have shown that people who eat a higher-fibre diet tend to weigh less than people who don't. Most likely this is because high-fibre foods fill people up, so they tend to be satisfied with less food. These foods also tend to be low in fat and calories. Some tasty whole grains are bulgar (cracked wheat), quinoa, buckwheat, pearl barley and brown rice.

Beans. I usually count beans as a serving of protein in my daily eating plan. It's important to remember, however, that they are also an excellent source of complex carbohydrates and have plenty of soluble fibre (4 to 7 grams per 100 grams), which may help lower cholesterol and may prevent or control heart disease and diabetes. Studies show that 110 to 225 grams (4 to 8 oz) of beans eaten daily can significantly reduce blood cholesterol levels and control blood sugar in people with diabetes. Beans are a great source of vitamins including thiamin, riboflavin, niacin and folate, and minerals including calcium, iron,

(continued on page 72)

LIVING A REAL FOOD LIFE

How Susan Learned the Truth about Carbohydrates

Name: Susan

Real Food Life Issues: Put on weight after moving in with boyfriend, high-protein diet/fear of carbohydrates

Susan is a computer programmer in her late twenties. She works hard but cherishes her time off, when she can relax with her boyfriend and their dog, a sweet black and brown mongrel named Otis. She was thrilled when she moved in with her boyfriend two years ago, but she has gained about 4.5 kg (10 lb) since then – that hasn't thrilled her much. Here's where I found her:

27 January

OK, I know I have to do something about my diet. I'm craving carbohydrates so badly, it's got to the point where Otis's dry food is looking good to me. Every time I pass the bakery section at the supermarket, I feel like I'm going to pass out with bread lust.

On this score, Jason is no help. I tell him I miss carbs and he brings home a giant bag of tortilla chips and a vat of salsa. He thinks that's helping! He's a sweetie, but I feel like crying in frustration. I'm still struggling with these last 10 pounds and I feel like I'm one chip away from blowing up into a ball of fat and bloat.

Jason thinks an all-meat diet is as close to heaven as we're going to get. As close as we've become, I don't think he wants to hear about how my toilet visits have become few and far between lately. For the first time in my life, I'm actually craving things like raw broccoli and cabbage. Oh, to eat something crunchy!

When I met Susan, she hadn't regularly eaten fruit, vegetables or whole grains for months. While she lost a few pounds on high-protein/low-carbohydrate plans, they were not the miracle diets she read about and was hoping for. On top of that, eating almost no carbs, simple or complex, caused her to experience major mood swings. She also had lower energy levels, constipation and slight depression, and she felt that she hadn't had a good, focused, strong workout in months.

Since most of her diet consisted of meat, fish and cheese, she began feeling physically ill at the sight of these foods. Also, she would have obsessive, uncontrollable urges for doughnuts and crisps. She would then end up bingeing – eating an entire loaf of French bread or large bag of crisps at one sitting. Because she read about the 'evils of carbohydrates', she was scared to eat them. She believed if she started eating carbs, they would make her put on more weight. Nevertheless, she missed fruit and vegetables and was ready to add them back into her diet. That's why she found me.

The first thing I did with Susan was re-educate her about the basics of a nourishing food plan. I explained that the body needs carbohydrates and cannot function properly without fruit, vegetables and whole grains. I told her that she couldn't get her requirement of vitamins and minerals, much less important antioxidants and phytochemicals, without fresh produce in her diet. We worked hard to dispel her fears about carbohydrates and endeavoured to add them back into her diet gradually.

Susan started off by adding one piece of fruit, a slice of wholegrain bread and a serving of vegetables to her daily diet. She did this for a week, but the bulk of her diet was still protein. The following week, she added more carbohydrates to her daily eating plan. Slowly, she continued upping the amounts of fruit, vegetables and whole grains she ate, until she was eating a healthier balance of protein and carbohydrates.

Susan started eating more essential fatty acids, too. She also started cutting back on fattier cuts of meat and full-fat dairy foods. Susan had got used to the taste of whole milk, but she found that cutting back to semi-skimmed wasn't that bad and soon she drank skimmed effortlessly. She replaced the hamburgers she had been eating with veggie or turkey burgers and started eating the buns as well. She ate fish a few times a week for the omega-3s as well as its clean taste. By week 4, she experienced fewer mood swings and had more energy. She noticed that her workouts were feeling better, that she was stronger when she lifted weights and had more stamina on the rowing machine.

By week 8, Susan was noticeably less depressed and less obsessed with food. She realised she had missed carbohydrates and that they did make her feel better. Since she was more educated about her food choices, she was able to pick foods that her body really wanted. Subsequently, she got over the constipation and did not put on weight. In fact, after 8 weeks, she found that she had lost the weight she had put on since moving in with her boyfriend.

copper, zinc, phosphorus, potassium and magnesium. Beans are also a great anti-cancer food because they contain phyto-oestrogens. Soyabeans, in particular, are extremely rich in the phyto-oestrogen isoflavone, which may decrease the risk of certain hormone-dependent cancers like breast and prostate cancer.

In addition, beans are a good source of protein. Soyabeans are unique in that they're a complete protein. To make other beans even more nutritious, eat them with (or within a few hours of) whole grains. (See page 76 for more on protein.)

If you avoid eating beans because you're afraid they're going to cause flatulence, there's a simple solution. Just add a few drops of a product called Beano to the bean dish. Beano is an enzyme that helps the body digest the sugars found in beans that lead to this problem. If you can't find Beano, the way you prepare beans can also eliminate this problem. First, soak beans for 4 to 5 hours, then drain and throw out the water. Add fresh water – 2 litres (3½ pt) to 450 g (1 lb) of beans – and boil for 10 minutes; simmer for half an hour and throw out the water again. If the beans need more cooking, add fresh water and cook until soft. Don't worry; this cooking process won't harm the nutrients. You can also use tinned or frozen beans to save time on cooking. Just rinse them well to reduce the sodium level.

Simple Carbohydrates

Simple carbohydrates are made up of short chains of only one or two sugars. They're also referred to as simple sugars and include fructose (fruit sugar), sucrose (table sugar) and lactose (milk sugar). Fresh, frozen or dried fruit is one of the most healthy sources of simple carbohydrates.

Sucrose. We all love our sugar, but it's a love that could lead to obesity. The consumption of sugar in the UK, for example, has taken a massive leap in the past 180 years. In the 1820s, each person consumed a mere 2 teaspoons of sugar daily. Today, the average person takes in a whopping 20 teaspoons daily.

The Dietary and Nutritional Survey of British Adults shows that major contributors of sugar to the adult diet are table sugar, confectionery and preserves (29 per cent), cereal products including cakes, biscuits and puddings (23 per cent) and soft drinks (17 per cent).

The average person drinks 310 cans of soft drinks each year. With 4 teaspoons per can, that's 1,240 teaspoons of sugar from soft drinks alone.

A recent study in the US found that if a child increased his or her soft drink consumption by just one extra drink per day, the child was 60 per cent more likely to become obese later in life. These researchers concluded that the body may have trouble adapting to intense concentrations of sugar taken in liquid form.

People are usually less concerned with the amount of sugar in their diets than the amount of fat. Just look at the boom in fat-free sweets on the market. But it's dangerous to think that sugar is innocent when it's not accompanied by lots of fat. Ironically, most fat-free foods contain more calories than regular-fat foods, because they substitute sugar for fat. Eating these products could lead to weight gain, since every 3,500 calories that go unused by the body turns into 450 g (1 lb) of fat. Consuming large amounts of sugar is not only bad for your teeth, but it may well be a factor in the development and progression of obesity. Sugar is also linked to premenstrual syndrome, food cravings, fatigue, depression and seasonal affective disorder (SAD).

Make sure you look at the Nutrition Information label on food. If the product is high in sugar it should be avoided or eaten only occasionally. (Note: If you have diabetes, your doctor or dietitian will probably give you an eating plan that is different to the one described in this chapter.)

The UK Department of Health recommends that you limit your added sugar intake to no more than 9 teaspoonfuls a day if you eat 1,800 calories or 12 teaspoonfuls a day if you eat 2,200 calories. What this means is that added sugar should constitute around 11 per cent of your total daily calories. Currently, 17 per cent of the average adult's daily calories come from added sugar.

Lactose. For the past few years, lactose has been enmeshed in controversy. Many adults suffer serious stomach problems such as bloating, wind, diarrhoea and cramps when they consume dairy foods containing lactose. Tummy troubles arise because many adults stop producing lactase, the enzyme needed to digest lactose. While most Northern Europeans and their descendants produce lactase for their whole lives, many Asians and Africans and their descendants stop producing lactase after infancy.

If you think you suffer from lactose intolerance, you can try Lactaid (a dietary supplement that helps the body process lactose), drink lactose-free milk or substitute soya products for dairy ones. There are many soya foods available at the supermarket that resemble dairy foods and taste very much like their dairy counterparts. Try soya milk, soya yogurt and soya cheese. Try to make sure that the soya foods have had the bone-strengthening mineral calcium sulphate added to them, so that you get all the benefits you would if you had the dairy foods. If you don't think you're getting enough calcium from your diet, try a supplement. (For more information on calcium, see page 102.)

Fibre

Dietary fibre is a crucial part of our diet. It's a form of carbohydrate (often referred to as roughage) that comes from the structural part of fruits, vegetables, grains and other plant foods. We're unable to digest dietary fibre. Most fibre travels through the gastrointestinal tract and ends up in the stool.

There are two types of dietary fibre: insoluble and soluble fibre. Most plant foods contain both types of fibre in varying amounts. Insoluble fibre doesn't dissolve in water, thus it attracts and retains water in your intestinal tract. This increases the bulk of stools and makes them softer and easier to eliminate. Insoluble fibre is found in high amounts in wheat bran and other whole grains. Soluble fibre forms a gel in water that helps to bind acids and cholesterol in the intestinal tract, preventing their reabsorption into the body. This may be why soluble fibre helps to lower cholesterol levels (and decreases the risk of heart disease) and also maintains steady blood sugar (glucose) levels. Soluble fibre is found in oats and oat bran, barley, brown rice, beans, apples, carrots and most other fruits and vegetables.

Why Do You Need Fibre?

Even though fibre is not digested per se, it still has vital health benefits. Fibre may reduce the risk of colon cancer by either combining with or diluting cancer-causing agents or altering the natural bacteria of the intestines. Fibre also speeds up the rate at which stools pass through the body, keeping the digestive tract clean and healthy and preventing constipation and haemorrhoids.

Fibre-rich foods tend to be bulky and lower in fat and calories. These foods help with weight control because they're naturally filling and they're chewy, so they take longer to eat. This will make you less likely to overeat and you will feel fuller longer.

Complex carbohydrates are usually high in fibre and are great choices for active people needing high-endurance, long-burning foods. The carbohydrates provide the fuel needed to power the muscles used during activity. This is why low-carb diets aren't helpful. Foods with a lot of soluble fibre, such as oatmeal, lentils and pasta, become great sources of long-term fuel because they release sugar into the bloodstream slowly. Fibre can enhance stamina during a marathon, a long bike ride or any endurance activity.

How Much Fibre Do You Need?

For the greatest health benefits, adults should consume at least 18 to 25 grams of fibre each day. Most of us consume just a third to a half of this recommended amount. It is especially important for elderly people and pregnant women to consume plenty of fibre (along

High-fibre Foods

With delicious foods like those listed below, there's no reason why getting more fibre in your diet needs to be unpleasant! All of the following are excellent sources of dietary fibre.

Cereals. Breakfast cereals are a quick and easy source of fibre. By eating a variety of grains such as wheat, corn, oats and rice, you'll get both soluble and insoluble fibre. Mixing cereals is a way of adding a variety of tastes and fibres to your meal or snack. Try 1 bowl (approximately 40–50 g/1½–2 oz) of any of the following: All-Bran (11 grams of fibre), Bran Flakes (6 grams), Shredded Wheat Spoon Size (4.5 grams), Weetabix (3.8 grams), Quick Quaker Oats (2.8 grams), Puffed Kashi (2 grams).

Fruits. Fibre is usually concentrated in the skin and outer layer of the fruit, so opt for fruit with edible skins and seeds. Try one kiwifruit (5 grams of fibre), pear (4.5 grams), orange (4 grams) or apple (2.5 grams); 150 g (5 oz) of blackberries (7 grams) or raspberries (6 grams); or two figs (4 grams).

Vegetables. Vegetables with edible skins are the best high-fibre choices, but almost every vegetable has a decent fibre content. The difference between raw and cooked is minor. Try 2 servings of winter squash (6 grams), kale (5 grams), broccoli (4 grams), spinach (4 grams), carrots (3.5 grams), cauliflower (3 grams) or green beans (3 grams).

Breads and crackers. Those with the most fibre are made from wholegrain flours; check the ingredients list. Be aware that most breads contain moderate amounts of fat, so if you're following a low-fat diet, check the label and choose breads with a lower fat content. Brands of high-fibre bread to look for include: Allinsons Hi Bran (2.9 grams of fibre per slice), Kingsmill Crusty Wholemeal (2.9 grams), Allinsons Wholemeal (2.7 grams), Hovis Hearty Wholemeal (2.6 grams). As for crackers, I recommend Finn Crisps (1.9 grams per slice), Ryvita Multigrain (1.8 grams) and Ryvita Dark Rye (1.7 grams).

Beans and legumes. The following are all tops in fibre (per 50 g/2 oz, uncooked): kidney beans (10 grams), chickpeas (7 grams), lentils (4.5 grams), split peas (4.5 grams).

Snacks. Try 40 g (1½ oz) or 3 large handfuls of unsalted and unsugared popcorn (4.5 grams of fibre), or a handful of pistachio nuts (2 grams), or 40 g (1½ oz) dried fruit (amount of fibre varies, but generally it's high).

with adequate fluid) because of their tendency towards constipation.

It's best to increase your fibre intake gradually so that your stomach has time to adjust. Expect softer and more frequent bowel movements. You may also notice that you become a bit more 'windy' – this is natural and a sign that you're getting adequate fibre from your diet. Since fibre acts like a sponge and attracts water into the intestines, drinking plenty of water – at least eight 225-ml (8-fl oz) glasses a day – is important to keep the stool soft. Too little water combined with increased fibre can result in constipation.

The best way to get the fibre you need is from foods, not from laxatives or stool softeners. The most sensible way to increase your fibre is to eat a variety of fibre-rich foods including fruit, vegetables, beans and whole grains. Try to eat these foods as close to their natural state as you can (that includes keeping skins on fruit and vegetables where possible), since a lot of fibre gets lost through processing (including juicing). Dried fruits are good because they offer concentrated fibre compared to their fresh counterparts.

Protein

Protein is an essential building block of life. It's also one of the most satisfying food groups you can eat. Most Westerners get their proteins in the form of meat and dairy, but there are other, more healthy protein choices that you should try to work into your diet.

Why Do You Need Protein?

Every organism in our world – from the tiniest microbe to the largest animal – is made of protein. Protein is the primary building material for the brain, heart, muscles, blood, skin, hair and nails, and it's essential for growth and development.

Proteins help the body to regulate water balance, aid in the formation of hormones and enzymes that control the metabolism, help maintain skin moisture levels and regulate skin pigment. Antibodies – an important part of the immune system – also require protein to function properly.

Protein is made up of 22 different amino acids. When protein is metabolised, it gets broken back down into amino acids. Some amino acids are termed 'non-essential'. This doesn't mean that they aren't important; it simply means that the body can produce them from other amino acids, so they don't need to come from the diet. Other amino acids are termed 'essential', which means the body can't produce them and they must come from the foods we eat.

When the body builds muscle or makes cells, it needs a variety of amino acids. If the body is chronically low in amino acids (which will happen if a diet is deficient in essential amino acids), it can't function properly. This is why it's important to consume foods that contain all the essential amino acids.

Complete or Incomplete?

Proteins can be divided into two groups depending on the amino acids they contain:

Top Tips to Strengthen Your Nails

Have you been hiding your hands so no one sees your broken, jagged fingernails? Do you have white bands across your nails? Read on for ways to pamper your nails.

- Protein provides building material for new nails and prevents white bands across the nails, so to have good nails, you need to consume an adequate amount of protein. Be sure you're getting enough meat, eggs, soya foods or tofu.
- Vitamin C helps prevent hangnails. Try berries, citrus fruits, broccoli and peppers.
- Vitamin A and calcium help prevent dry and brittle nails. Try eating some carrots, peaches, squash, low-fat dairy foods, dark green, leafy vegetables or tinned fish.
- The B vitamins – including folate and B_{12} – help strengthen nails and prevent ridges and dryness. Eat some asparagus, barley, bran, root veggies, sea vegetables, eggs, seafood or soya foods.
- Zinc helps prevent white spots. Eat some lean meat, legumes, mushrooms, oysters or whole grains.
- Essential fatty acids – found in pumpkin seeds, walnuts, flaxseed, and fish and fish oils – help to nourish the nails.

complete proteins or incomplete proteins. Complete proteins – also referred to as high-quality proteins – contain plenty of the essential amino acids and are found most readily in animal products like eggs, meat, poultry, fish and dairy products; tofu and other soyabean products are pretty much the only non-animal sources of complete proteins.

Incomplete proteins contain only some of the essential amino acids. Sources include beans, peas and other legumes, grains and green leafy vegetables. In the past, it was thought that incomplete proteins needed to be combined with other complementary (incomplete) protein foods in the same meal to make them complete. But now we know that if you eat incomplete proteins at different meals, your body is usually able to make complete proteins using its store of bacteria found in the digestive tract. Your body will take care of the food combining it needs to do to get the maximum amount of nutrients from the food you eat.

How Much Protein Do You Need?

The risk of protein deficiency is almost non-existent in the Western diet. Even pregnant women and athletes are not usually at risk of protein deficiency, since a balanced food intake provides plenty of protein. Growing children, women who are breastfeeding and people recuperating from major injury or illness typically require a little more protein, but even they can usually get it from a normal diet.

Fifteen to 20 per cent of your daily calories should come from proteins. The average person really needs only 50 to 60 grams of protein per day, with 100 grams as the ceiling. That means you need no more than 200 to 225 grams (7 to 8 oz) of protein-rich foods a day.

Animal Protein

Meat and poultry. Our bodies absorb certain nutrients, such as iron and zinc, better when they come from meat than from plant foods. Women, in particular, tend to be low in these minerals, so eating moderate amounts of meat can be beneficial. On the other hand, diets that are very high in animal proteins tend to be lower in phytochemicals and fibre (both of which come from plant-based foods) and can lead to diet-related diseases. The bottom line? If you choose to eat meat, stick to moderate amounts. Remember that most people need no more than 225 grams (8 oz) of protein-rich foods each day. Also, since meat is loaded with protein, eat it with a lot of veggies to be sure you're getting adequate amounts of phytochemicals and fibre and a wide variety of nutrients.

If you eat meat, you should look for the leanest cuts available. Chicken breast and turkey breast, both with the skin removed, are good poultry choices. Fillet and sirloin steak are my favourite lean cuts of beef.

Dairy. Dairy foods like yogurt, milk and cheese are nutritional powerhouses. They're great sources of high-quality protein and are rich in minerals and vitamins like calcium, zinc, magnesium, phosphorus, vitamins A, D and K, and some B vitamins. Dairy foods are very high in the amino acid lycine, which plant foods lack, so the protein in dairy complements the protein in plant-based foods like legumes and grains.

When choosing dairy foods, stick with low-fat or fat-free options. These products have as much protein and calcium as their full-fat counterparts but are, of course, much lower in saturated fats (which are directly related to higher blood cholesterol levels). I often buy organic dairy products: they're much more flavoursome and 'richer'-tasting than conventional dairy products and there's the added peace of mind of knowing that they're free of chemicals.

Eggs. Eggs are a great source of high-quality protein and nutrients, but they are high in cholesterol. A single large egg contains 6 grams of protein, 5 grams of fat (most of it unsaturated), good amounts of vitamins B_{12} and E, riboflavin, folate, iron and phosphorus, but two-thirds of the daily recommended amount of cholesterol. If eaten occasionally (no more than 5 a week), eggs won't raise your cholesterol levels. Egg whites, though, are fat-free and cholesterol-free and are still an excellent source of protein – so feel free to enjoy as many egg whites as you like. Just be sure that you always cook eggs (both the whites and the yolks) thoroughly before eating them.

As for egg substitutes and pasteurised bottled egg whites, they're quick and easy, but I prefer eating things closer to nature, such as fresh whole eggs or fresh egg whites.

Fish. Fish is an excellent source of high-quality protein and certain varieties contain omega-3 fatty acids (a good kind of fat). Studies have shown that in countries where fish is a mainstay of the diet, people tend to be healthier and live longer. Fish is also high in water content, so it helps to flush you out, makes you feel full without feeling 'stuffed', and keeps you feeling satisfied longer. Varieties of fish that are high in both protein and omega-3 fatty acids include salmon (smoked salmon is fine if there are no additives), tuna (including tinned varieties packed in water), herring, sardines, mackerel, trout, anchovies and shellfish.

Plant Protein

Grains. The United States is one of the largest producers of grains in the world, but the grains harvested there contribute to only a quarter of the calories in the American diet. More than half the grains grown there are used for animal feed. In Asia, on the other hand, grains (in the form of rice) make up 65 per cent of the citizens' diet and in less developed countries, grains constitute 80 to 85 per cent of the diet.

Grains are a good source of low-fat protein. Barley, quinoa, rye, wholemeal bread, buckwheat noodles and spaghetti (made from semolina flour) are all good grain sources of protein, especially if you bulk up dishes with beans.

Beans/legumes. Beans, too, are a good source of low-fat protein. The most filling way to enjoy them is with grains or flour products, such as rice and beans, tortillas and fat-free refried beans or pasta and bean soup. Beans are also cholesterol-free and high in complex carbohydrates and fibre. They come in a huge variety of sizes, shapes and colours, but most are nutritionally similar. Dried beans are often referred to as legumes (which are defined as vegetables

Jumping for Soya

Soyabeans and foods made from soyabeans are 'super foods'. They're the only plant-based food equivalent to animal products in terms of protein quality. Soyabeans are packed with energy-producing complex carbohydrates and B vitamins, zinc, potassium, magnesium and iron. They're also loaded with fibre – 50 grams (2 oz) of dried soyabeans have an amazing 11 grams of fibre. Their calcium levels can hardly be beaten either, with 29 milligrams of calcium per 25 grams (1 oz). (Fat-free milk has 38 milligrams per 25 ml/1 fl oz.) They contain 9 grams of fat in a cooked 110 gram (4 oz) serving, but it's the good, unsaturated kind.

Soya foods contain isoflavones – phytochemicals that have hormonal effects and may protect people from certain cancers. Soya also contains a huge amount of anti-cancer compounds called phyto-oestrogens (plant-based oestrogens), which may raise natural oestrogen levels in menopausal women and lower high oestrogen levels in younger women. The high fibre in soya also may lower cancer risks. Some studies have shown that isolated soya proteins are helpful in preventing osteoporosis and heart disease and may help with symptoms of menopause.

To get the fullest benefits of soya, try to take in at least 40–50 grams (1½–2 oz) of soya foods each day. By upping the amount of soya in your diet, you'll also increase your intake of fibre, phytochemicals and omega-3 fatty acids (which protect against heart disease and other diseases). When you increase your soya intake, you'll probably lower your saturated fat intake because by eating more soya protein, chances are you'll be eating less animal protein.

Soyabeans are among the oldest cultivated crops, dating back about 10,000 years. They have

that grow in pods), and include black beans, butterbeans, chickpeas, kidney beans, split peas and lentils.

Beans are a good source of water-soluble vitamins such as thiamin, riboflavin, niacin and folate. These vitamins are stored in the body only for a short time and then quickly excreted through urine, so you need to take in water-soluble vitamins on a daily basis. Tinned beans tend to be lower in these vitamins due to processing, but they still provide a good amount. Be sure to rinse tinned beans very well (in a bowl of cold water for 3 to 5 minutes), which will help remove the excess salt. All beans – tinned or freshly prepared – are also a very good source of minerals such as calcium, iron, copper, zinc, phosphorus, potassium and magnesium.

Nuts and seeds. Nuts and seeds are tasty and healthy. They provide good amounts of protein, fibre, iron, potassium, calcium, magnesium, zinc, copper, selenium, vitamin E and B vitamins. But despite their deliciousness, they are too high in fat to be a primary source of protein. When eating nuts and been a staple food in Asian diets for centuries. Today, soya is available in a huge variety of forms, including tofu, miso, soya milk, soya cheese and soya yogurt.

When the by-product of soya milk is dried, it forms the basis of mock meat products like soya burgers, soya hot dogs and soya 'chicken'. When a culture is added to cooked soyabeans, it binds them into solid cakes called tempeh, which can then be flavoured and used like meat. Roasted soyabeans are the basis of a very new product called soya nuts, which are a tasty nibble and have much more omega-3 than peanuts do. Soya has also recently become an important ingredient in some baby foods.

A great new way to get children (or even adults) to eat their soya is with fresh soyabeans – sometimes called edamame. They're available whole (in their pods) or shelled frozen (boil either variety for 5 minutes). Occasionally, you can find fresh soyabeans at specialist Asian food shops (they still require a 5-minute boil). They're a healthy, earthy-tasting snack. (They taste similar to green beans.) In their whole form, they're fun to eat since you scrape the beans out of their pods much as you would with peanuts and children, particularly, think this is great fun. But they're easier to use if you buy them already shelled.

Soya milk is a great addition to your eating plan. Soya milk is wholesome and nutritious and mixes well with other flavours – it's especially good in shakes and smoothies. Experiment with the different flavours available, but make sure the brand you buy is processed with calcium sulphate, so you get all the calcium benefits you would if you used cow's milk.

seeds, enjoy them sparingly – no more than a handful or so each day.

Protein Supplements

In my opinion, protein bars are expensive, glorified sweets. I also believe that protein powders and supplements are a complete waste of money. Most Westerners get more than enough protein from their regular diets and don't need extra. If you enjoy protein shakes, however, an occasional one will do no harm. Just be sure to buy a soya-based one with 100 calories or fewer per scoop.

Fats

In the past 10 years, there has been a lot of noise made that people should reduce the amount of fat in their diets or eliminate it completely, since saturated fats are associated with an increased risk of heart disease. The truth is, though, that the human body requires fat to function properly. Fat acts as an intestinal lubricant and protects the internal organs. It also helps generate body heat and helps to absorb the fat-soluble vitamins A, D, E and K – without fat, we would be deficient in these vitamins.

All cell membranes are composed of fat, as are the myelin sheaths that protect nerve fibres. Infants and children need fat for brain development and adults need fat throughout their lives for energy and growth. In fact, fat is the most concentrated energy source available to the body.

Dietary fat makes foods taste delicious; without it, food would be less tender and flavoursome, since fat is a flavour carrier. Fats also delay the emptying of the stomach, so they keep you feeling satisfied and 'full' longer. Of course, excessive fat intake and eating the wrong types of fat are major factors in high cholesterol (see page 84) and blood pressure, obesity, heart disease, colon cancer and diabetes.

What Kinds of Fat are Healthiest?

Fats are made up of building blocks called fatty acids. There are three main categories of fatty acids: saturated, monounsaturated and polyunsaturated. These classifications are based on the number of hydrogen atoms within the chemical structure of the fatty acid itself.

Saturated Fatty Acids

Saturated fats are fats that are solid at room temperature and get harder as they chill. They're usually found in animal products such as dairy foods, including whole milk, cream, butter and cheese, and meats such as beef, lamb and pork (the marbling of fat that makes meat so tasty is pure saturated fat). There are some plant-based saturated fats, too, notably palm kernel oil, coconut oil and white vegetable fat.

The liver uses saturated fat to make cholesterol, so eating foods with too much saturated fat can increase cholesterol levels, especially low-density lipoproteins (LDL) – the bad cholesterol. Even more than the cholesterol content, it's important to pay close attention to the saturated fat content in food.

Not all saturated fats are alike, however. Stearic acid, a saturated fat found in both meat and chocolate, doesn't raise your LDL cholesterol but can increase the risk of blood clots. The saturated fat that does the most physical harm, myristic acid, is found in full-fat dairy products, so stick to low-fat or fat-free dairy products.

Monounsaturated Fatty Acids

Monounsaturated fats are liquid at room temperature and get more viscous when they're chilled. Good sources of monounsaturated fats include olive oil, rapeseed oil, avocados, avocado oil, olives (be careful, though, since these can be very high in salt), and high oleic (a fatty acid that is lower in omega-6, is light tasting and can stand up to high cooking temperatures) safflower and sunflower oils. These fats may actually help to raise levels of HDL (good cholesterol) while reducing levels of LDL (bad cholesterol). Olive oil can also help decrease the risk of blood clots because it contains squalene, a substance that has anti-clotting properties and can also lower cholesterol.

Polyunsaturated Fatty Acids

Polyunsaturated fats are liquid at room temperature and stay liquid even when chilled. Large amounts of polyunsaturated fats are found in corn oil, soyabean oil, safflower oil and sunflower oil. Polyunsaturated fats may help to lower total cholesterol, but the downside is that if you have too much of them, they may also lower your high-density lipoproteins (HDL) – the good cholesterol.

Essential fatty acids (EFAs).
Polyunsaturated fatty acids can be further classified into omega-6 fatty acids and omega-3 fatty acids (there are others as well but these are the most important). These fatty acids are called essential fatty acids (EFAs) because they are necessary for normal human growth and development, including rebuilding and producing cells. Our bodies can't produce them, so they must come from our diets.

EFAs also help reduce blood pressure, aid in the prevention of arthritis, aid in nerve impulse transmission, are needed for normal brain functioning and are beneficial for skin and hair.

Both omega-3 and omega-6 fatty acids

are converted into hormonelike substances called eicosanoids, which can profoundly affect health and well-being. Omega-3 and omega-6 produce opposite functions; this is why choosing the right fat is crucial. Eicosanoids affect blood pressure and the immune system, influence the perception of pain and can make you more or less prone to allergies and inflammation. When you have more omega-6 in your diet than omega-3, your body produces more eicosanoids, which then increases your risk of asthma, allergies, arthritis, psoriasis and colitis. Most of us eat too much omega-6 and too little omega-3, so it's important to become more aware of these fats and to find a healthier balance in consuming them. Sources of omega-6 include corn oil, safflower oil, sunflower oil, soyabean oil, peanut oil, sesame oil, grapeseed oil, borage oil and primrose oil.

Omega-3 can reduce blood pressure, may help decrease the risk of heart disease, reduces the risk of heart attacks, decreases blood clot formation and helps to stabilise the heartbeat. Omega-3 may also decrease the incidence of depression and can lessen the severity of several inflammatory and autoimmune diseases such as asthma, allergies, arthritis, psoriasis and colitis, as well as heart disease and high blood pressure.

Fish is a primary source of omega-3. A study published in the *Journal of the American Medical Association* found that women who ate seafood two to four times a week had half the risk of strokes caused by blood clots as women who ate seafood less than once a month. The scientists concluded that the omega-3 fatty acids from the seafood appeared to protect the women against stroke.

Excellent sources of omega-3 are mackerel, herring, salmon, fresh tuna and sardines. Good sources include trout, shellfish, flaxseed oil and flaxseed, rapeseed oil, walnut oil, walnuts and brazil nuts.

Trans fatty acids (TFAs). Trans fatty acids are polyunsaturated vegetable oils that have been hydrogenated to increase shelf life. Hydrogenation is a process in which oils are heated to become solid at room temperature; margarine and white vegetable fat are prime examples.

These fats are different from other polyunsaturated fats in that they act like saturated fats in the body: they increase the risk of heart disease, stroke and diabetes by raising LDL cholesterol and decreasing HDL cholesterol. Even if you don't use margarine or vegetable fat, you may be consuming trans fatty acids in processed foods. They're found in large amounts in foods fried in deep fat, commercial pastries, biscuits, crackers, crisps and many other snack foods. Because of their health risks, you should actively try to avoid these fats in your diet. By reading food labels, you can see if

products contain 'hydrogenated oil', which is another term for trans fatty acid, and you can make a better food choice.

How Much Fat Do You Really Need?

Fats should make up 30 per cent of your diet. The average person requires only one or two servings of good fatty acids per day. Most of the dietary fat we consume should come from a variety of omega-3 fatty acid sources or monounsaturated fatty acids. But remember that our bodies need fat (the good kind), so don't eliminate it from your diet.

Cholesterol

Cholesterol is a fat-like substance – called a sterol – found only in animal-based foods. Cholesterol is also naturally found in the brain, nerves, blood and bile, and is necessary for the proper functioning of the body. It's used to build membranes and produce sex hormones. The liver uses cholesterol to make bile acids, which help you digest food. Eighty per cent of total body cholesterol is manufactured in the liver; the remaining 20 per cent comes from the diet. While cholesterol is necessary, elevated cholesterol levels can be dangerous and can lead to plaque-filled arteries, which inhibit the flow of blood to the brain, kidneys, genitals, extremities and heart, and can promote heart disease.

How Does Cholesterol Work?

Cholesterol travels from the liver through the bloodstream to various tissues and cells by a special class of proteins called lipoproteins. The cells take what cholesterol they need and the remainder stays in the bloodstream until other lipoproteins pick it up and take it back to the liver.

There are two types of lipoproteins: low-density lipoprotein (LDL), the bad form of cholesterol, and high-density lipoprotein (HDL), the good form. LDLs carry a lot of cholesterol from the liver to all the cells of the body. HDLs carry very little cholesterol, circulate in the bloodstream and remove excess cholesterol from the blood and tissues. After HDLs travel through the bloodstream and collect the excess cholesterol, they return it to the liver, where it's incorporated into LDLs for delivery to the cells. If everything is functioning properly, this system remains in balance.

If there is too much cholesterol for the HDLs to pick up in time or if there isn't enough HDL in the body to do the job, cholesterol forms plaque that sticks to artery walls and may cause heart disease. That's why it's beneficial to have high HDL levels and low LDL levels.

Diet and Cholesterol

Since 20 per cent of total body cholesterol comes from what you eat, diet and cholesterol are linked. Decreasing your intake of animal foods that contain a lot of cholesterol (and saturated fats) is important, but it's not the whole story.

It has been shown that saturated fats increase blood cholesterol even more than cholesterol does. This is because saturated fat lowers LDL receptors, so more LDL remains in the blood. So when a food product claims that it contains 'no cholesterol', the product may still negatively affect your cholesterol level if it's high in saturated fats like palm oil, coconut oil or hydrogenated oils. Sugar and uncontrolled alcohol intake may also raise the level of natural cholesterol that your body produces. Stress, too, can raise cholesterol levels.

Reducing your risk of heart disease requires reducing the amount of animal foods you eat, removing saturated fats from your diet, reducing your sugar intake, moderating your alcohol consumption (but not necessarily completely eliminating it, since drinking one 150-ml (5-fl oz) glass of red wine a day may actually raise your HDL), and reducing stress.

Reducing Cholesterol

You can lower your LDL cholesterol level by modifying your diet. Using monounsaturated fats instead of saturated ones helps to lower LDL. Physical exercise and consuming foods rich in omega-3 fatty acids will

(continued on page 88)

LIVING A REAL FOOD LIFE

High Cholesterol Prompted Robert to Overhaul His Diet

Name: Robert

Real Food Life Issues: High cholesterol, high blood pressure

At 64, Robert was looking forward to retirement. He had worked hard his whole life, his grown-up children had left college years ago, and now he was getting ready to travel with his wife, play golf and do some part-time voluntary work. When I met Robert, he got practically no exercise and ate whatever he felt like, particularly fatty meats and fast foods. He especially loved doughnuts. Only when his wife forced him would he eat fresh fruit and vegetables. Here's where I found him:

14 July

I'm half inclined to look into my doctor's credentials. He looks as if he graduated from medical school the same day I qualified for early retirement. I went in for a checkup and he told me I had to change everything - stop eating red meat, stop putting salt on my food, stop eating doughnuts. I didn't know whether to thank him or punch him!

I suppose I knew it would happen. I'm getting to that age . . . even though I'll be damned before I admit that to anyone. God knows, I don't want to give my wife any more ammunition to tell me how to eat. But I have to admit, she's been saying the same things for about 10 years. Of course, I'll never admit that to her - that would give her too much pleasure. (Just kidding.) I know she has my best interests at heart - I just wish my best interests tasted a little better.

Who wants to live to be 100 if you can't eat a big slab of beef when you want to? And where's the harm in a couple of martinis in the afternoon? They don't have any of this 'saturated fat' everyone seems to be terrified of. Sometimes I think it's just all a big conspiracy to drain the joy out of our best years . . .

Robert had very high cholesterol and high blood pressure along with slightly elevated blood sugar levels. His doctor told him if he couldn't change these levels through diet and exercise in a few months, he would have to be put on medication. His father died at 65 and Robert was afraid the pattern would repeat, so that's why he came to see me.

We overhauled Robert's food life to reduce his cholesterol levels. First, he cut out almost all saturated fats and hydrogenated oils from his diet. This meant eating leaner meats, including more chicken and fish. He had lean beef only two or three times a week. He indulged in doughnuts only on rare occasions. He also added more fresh fruits and vegetables into his diet – a particularly healthy step for him because the potassium in fresh produce can help reduce blood pressure. These changes were hard at first – after all, Robert had eaten his old diet for more than half a century. But with support from his wife, his children, his doctor and me, coupled with the memory of his own father's early death, he made an effort to make these changes.

Robert also joined his local gym and began taking exercise classes specially for older people. Within a few weeks, he felt physically better and stronger than he had in years. And during his golf games, he began walking round instead of using the buggy.

Robert also began drinking 8 glasses of water and 1 cup of green tea each day. I coached him on how to reduce his sodium intake by reading food labels carefully and cooking dishes without added salt; he shared these techniques with his wife as well. He began adding tinned beans (no salt added and well rinsed) to his salads and eating porridge for breakfast because the soluble fibre in both foods can help reduce cholesterol levels. He also took a daily B-complex vitamin to help keep his homocysteine levels down.

He started eating more foods that are high in essential fatty acids, since these acids can help reduce cholesterol. In addition to eating olive oil, flaxseed oil, and nuts and seeds, he also started eating fish three times a week. I also got him to try a variety of soya-based foods to further help reduce his cholesterol. He was surprised that he actually liked flavoured tofu and soya sausages.

By the end of 8 weeks, Robert's blood pressure was heading towards the normal range, his cholesterol level had come down significantly and his blood sugar level had returned to normal. Thrilled to see these improvements, his doctor held off prescribing medications and told him to continue eating this way and to continue exercising. Today, Robert continues with his new food life, is still medication-free and is healthily and happily enjoying his retirement.

also help in this regard. A diet rich in foods that have high amounts of soluble fibre, such as barley, beans, peas, brown rice, alfalfa, fruit and oats, can also help to decrease LDL levels.

If you have high cholesterol, you should see your doctor about changes in the recommended levels of dietary fat you should consume. In the UK people with high cholesterol are advised to obtain less than 30 per cent of their total calories from fat. Of this, no more than 10 per cent should be from saturated fat, no more than 6 per cent should be from polyunsaturated fat and up to 15 per cent should be from monounsaturated fat. A higher intake of total fat, mostly in the form

of unsaturated fat, can help to reduce triglycerides and raise HDL cholesterol in persons with high cholesterol.

The traditional advice for people with high cholesterol was to avoid shellfish because it was thought to be too high in cholesterol. This advice is outdated. The cholesterol from seafood will probably not raise your cholesterol level. In addition, shellfish is low in fat and a great source of protein and omega-3s. In one study, volunteers ate 300 grams (10 oz) of prawns each day for 3 weeks. While their LDL did increase by 7 per cent, they also had a 12 per cent increase in their HDL, which more than cancelled out the rise in LDL.

Decoding Cholesterol

When you get your cholesterol levels checked, your doctor will take some blood and send it to a lab for analysis. The lab will check for levels of HDL cholesterol, LDL cholesterol, total cholesterol (which includes both HDL and LDL) and triglycerides. Here's what those numbers mean.

- A normal, healthy *total cholesterol level* is less than 5.0 mmol per litre (mmol/l). A reading above this level indicates the potential for developing heart disease.
- *HDL levels* above 1 mmol/l protect against heart disease and a level below 1 mmol/l is an independent risk factor for heart disease.
- For men and women, the optimal *LDL level* is 3 mmol/l or less. Above this is considered to be an increased risk.
- *Triglycerides* are blood fats that play a role in heart disease. They are also associated with obesity, diabetes, hypertension and low HDL levels. A reading of 0.7 to 1.8 mmol/l is in the healthy range. A reading above this range is associated with increased risk of heart disease.

Finally, taking antioxidant vitamins like vitamins C, E and beta-carotene has been shown to reduce cardiovascular risks and plaque buildup in the arteries.

Homocysteine

Several B vitamins are associated with a reduced incidence of heart disease. Vitamins B_6, B_{12} and folate are essential in controlling a compound called homocysteine, an amino acid that can injure the walls of the coronary arteries. Levels of homocysteine rise when your diet is low in these vitamins. Higher levels of homocysteine mean an increased risk of heart disease even if your blood cholesterol levels are low. Eating plenty of fruit and vegetables daily – 5 or more servings a day – will keep your homocysteine levels in line. I also recommend taking 400 micrograms of folic acid, 3 micrograms of B_{12} and at least 2 milligrams of B_6.

CHAPTER 4

THE ABCs OF VITAMINS AND MINERALS

Get your vitamins and minerals. It sounds like such a cliché. But for good health, you really do need to make sure you're getting enough of these powerful substances, whether you get them from the foods you eat or the supplements you take. In the following pages, I've provided sketches of several essential vitamins and minerals. You'll discover why they're necessary for good health and well-being, what can happen if you're deficient in them, what the top food sources are for each and how much you need to be getting each day.

Vitamins are organic substances that the body needs in tiny amounts to help regulate cell functions necessary for good health. We usually get the majority of the vitamins we need through food – except for vitamin K (which the body can produce from bacteria in the intestines).

Vitamins are categorised as either fat-soluble (vitamins A, D, E and K) or water-soluble (all the B vitamins, biotin, folic acid and vitamin C). The body stores fat-soluble vitamins in the liver and in body fat for long periods of time; they get released and used slowly. Water-soluble vitamins are stored in tissues, stay in the body for short periods of time and need to be replenished daily.

Minerals are inorganic basic elements from the earth's crust that are used in many bodily functions, from bone formation to the effective working of the digestive system. Minerals are also vital for the activity of enzymes (protein molecules that are necessary for almost every biochemical activity in the body). While there are more than 60 minerals in the body, only 22 are considered essential.

Both vitamins and minerals are essential nutrients and dietary guidelines for their recommended intakes have been used in the UK for over 40 years. Until recently they took the form of a single figure, the Recommended Daily Amount (RDA). However, the limitations of having just one set of figures for each nutrient soon became apparent. In 1991 the Department of Health published Dietary Reference Values (DRVs), a set of standards for use in different applications. One subset of these standards are the Reference Nutrient Intakes (RNIs), which are the amounts of a vitamin or mineral which should meet the requirements of virtually every healthy person within a defined group. These are the most useful way to look at requirements for these micronutrients and will be used in this chapter.

Sometimes food labels in the UK will state that a serving of the food meets a percentage of the recommended daily intake for a particular vitamin, which can be helpful in showing how individual foods contribute to your total diet.

Vitamin and mineral requirements vary with age, sex and physiological states such as pregnancy and breastfeeding. The standard recommendations are widely considered to be inadequate and do not take into account illness, stress or high levels of physical activity, when needs may be higher.

A Prescription for Vitamins and Minerals

The best way to get the nutrients your body needs to maintain great health and protect and heal itself is to eat several servings of fruit and vegetables every day. But even if you eat a wholesome diet with an emphasis on fruit, vegetables, whole grains and high-quality proteins, you may not be getting enough vitamins and minerals. So I recommend taking a multivitamin every day to ensure you're getting all the nutrients you need.

You may also want to take additional vitamin C at certain times to help boost your immune system. I recommend taking up to 500 milligrams of vitamin C daily if you feel under par or are suffering from stress.

Many people, especially women, don't get enough calcium. While the best source of calcium is food, you may not be getting enough through your diet alone. I recommend taking a calcium supplement with added vitamin D, which helps the body absorb the additional calcium. You should try to take 700 milligrams a day and I recommend 1,200 milligrams if you're aged 50 or over. For best absorption, don't take more than 500 milligrams at a time.

My female clients and I take vitamin B_6 (50 to 100 milligrams) a few days before our periods and during the first few days and then stop until the next cycle. We feel it helps with irritability and bloating.

If you plan on becoming pregnant, you should take only special prenatal multivitamins (which have higher levels of vitamins and minerals, such as iron and folic acid, than 'regular' multivitamins). You may also want to take a B-complex vitamin that contains at least 400 to 600 micrograms of folic acid to protect against neural tube defects. It also protects against high blood levels of homocysteine, a protein that can cause heart disease.

Vitamins
Vitamin A and Carotenoids

Why vitamin A is important: Especially when it comes from carotenoids, vitamin A is an all-star antioxidant, which means that it helps protect cells against cancers. It is also needed for new cell growth and for the formation of teeth and bones. Vitamin A enhances the immune system, supports reproduction and growth, maintains healthy skin and helps the body to fight infections. In addition, it helps prevent night blindness and it may slow down the ageing process. Surplus vitamin A is stored in the body and if it's taken in extreme quantities it can be toxic, causing liver damage. High intakes of vitamin A can potentially damage a developing foetus, so pregnant women should avoid high-dose supplements as well as foods

such as liver which contain high levels.

Carotenoids are a class of compounds related to vitamin A. There are believed to be more than 600 carotenoids in existence; 400 have been identified and named. Of those 400, 50 are precursors to vitamin A, which means the liver will convert them into vitamin A as the body needs it. After they're converted, these carotenoids perform all the functions of vitamin A, such as having antioxidant properties and disease-preventing potential.

Carotenoids taken in extreme quantities aren't believed to be toxic but may turn the skin orange. The best-known carotenoid is beta-carotene, but there are many more, including lycopene and lutein. Lycopene is a potent antioxidant that may help to prevent prostate and other cancers; it is naturally abundant in tomatoes, pink grapefruit and watermelon. Lutein is also an antioxidant and may protect against vision disorders that can occur with age. These and other carotenoids are abundant in dark green, leafy vegetables (like spinach and spring greens), and dark orange fruits and vegetables (like carrots, squash and papayas).

Symptoms of deficiency: Dry hair and skin, poor growth and night blindness. Also may lead to problems with reproduction, painful joints, insomnia, lowered resistance to infection, frequent colds and skin disorders.

Symptoms of toxicity: Hair loss, skin rashes, fractures, haemorrhaging and liver

Find an Oasis for Dry Skin

Skin that's dry, flaky and itchy not only is irritating but can be unsightly. Rehydrate with these all-natural remedies.

- Foods rich in beta-carotene – including yellow and orange vegetables – can help prevent and may remedy dry, flaky skin.
- Foods high in B vitamins also help relieve itchy skin. Try some fish, legumes, nuts, eggs and whole grains – and take a B-complex supplement.
- Vitamin C helps the production of collagen and can strengthen the capillaries that feed the skin. Eat plenty of dark green vegetables, sweet potatoes, berries and oranges.
- Foods that contain sulphur can help keep skin smooth. Eat some garlic, onions, eggs, asparagus or wheat germ at your next meal.
- Drink at least 8 glasses of water a day. Water naturally hydrates your body and skin. Avoid alcohol and caffeine. Both dehydrate the skin (and the body).

failure can all result from too much vitamin A. Women taking more than 3,000 micrograms daily can experience reproduction complications.

Foods rich in vitamin A and carotenoids: Animal and fish liver; egg yolks; milk fortified with vitamins A and D; red peppers; and green, yellow and orange fruits and veggies, including apricots, asparagus, broccoli, cantaloupe melon, carrots, kale, papayas, peaches, spinach, sweet potatoes, watercress and yellow squash.

How much do you need a day? 700 micrograms for men, 600 micrograms for women.

B-complex Vitamins

The B-complex family of vitamins help to maintain the health of the nerves, skin, eyes, hair, liver, muscles, gastrointestinal tract and brain functions. They also help prevent mouth ulcers and other mouth sores. In addition, the Bs help produce and maintain energy and they may help alleviate anxiety and depression. They're water-soluble vitamins, which means they need to be replenished daily.

Vitamin B_1 (Thiamin)

Why vitamin B_1 is important: It enhances circulation and assists in blood formation. It also aids in digestion, helps with brain functions and helps the body to use carbohydrates. B_1 has positive effects on energy, growth, appetite and learning capacity. It's also needed for muscle tone of the intestines, stomach and heart.

Symptoms of deficiency: Constipation, oedema, fatigue, forgetfulness, stomach problems, irritability, muscle atrophy, nervousness, numbness in the limbs and general weakness.

Foods rich in vitamin B_1: Brown rice; egg yolks; fish; fortified grain products such as bread, rice and whole grains; legumes; oatmeal; peanuts; peas; pork; poultry; rice bran; sunflower seeds; wheat germ and yeast extract.

How much do you need a day? 1 milligram for men, 0.8 milligrams for women.

Vitamin B_2 (Riboflavin)

Why vitamin B_2 is important: It's necessary for red blood cell formation, antibody production and cell repair and growth. Vitamin B_2 also helps in the prevention and treatment of cataracts and helps metabolise carbohydrates, fats and protein.

Symptoms of deficiency: Sores and cracks in the corners of the mouth, eye disorders, skin lesions, skin rash, dizziness, hair loss, insomnia, light sensitivity and slowed growth and mental response.

Foods rich in vitamin B_2: Cheese, egg yolks, fish, legumes, meat, milk, poultry, sardines, spinach, whole grains, yeast extracts and yogurt.

How much do you need a day? 1.3 milligrams for men, 1.1 milligrams for women.

Niacin or Nicotinic acid (Vitamin B_3)

Why niacin is important: It's necessary for good circulation and healthy skin. It also helps the nervous and digestive systems function properly and helps to metabolise carbohydrates, fats and protein. Plus, it can be used to lower LDL (bad) cholesterol – under the supervision of your doctor – and may help to enhance memory.

Symptoms of deficiency: Depression, diarrhoea, halitosis (bad breath), indigestion, insomnia, mouth ulcers, weakness, and skin bumps and inflammation.

Symptoms of toxicity: Niacin flush – a burning, tingling and itching sensation. Diarrhoea, heartburn, nausea, ulcers, vomiting and headache.

Foods rich in niacin: Broccoli, carrots, cheese, chicken breasts, cornflour, dandelion greens, dates, eggs, fish, milk, oatmeal, peanuts, potatoes, tomatoes, tuna, turkey, wheat germ, wholewheat products and yeast extract.

How much do you need a day? 7 milligrams for men, 13 milligrams for women.

Pantothenic Acid (Vitamin B_5)

Why pantothenic acid is important: Known as the anti-stress vitamin, this is needed to form antibodies and for the proper functioning of the gastrointestinal tract. It helps the body use other vitamins and helps to convert fats, proteins and carbohydrates into energy. It also enhances stamina, helps to prevent certain forms of anaemia and is proving helpful in treating depression and anxiety.

Symptoms of deficiency: Fatigue, headache and nausea.

Foods rich in vitamin B₅: Avocados, beef, eggs, fish, legumes, mushrooms, nuts, poultry, sea fish and whole grains including whole rye flour and whole wheat.

How much do you need a day? There is no RNI for pantothenic acid but 3 to 7 milligrams is believed adequate to prevent deficiency.

Vitamin B₆ (Pyridoxine)

Why vitamin B₆ is important: This vitamin is involved with more bodily functions than almost any other single nutrient. It helps produce serotonin and other neurotransmitters (brain chemicals that are important for good mental balance). It also helps protect against heart disease by reducing the level of homocysteine (a protein that can injure the walls of the coronary arteries) in the blood. It helps to maintain the balance of sodium and potassium and helps the production and digestion of fats and proteins. It also promotes the formation of red blood cells and the production of antibodies. It is needed for proper functioning of the brain, nervous system and immune system, and helps to prevent kidney stones. B₆ is also a mild diuretic, so it is great for relieving water retention and may help with symptoms of PMS.

Symptoms of deficiency: Anaemia, convulsions, headaches, nausea, acne, depression, fatigue, irritability, inflammation of the mouth and hair loss.

Symptoms of toxicity: Bloating, fatigue, headaches and bone pain.

Foods rich in vitamin B₆: Avocados, bananas, carrots, chicken, eggs, fish (especially oily fish such as salmon and tuna), liver, nuts, peas, pork, potatoes, pulses, spinach, sunflower seeds and wheat germ.

How much do you need a day? 1.4 milligrams for men, 1.2 milligrams for women.

Vitamin B₁₂ (Cyanocobalamin)

Why vitamin B₁₂ is important: B₁₂ will prevent anaemia and nerve damage and it works with folic acid to regulate red blood cell formation. It helps the body to use iron, protein, carbohydrates and fat, and aids in digestion. It will also promote growth, helps to maintain fertility and may help with memory and learning.

Symptoms of deficiency: Anaemia, constipation, depression, problems with digestion, drowsiness, fatigue, eye disorders, moodiness and heart palpitations.

Foods rich in vitamin B₁₂: Dairy products, eggs, fortified cereals, fortified soya-beans and soya products, herring, mackerel,

Curb the Symptoms of PMS

Just because your period is due doesn't mean that you have to feel bloated, irritable and crampy. These remedies will gently soothe the symptoms of PMS.

- A daily B-complex vitamin supplement can help relieve irritability, moodiness, swelling and bloating.

- Calcium can help decrease bloating and irritability, muscle cramps, pelvic pain and nervousness. Take a 500-milligram supplement twice a day and make sure you eat at least two or three calcium-rich foods a day. Good options include low-fat yogurt, skimmed milk and tinned sardines or salmon.

- Magnesium helps with cravings, mood swings, bloating and breast tenderness. Zinc helps with headaches, irritability, depression and cramps. Try eating foods rich in both minerals, including whole grains, soyabeans, nuts and seeds, and dark green, leafy vegetables.

- Exercise helps with cramping and helps your system to flow properly.

- Iron prevents fatigue and anaemia, so eat some eggs, fish, meat, poultry, beans, legumes or dried fruit to prevent iron-poor blood.

- If you slightly increase your protein intake and slightly decrease your carbohydrate intake, you can reduce that bloated feeling often associated with PMS.

- If you have sweet cravings that you just can't ignore, eat a few boiled sweets.

- Don't forget: stay away from salty processed foods because they make your body retain more fluid and therefore increase PMS symptoms.

meats, milk, seafood and sea vegetables (including dulse, kelp, kombu and nori).

How much do you need a day? 1.5 micrograms. (Vegetarians – especially vegetarian women who are breastfeeding – need to be sure they get this daily requirement, usually from a multivitamin.)

Folate (folic acid)

Why folate is important: This vitamin is crucial for women who are or plan on becoming pregnant. They should start taking an additional supplement of 400 micrograms of folic acid per day in addition to getting 200 micrograms from their diet. Why? Because

(continued on page 100)

LIVING A REAL FOOD LIFE

A Diet Packed with Vitamins and Minerals – Instead of Takeaways – Turned Julia's Life Around

Name: Julia

Real Food Life Issue: Social isolation, using food for comfort/activity, frequent colds and depression

When I met Julia, she was a college student living away from home for the first time. She was depressed because she missed her family terribly, she was overweight and she caught colds all the time. Plus, she felt isolated because she didn't live on campus. She used food as a source of comfort and for company – especially when she was bored and lonely. At that point, Julia's days revolved around going to lectures, eating, coming home, eating, studying, eating and sleeping. Here's where I found her:

10 October

The days are getting darker earlier now. I can't wait to get home in the afternoons - I just want to be inside all the time. I've got into a ritual lately: I get off the bus from college, head straight to my flat, turn on the TV and check my answerphone (usually empty). Then I grab the phone, stick my hand in the top kitchen drawer and pull out a takeaway menu at random. Sometimes I spend the bus trip thinking about what's going to come out of the drawer that night.

I have a favourite meal at each place: pepperoni pizza, deep-fried shredded beef with chilli, chicken curry. Everyone delivers around here. My favourite dessert is chocolate chip cookie ice cream. I know all the delivery people by name and I think they like me - probably because I tip them well. They always say hello, but I just throw the money at them and grab the bag out of their hands. Then I settle in front of the TV - although these days, I have to limit my TV because I've got to revise for exams. I let myself watch only while I eat. I'll dawdle over dessert, because I know as soon as I've finished, the TV goes off and the books get opened.

Most days, I feel like I'm on autopilot. I wonder what would happen if I just stopped going to lectures. I'm terrified I'm going to fail ...

At her off-campus flat, Julia ordered in most of her meals. Her tastes ran to foods that are very high in saturated fat, such as pizza and curries. She would also have a tub of ice cream almost every night. She ate no fruit, vegetables, whole grains or foods high in essential fatty acids, such as fish and nuts. Her depression made her not care about what she ate or looked like and that made her even more depressed.

Our first plan of action was to go food shopping. I showed Julia how to stock up on healthy foods for quick and nourishing meals and snacks. We bought a variety of whole grains (crackers, easy-cook brown rice, cereals), high-quality proteins (veggie burgers, frozen prawns, tinned beans), essential fatty acids (olive oil, nuts and seeds) and some fresh and dried fruits, and frozen and fresh vegetables. We even got her some treats.

I started her on vitamin supplements, including a B-complex to help with her depression, and vitamins C and E to help her immune system. I also recommended – and she embraced – eating fish three times a week (usually grilled salmon or tinned tuna). She also started eating salads daily, topped with a few walnuts and dressed with olive oil and lemon juice.

We pored over all of her takeaway menus and I pointed out delicious and wholesome choices in each one; I also showed her which dishes she'd do best to avoid. Julia soon replaced her tubs of ice cream with a small piece of high-quality dark chocolate, and she came to realise that sometimes she didn't even need her nighttime sweet. By week 4, she was drinking 8 glasses of water a day and her colds had cleared up.

Instead of rushing home to study and mope and eat, she also started going to the gym at college. She began taking a few exercise classes there each week, which allowed her to start feeling better about her body and meet more people at the same time. She also began helping out at the nearby soup kitchen once a week, serving the needy. This really improved her self-esteem because she was doing something for someone other than herself and making a small contribution to bettering her new community (and she met even more new people).

By the end of 8 weeks, Julia's depression had improved tremendously. Between her involvement at the soup kitchen and her new-found workout schedule, her energy increased significantly and she felt much better about herself and her situation. Even her grades improved. And, much to her pleasure and surprise, she lost a little weight, even though that was not her main goal.

folate protects against neural tube defects such as spina bifida and anencephaly and it may also help prevent premature birth. Folate is also needed for healthy cell division and replication, energy, and the formation of red blood cells. It can strengthen the immune system and may help alleviate depression and anxiety. It may protect against colon and lung cancer and it decreases homocysteine (a protein that causes heart disease).

Symptoms of deficiency: Anaemia, apathy, gastrointestinal disturbances, fatigue, growth impairment, memory problems, general weakness and birth defects.

Foods rich in folate: Asparagus, barley, bran, brown rice, cheese, chicken, chicory, dates, green leafy vegetables, lamb, legumes, lentils, milk, mushrooms, nuts, oatmeal, oranges, root vegetables, salmon, seaweed, split peas, sunflower seeds, tuna, wheat germ, whole grains and whole wheat.

How much do you need a day? 200 micrograms.

Vitamin C

Why vitamin C is important: This may be the most well known of all the vitamins, due to its ability to strengthen the immune system (which is why it's often taken just before or during a cold) and the fact that it's a powerful antioxidant that helps rid the body of free radicals. Needed for tissue growth and repair, vitamin C is also necessary for proper functioning of the adrenal glands (which regulate hormones) and for healthy gums. It protects against damage from pollution, cancer and infections. Essential for the formation and repair of collagen (which gives skin its suppleness and strengthens bones and blood vessels), it promotes the healing of wounds and burns. It also increases absorption of iron and reinforces and strengthens vitamin E's antioxidant properties. Vitamin C also helps to reduce LDL (bad) cholesterol and high blood pressure and may help to prevent osteoporosis.

Symptoms of deficiency: Scurvy (symptoms include soft and spongy bleeding gums and loose teeth), oedema, bleeding gums, increased susceptibility to infections, slower wound healing, lack of energy, poor digestion, bruises and tooth loss.

Symptoms of toxicity: Nausea, abdominal cramps, diarrhoea and kidney stones.

Foods rich in vitamin C: Asparagus, avocados, berries, blackcurrants, broccoli, Brussels sprouts, cantaloupe melon, citrus fruits, green leafy vegetables, kiwifruit, mangoes, papayas, potatoes, red and green peppers, spinach, strawberries and tomatoes.

How much do you need a day? 40 milligrams – although regular smokers may need twice this amount. (Look for a buffered variety if you're taking a supplement, since it's easier on the stomach.)

Vitamin D (Cholecalciferol)

Why vitamin D is important: It helps the body absorb – and efficiently use – calcium and phosphorus and is necessary for growth, particularly of children's teeth and bones. Vitamin D also strengthens muscles, enhances immunity and thyroid functions, regulates the heartbeat and prevents and may remedy osteoporosis. Vitamin D is stored in the body's fat.

Symptoms of deficiency: Bone disorders, diarrhoea and insomnia.

Symptoms of toxicity: Kidney stones, hardening of blood vessels, nausea, vomiting and loss of appetite.

Foods rich in vitamin D: Sunlight converts vitamin D in the skin to its active form, so if you're outside for just 10 to 15 minutes of midday sun 2 or 3 times a week, you get all the D you need. During the winter months, you'll need a supplement if you live in cold climates or are housebound. Vitamin D is also found in dairy foods, eggs, fortified cereals and oily fish like salmon, mackerel and tuna.

How much do you need a day? If you get some skin exposure to sunlight during the year, you shouldn't need a dietary source of vitamin D. There is an RNI of 10 micrograms per day for adults over 65, pregnant and breastfeeding women, and for people who get little exposure to sunlight. (Note: If you drink at least 2 glasses of milk per day, you don't need a vitamin D supplement.)

Vitamin E

Why vitamin E is important: It promotes healthy skin, hair, nerves and muscles. It also stabilises cell membranes, enhances the immune system and may help to prevent certain cancers and heart disease. Vital for healing, vitamin E repairs tissues, clots blood and reduces scarring. It slows tumour growth, decreases blood pressure and strengthens coronary arteries to repair the effects of heart disease. It also helps relieve leg cramps and helps treat PMS, hot flushes and breast tenderness. Plus, it's an important antioxidant.

Symptoms of deficiency: Potential nerve and red blood cell damage, infertility, menstrual problems, miscarriage and heart disease.

Foods rich in vitamin E: Avocados, brown rice, 100 per cent wholegrain cereals and breads, eggs, extra-virgin olive oil, fish, green leafy vegetables, legumes, meat, milk, nuts, oatmeal, rapeseed oil, seeds, soyabeans and wheat germ.

How much do you need a day? There is no RNI but to prevent deficiency men need at least 4 milligrams and women 3 milligrams. (Buy vitamin E labelled 'd-alpha tocopherol', which is the best source of natural vitamin E. Vitamin E labelled 'DL' is synthetically derived and not as good.)

Vitamin K

Why vitamin K is important: Necessary for proper blood clotting and bone formation and repair, vitamin K is also used by our bodies for making bone protein, which helps prevent osteoporosis. It also helps to increase our resistance to infection, particularly in children. Like vitamins A and D, K is fat-soluble.

Symptoms of deficiency: Abnormal and/or internal bleeding.

Foods rich in vitamin K: Asparagus, broccoli, Brussels sprouts, cabbage, cauliflower, dark green, leafy vegetables including kale, spinach and Swiss chard, dried seaweed, eggs, oatmeal, oats, onions, rye, soyabeans and wheat. Green tea has some, too.

How much do you need a day? 1 microgram should be adequate to prevent deficiency in adults.

Coenzyme Q_{10}

Why coenzyme Q_{10} is important: Coenzyme Q_{10} isn't an actual vitamin. Rather, it's a vitamin-like substance that resembles vitamin E. It's a powerful antioxidant that has enormous anti-ageing properties. For this reason, it's often used in skin creams. It also is critical for energy production, aids in circulation, stimulates the immune system and alleviates allergies, asthma and respiratory diseases. Finally, coenzyme Q_{10} is used in the treatment of some cancers and heart disease (because it helps strengthen the heart muscle).

Foods rich in coenzyme Q_{10}: Beef, mackerel, peanuts, salmon, sardines and spinach.

How much do you need a day? No RNI.

Minerals

Calcium

Why calcium is important: Ninety-nine per cent of your body's calcium is found in your bones and teeth: this mineral is vital for forming and growing strong bones and teeth. Calcium also helps to maintain healthy gums and a regular heartbeat. Plus, it aids in neuromuscular activity, helps keep skin healthy, protects against pre-eclampsia and can help with symptoms of PMS. Calcium is needed for blood clotting and may help to protect against colon cancer, prevent heart disease, prevent muscle cramps and lower both blood pressure and cholesterol levels. Because of its bone mass-building properties, it's also beneficial in the prevention of osteoporosis.

Symptoms of deficiency: Aching joints, osteoporosis, brittle nails, high blood cholesterol, eczema, heart palpitations, high blood pressure, insomnia, muscle cramps, nervousness, pasty complexion and depression.

Symptoms of toxicity: Constipation, interference with absorption of other minerals, urinary stone formation and kidney dysfunction.

Foods rich in calcium: Low-fat or fat-free yogurt, milk and cheese ('reduced-fat' cheeses can be almost as high in fat and calories as normal cheese, so it's best to stick with low-fat or fat-free varieties). Other good sources include almonds, asparagus, broccoli, cabbage, calcium-fortified orange juice, cereals, figs,

Easy Ways to Boost Your Calcium Intake

Having trouble getting enough calcium in your diet? Try these simple – and delicious – strategies for boosting your daily calcium consumption.

- Eat more yogurt (225 ml/8 fl oz of yogurt has 100 milligrams more calcium than the same amount of milk.)
- Have cereal with milk and cook porridge oats in skimmed milk instead of water.
- Choose calcium-fortified orange juice.
- Have a big serving of broccoli.
- Add fat-free powdered milk to mashed potatoes, casseroles, sauces and soups.
- Add calcium-fortified tofu to smoothies, sauces, soups, salads and chilli.

goat's milk, green leafy vegetables, oats, prunes, sardines and salmon (tinned), sesame seeds, shellfish, and fortified soya products, including soya milk, soya yogurt, soya cheese and tofu processed with calcium sulphate.

How much do you need a day? 700 milligrams for adults; 800 to 1,000 milligrams for teenagers.

Chromium

Why chromium is important: Chromium helps metabolise glucose (blood sugar), which gives us energy. It's also vital for burning fats and proteins and the body needs it to use insulin properly and to maintain stable blood sugar levels. Without chromium, insulin can't make glucose available to cells. Chromium may be especially helpful to people with diabetes and hypoglycaemia.

Symptoms of deficiency: Anxiety, fatigue and insulin resistance (when the body doesn't use glucose as it should), particularly in people with diabetes. May lead to arteriosclerosis (hardening of the arteries). A diet high in processed foods can decrease chromium levels and wreak havoc with blood sugar levels.

Foods rich in chromium: Brewer's yeast, brown rice, cheese, eggs, legumes, meat, nuts, seafood and whole grains.

How much do you need a day? No RNI.

Copper

Why copper is important: Copper aids in bone and red blood cell formation and has anti-inflammatory properties. It plays a role in the healing process, energy production, the sense of taste, and hair and skin pigmentation. It also increases the strength of collagen, a protein that gives strength and elasticity to skin and connective tissues.

In the body, levels of copper are directly related to levels of vitamin C and zinc. If too much vitamin C or zinc is consumed, copper levels drop; if copper levels are too high, vitamin C and zinc levels drop, so it's important not to take too much of either supplement.

Symptoms of deficiency: Osteoporosis, anaemia, diarrhoea, impaired respiratory functions, impaired immunity and sores.

Foods rich in copper: Almonds, avocados, barley, beans, beetroot, broccoli, garlic, lentils, mushrooms, oats, oranges, oysters, pecans, sardines and sunflower seeds.

How much do you need a day? 1.2 milligrams.

Iodine

Why iodine is important: It's vital for maintaining healthy thyroid glands (which control metabolism and growth) and it prevents goitre (enlargement of the thyroid caused by lack of iodine). Iodine is important for mental and physical development in children. It's also essential for the absorption of carbohydrates and necessary for reproduction.

Foods rich in iodine: Dairy foods, eggs, iodised salt, kelp, sea fish and seafood.

How much do you need a day? 140 micrograms.

Iron

Why iron is important: An essential part of haemoglobin (a protein that gives blood its red colour and carries oxygen to all the cells), iron is also part of myoglobin (which stores oxygen in the muscles to provide energy for muscle contractions). Iron is important for growth, a healthy immune system and energy production.

There are two kinds of iron, haem and non-haem. Haem is found mostly in animal-based foods and is absorbed much more efficiently than non-haem; non-haem is found mostly in plant-based foods and is poorly absorbed by the body. Vitamin C increases non-haem iron absorption by up to 30 per cent. For this reason, it's best to eat foods that are high in vitamin C along with iron-rich foods to increase iron's absorption. For example, drink orange juice along with your tofu or rice and beans. You might also cook acidic foods such as tomatoes in cast-iron pans because the iron leaches into the food.

Symptoms of deficiency: Anaemia, brittle hair, digestive problems, inflammation of the mouth tissues, nervousness, slowed mental reactions, intestinal bleeding, weakness and fatigue. Too much phosphorus in the diet, poor digestion, eating too many antacids or drinking too much coffee or tea could prevent you from getting enough iron. Strenuous exercise and heavy perspiration also deplete iron.

Symptoms of toxicity: Upset stomach, diarrhoea, constipation, fatigue, haemosiderosis (a genetic disorder that enhances iron absorption) and possibly kidney damage. Excessive iron may also lead to heart disease and cancer.

Foods rich in iron: Beans and legumes, dried fruit, eggs, fish, fortified cereal products and bread, green leafy vegetables, liver, poultry, red meat, seeds, tofu and whole grains.

How much do you need a day? 14.8 milligrams for women aged 19 to 50, 8.7 milligrams for men and women over 50.

Magnesium

Why magnesium is important: The main function of magnesium is energy production. Magnesium is a major component of bones and teeth and helps to regulate heart rhythm and calcium and potassium metabolism. In addition, it enhances the immune system and may help to increase HDL (good) cholesterol and prevent cardiovascular disease and osteoporosis. It also helps ensure good sleep. Magnesium can help prevent depression, PMS, dizziness, muscle weakness and twitching, and premature labour and convulsions in pregnant women.

Symptoms of deficiency: Too little magnesium could interfere with the transmission of nerve and muscle impulses and cause irritability, tiredness and nervousness. Too little of this mineral could also result in loss of appetite, cramps, abnormal heart rhythms and feelings of 'weakness'.

Foods rich in magnesium: Apples, apri-cots, avocados, bananas, brown rice, butter-beans, cantaloupe melon, dairy products (fat-free or low-fat), figs, fish, garlic, grapefruit, green leafy vegetables, lemons, meat, nuts (especially Brazil nuts), potatoes, pumpkin seeds, salmon, sardines, sesame seeds, shellfish, soyabeans, sunflower seeds, tofu, watercress, whole wheat and whole grains including quinoa and amaranth.

How much do you need a day? 300 milligrams for men, 270 milligrams for women.

Manganese

Why manganese is important: Manganese metabolises protein and fat and it is also needed for healthy nerves, a strong immune system and the regulation of blood sugar. It's required for reproduction and for normal bone growth and for the formation of cartilage and synovial (lubricating) joint fluids. Pregnant women need manganese for the production of breast milk. When taken with B-complex vitamins, manganese helps to give an overall sense of well-being.

Symptoms of deficiency: Hardening of the arteries, confusion, eye problems, hearing problems, high cholesterol, high blood pressure, memory loss, profuse sweating, rapid pulse and teeth grinding.

Foods rich in manganese: Avocados, blueberries, dried peas, egg yolks, green leafy vegetables, legumes, nuts and seeds, pineapples, seaweed, tea and whole grains.

BEST BITES

Foods to Keep You Loving All Night Long

Choosing the right foods can enhance all aspects of your life – including your love life! Before a night of romance, have a look at the following tips.

- Carbohydrates provide energy and stamina, so try some sexy fruits such as pomegranates, cherries, passion fruit, blood oranges, mangoes, papayas and figs.
- Zinc is great for sex hormones. Indulge in some shellfish (especially oysters), lean beef, whole grains, wheat germ, beans, cashews, chicken or turkey.
- Essential fatty acids help regulate hormones – including the sex hormones. To get more of these good fats in your diet, sprinkle walnuts on a salad and drizzle with olive oil.
- Vitamin C helps with sperm production. So try some melons, berries, sweet potatoes, red and green peppers, and citrus fruit (and be careful).
- Avoid wind-producing foods like beans and legumes.
- Hot peppers help with circulation. Spice up your meals with cayenne or other hot peppers.
- Dark chocolate is a good source of antioxidants and is just plain sensual – especially when melted on strawberries!

How much do you need a day? There is no RNI but safe levels to prevent deficiency are considered above 1.4 milligrams for adults.

Phosphorus

Why phosphorus is important: It's needed for bone and tooth formation, cell growth, heart contractions and proper kidney functioning. Phosphorus also assists in the utilisation of vitamins and helps convert food to energy.

A proper balance of magnesium, calcium and phosphorus needs to be maintained at all times. If the body has too much or too little of one of these minerals, it won't function properly.

Symptoms of deficiency: Since phosphorus is found in most foods, deficiency is rare, but prolonged use of antacids can cause it.

Symptoms of toxicity: Interferes with calcium and iron uptake. Excessive phosphorus may be a problem for people who drink more than 1 litre (1¾ pt) of soft drinks a day.

Foods rich in phosphorus: Most foods contain some phosphorus. The following foods, however, are top sources: asparagus; bran; corn; dairy products; eggs; fish; fruit (dried); garlic; legumes; meats; nuts; poultry; pumpkin, sesame and sunflower seeds; salmon; and whole grains.

How much do you need a day? 550 milligrams.

Potassium

Why potassium is important: Vital for a healthy nervous system, potassium also regulates the heartbeat, prevents strokes, aids in muscle contractions, maintains stable blood pressure and works with sodium to control the body's water balance.

Symptoms of deficiency: Critically dry skin, acne, chills, constipation, diarrhoea, erratic heartbeat and depression.

Foods rich in potassium: Apricots, avocados, bananas, brown rice, dairy foods, dates, figs, fish, fruit (including dried), garlic, legumes, meat, oats, potatoes, poultry, raisins, vegetables, wheat bran, whole grains, winter squash and yams.

How much do you need a day? 3,500 milligrams.

Selenium

Why selenium is important: Selenium and vitamin E work together to help produce antibodies and maintain a healthy heart and liver. Alone, selenium enhances the immune system and has antiviral and anti-inflammatory properties and is necessary for both pancreatic functioning and tissue elasticity. It also has antioxidant properties, which means that it helps to prevent the formation of free radicals that can damage the body.

Symptoms of deficiency: Exhaustion, high cholesterol and infections. Also linked to cancer and heart disease.

Symptoms of toxicity: Arthritis, brittle nails, stomach upset, hair loss, irritability and skin problems.

Foods rich in selenium: Two Brazil nuts give you your daily requirement for selenium. Other sources include broccoli, brown rice, chicken, dairy foods, garlic and salmon.

How much do you need a day? 75 micrograms for men, 60 micrograms for women.

Sodium

Why sodium is important: Sodium is necessary for maintaining proper water balance and proper pH levels. It's also needed for stomach, nerve and muscle functions. The right balance of sodium and potassium is vital for good health; an imbalance could lead to heart disease.

Symptoms of deficiency: It's rare to have a sodium deficiency, but it can happen if someone has a kidney disorder, perspires excessively or takes too many diuretics.

Symptoms of toxicity: Water retention, high blood pressure, potassium deficiency and liver and kidney disease.

Foods rich in sodium: Sodium is found in virtually all foods and most people have

Kitchen CURES

A Natural Prescription to Soothe Acne

Whether you're a teenager or an adult, there's never a good time for a case of acne. Soothe your skin with the power of the following herbs and foods.

- Zinc helps prevent scarring and is necessary for oil-producing skin glands and tissue repair. So eat some zinc-rich foods, including shellfish, whole grains, sunflower seeds and nuts.

- Use tea tree oil, a natural antibiotic and antiseptic. Dab a little oil on a cotton swab and apply to affected areas up to three times a day.

- Beta-carotene helps heal and construct new skin. Have some dark green vegetables and orange fruit.

- Chamomile tea helps to nourish the skin, so make sure you have a cup or two each day.

- Add flaxseeds or flaxseed oil to your diet. Flax helps heal skin disorders, keeps the skin smooth and soft and repairs damaged skin cells.

adequate – or excessive – amounts of sodium in their diets.

How much do you need a day? No more than 2,400 milligrams (this is equivalent to 1 teaspoon of table salt).

Zinc

Why zinc is important: Needed for healing wounds, growth and bone formation, zinc also enhances the immune system and is a natural anti-inflammatory. It helps the prostate gland function properly and aids in the development of reproductive organs. Zinc also facilitates the senses of taste and smell. It may help prevent acne and regulate the activity of oil glands.

Symptoms of deficiency: Loss of taste and smell, fingernails can become thin and peel and develop white spots, wound healing slows, recurrent colds, impaired night vision, infertility and hair loss.

Foods rich in zinc: Butterbeans, dairy products, egg yolks, fish and shellfish, lamb and other meats, legumes, mushrooms, oysters, pecans, poultry, pumpkin seeds, soyabeans, sunflower seeds and whole grains.

How much do you need a day? 9.5 milligrams for men, 7 milligrams for women.

CHAPTER 5

HUNGER AND METABOLISM

You get hungry, so you eat. Simple, isn't it?

Not quite. There are two kinds of hunger: physical hunger and emotional, or 'head', hunger. In this chapter, you'll learn to distinguish between the two. You'll also learn about the role metabolism plays in your food life. And, best of all, you'll discover a fool-proof way to boost your metabolism, regardless of the genes you were born with.

How Do You Know You're Hungry?

Hunger is the body's mechanism to remind us to fuel it. The body needs food just as a car needs petrol. While most people won't ignore their fuel gauge when it hovers at empty, many don't pay attention to their body's hunger signals. But ignoring hunger signals can confuse the body's natural chemicals that activate the appetite and hunger.

Hunger more or less originates in the hypothalamus, an area in the brain partly responsible for eating behaviour. The hypothalamus sends signals to other areas of the brain, which then emit chemicals called neurotransmitters that help regulate how much we eat and what we eat.

When the body's levels of blood sugar and glycogen (the store of carbohydrates) are low, a neurotransmitter called neuropeptide Y (also known as NPY) is released from the hypothalamus. As NPY levels increase, so does the body's urge for sweet and starchy foods (carbohydrates).

For example, while you sleep, your glycogen and blood sugar levels naturally drop and then signal your brain to release NPY; that's why people naturally crave carbohydrates like breads, cereals, bagels and fruit for breakfast. If you don't eat breakfast, NPY levels will keep going up all day and eventually set you up for a carb-binge in the late afternoon. So, sometimes carb cravings and binges are not because you 'lack control'; rather, they're a natural function of your body's own chemistry. Not only does eating carbohydrates turn off the flow of NPY, but it also releases serotonin, a neurotransmitter that produces a feeling of satisfaction with your food and an overall sense of well-being.

Why Low-calorie Diets Don't Work

Another chemical important to hunger is cholecystokinin (CCK). CCK is a neurotransmitter whose function is to send signals to stop eating, to switch off the appetite and to activate feelings of fullness.

Some researchers believe that certain conditions, such as existing on very low-calorie diets, may cause CCK to become 'numbed'. As a result, the dieter is no longer able to recognise the signal to stop eating. Because very restrictive diets don't supply enough nutrients to the body and the body constantly wants to fuel up on nutrients, the 'stop eating' signal from the brain gets mixed messages and then fails to function properly.

For this reason, this dieting strategy will never be successful in the long term. Fortunately, when the person resumes eating a normal diet, CCK functions also return to normal.

Studies also show that those who engage in these extreme dieting practices lose their ability to recognise their natural hunger signals. Since these people have denied their hunger signals for so long, when they do eat, they're at risk of overeating because they can no longer register what 'fullness' feels like and they don't know when to stop.

Learning to Listen

So, what's the bottom line when it comes to hunger? Learn to listen to your body's hunger signals, eat and then acknowledge your body's feelings of fullness and satisfaction (rather than continuing to eat until you feel stuffed and uncomfortable). Try the following strategies, which will help you to tune in to your body's signals.

Get off the clock. Many people eat because of external circumstances, not because their bodies are telling them to eat. It could be the time of day ('It's noon, so I must have lunch'), or certain beliefs ('I have to finish this pizza because I don't want to be wasteful'), that lead to this sort of eating. These habits – especially when coupled with large portion sizes – contribute to people's

Blood Sugar and Hypoglycaemia

When people speak of blood sugar level, they're referring to the measure of the concentration of glucose in the bloodstream. (Glucose is the main source of energy for all bodily functions and comes from carbohydrates.) It's important to keep your blood sugar level stable, because if it gets out of balance, you won't feel your best. Also called hypoglycaemia, low blood sugar, in particular, is blamed for many conditions – from lack of energy to psychiatric disorders.

Hypoglycaemia is not a disease; rather, it's a set of symptoms that indicate blood sugar levels aren't normal. Symptoms may include one, some or many of the following: fatigue, irritability, lack of concentration, rapid heart rate, anxiety, hunger, shakiness and headaches. The only way to determine if you're actually hypoglycaemic is to get a blood sugar test.

Each individual has a different response to blood sugar levels. Some people may feel hypoglycaemic even when their blood sugar levels are in the normal range; others may not feel any symptoms even if their blood sugar levels have dipped into the clinically hypoglycaemic range. If you feel that you suffer from hypoglycaemia (and some of my clients do), you need to get your blood sugar levels tested by your doctor.

An acute episode of hypoglycaemia requires immediate treatment. If your blood glucose level is anywhere between 1.1 to 3.3 mmol/l, you should receive treatment. People with levels between 2.2 to 3.3 mmol/l should eat crackers or drink milk, while those with the lower end of 1.1 to 2.2 mmol/l should eat 2 to 3 teaspoons of simple sugar, such as honey or table sugar, followed by a well balanced meal in 10 to 15 minutes.

food lives spinning out of control. Instead, opt for flexible meal times and eat when your body tells you to, not when the clock does.

Slow down. After you've eaten, it takes the brain about 20 minutes to register that you're full. If you slow down while you eat, your body will have time to recognise that it's being fed and satisfied. Put your fork down between bites, chew your food for longer and drink plenty of water throughout the meal. All of these will force you to slow down while eating.

Eat when you're hungry, not starving. Don't allow yourself to get to the point of starving before you eat: you are much more likely to overeat or binge than if you eat when you're moderately hungry.

Recognise your thirst. It's easy to confuse your body's thirst signals with a desire for food. As a result, you may think you're hungry when you're actually thirsty. Instead of automatically reaching for food, first have a large glass of water to see if that's what your body really needs.

(continued on page 114)

LIVING A REAL FOOD LIFE

Mini-bar Raids Are a Thing of the Past for Ted

Name: Ted
Real Food Life Issues: Overweight, travels for work, human rubbish bin

Ted is in his early forties. He's married with three children ranging in age from 7 to 12. His demanding job requires long hours at work and about 2 weeks of business travel in the US each month. When we met, he was in a constant state of anxiety and felt so uptight that his stomach was chronically upset and he was able to sleep only 4 hours a night. Regularly travelling to different time zones didn't help matters. Here's where I found him:

> *5 June*
>
> *Can't write much today - flying to Houston tonight. Or Tulsa. Always get those confused because the hotels' mini-bars are exactly the same - on the small side, plenty of crisps and fizzy drinks, not too many chocolate bars. Not like Denver - those people know how to treat me right! Chocolate bars and a nice Danish pastry. My kind of people.*
>
> *Eating dinner tomorrow night with the head of construction on a major project. Last time we met, I hadn't eaten since 2 p.m. and I nearly ate the flower arrangement off the table. He said, 'You have to respect a man who relishes his dinner.' He offered me the rest of his steak - nice chap. Or at least I thought so. This time he wants to go for sushi ...*

One constant in Ted's life was his food. He always felt hungry and was afraid of food deprivation (even though he was never poor and was financially successful), so he always cleaned his plate because he never wanted to get hungry and be unable to feed himself. Not only did he always finish his own food, but he also finished all of his children's leftovers. They had nicknamed him 'the Human Rubbish Bin'.

All his life, Ted was overweight. But he had become so big over the past few years that he barely recognised himself any more. The stress of balancing his family and his career and the regular business travelling caused him to overeat even more than he previously had. Even though he was an experienced traveller, he felt that he never knew what to eat when he was away from home and he'd soothe his travel nerves with food. When he checked into his hotel, he would inevitably guzzle the whole contents of the mini-bar. Plus, he had a particular weakness for fried chicken sandwiches, sweets and crisps – cravings that were easy to satisfy on his many trips to various airports.

The way for Ted to get a Real Food Life was to set him up on an eating plan that he could easily follow when travelling. The first was to make sure he didn't go to the airport hungry. If he was hungry before he left, he ate a nourishing snack or meal. If he wasn't hungry before he left, he brought along some good snacks such as yogurt, low-fat cheese sandwiches or dried fruit and nuts – that way, he was prepared when hunger did strike. He also made sure to prearrange vegetarian or low-fat meals for his flights. To put an end to his mini-bar raids at the hotel, he always rang ahead and made the hotel empty the mini-bar before he even arrived so he couldn't be tempted.

Ted started eating fish four times a week with a salad or a cooked vegetable; this was easily achieved at business dinners. In the early years of his marriage, he used to do all the cooking, so he was fairly comfortable in the kitchen. When he was around at weekends, he cooked dinner for the whole family and made dishes to freeze for future meals.

Whether at home or travelling, Ted started drinking much more water. It surprised him that water helped to boost his energy, calm his stomach and subdue his hunger. He also started drinking a few daily cups of ginger or chamomile tea to soothe his stomach. In an effort to slow his pace, he tried to get at least 6 to 7 hours of sleep each night. A month into his new way with food, he felt much less anxious and much more energised.

Ted gave serious thought to his compulsive need to finish all the food in sight. We talked about hunger levels and I coached him to slow down while eating. At first, this was pretty hard for him. When he made a conscious effort, he slowed down, recognised how quickly he got full and eventually even learnt to leave his children's leftovers alone. He either saved them for another meal or threw them away (which drove him mad, but he knew he was doing his body a favour).

By the end of 8 weeks, Ted had lost 9 kg (20 lb). He also felt stronger, was sharper at work, had more energy and had greater patience with his children – and more balance in his life.

Buy small. Resist the come-ons from food manufacturers who want you to buy giant packets of their products. If you buy only small packets of foods you love and crave (like biscuits, crisps or sweets), you will eat less. Research has shown that people eat less of a food when it's in a small packet than when it's in a larger packet.

Eat often. Eating small but frequent meals throughout the day will keep your blood sugar levels more stable than if you eat three large meals. And stable blood sugar levels could mean fewer and less severe mood swings, fewer cravings and greater energy. Furthermore, eating regular meals and snacks throughout the day will help you get in touch with your true, biological hunger levels. If you retrain yourself to recognise feelings of hunger, you can acknowledge them and eat only when you're truly hungry.

Cravings

'Craving' is just another word for emotional hunger. When you're biologically hungry, many different kinds of food can quell your hunger and fill you up. But if you have a craving, you have an overwhelming desire for a very specific taste and only by eating that thing will you get satisfaction. If you're craving a chocolate bar, tuna won't satisfy you.

Ninety-seven per cent of all women and 68 per cent of all men experience cravings at some point. More women have cravings because hormones released during the menstrual cycle and pregnancy promote cravings. For most people, cravings hit the hardest between 3 p.m. and 6 p.m. and after 8 p.m.

On the other hand, perpetual dieters have cravings around the clock. Studies have shown that people who go on and off short-term, highly restrictive fad diets (with monotonous eating plans and many 'forbidden' foods) usually have intense cravings. They especially crave foods they aren't 'allowed' to eat – and end up thinking about them all day and ultimately become obsessed with them. Conversely, people who go on long-term eating plans tend to have fewer cravings. They have cravings less frequently because their diets are not only more sensible than restrictive ones, but these diets also tend to provide a wide variety of food options so they don't foster feelings of starvation or promote emotional eating.

If you are having a food craving, don't ignore it: acknowledge it and find a way to satisfy it. The more you fight a craving, the more it will become an issue. To move past your craving, you have to give yourself permission to satisfy it and enjoy the food you're craving – but do so in smaller quantities. Try eating a small portion of the food you crave and then end it. Stop eating and move on. After you've fed your craving, try not to focus on it any more. Recognise that you've indulged it and that you're satisfied and continue on with the rest of your day.

Metabolism

While hunger is our body's way of telling us that we need fuel, metabolism is the engine that burns and uses that fuel. We all need a minimum number of calories to keep our bodies operational and to maintain basic vital functions, including heartbeat, liver functions and breathing. The minimum number of calories required is measured by the Basal Metabolic Rate (BMR). This is what people are referring to when they talk about the 'base' metabolism or metabolism at complete rest. Body shape and size as well as activity levels also help to determine the

Restrictive Diets: Enemy Number One to Metabolism and Hunger

If you're on a restrictive diet and eat fewer than 1,000 calories a day, your metabolism will slow down and adjust itself to conserve energy and preserve bodily functions.

Why? When you restrict your calories, your body doesn't know it's dieting; it thinks it's starving because of famine. Your body will slow down all its basic physiological functions because it doesn't know when it will be fed again. First, your heart rate slows down. Next, your body temperature drops and your energy levels decrease. Then your metabolism slows down, causing you to become moody and sluggish. Your body does this to conserve energy and calories so that it can maintain basic body functions.

In one study, participants were placed on severe diets that would cause them to lose 25 per cent of their body weight (basically, it starved them). During this diet, the subjects became totally obsessed with food. They collected recipes and hung pictures of food on their walls; they also became irritable, moody, upset and lethargic. When they were allowed to put the weight back on, they binged and felt out of control with their eating and still the food obsessions lingered. Chronic dieters may be at risk of developing these same traits.

Another study weighed a group of chronic dieters and a group of non-dieters. The researchers told half the subjects they weighed 2 kg (4.5 lb) less than they actually did and told the other half they weighed 2 kg more. Both the dieters and non-dieters who were told they weighed 2 kg less were unaffected by what the researchers told them. However, unlike the non-dieters, the dieters who were told they weighed 2 kg more had a big drop in self-esteem, experienced bad mood swings and binged excessively on food, despite the hunger signals their bodies gave them. You don't need to be a scientist to analyse this data: chronic dieting is bad for your mind and body.

amount of calories a person needs for her day. Simply put, some people need a lot of fuel to keep them going, while others don't need as much, depending on their genes and activity level.

Lean muscle mass has a higher metabolism (that is, it burns more calories at rest) than fat does. So if you are more muscular, your metabolism will be higher than that of someone who has less muscle and more fat. Since a man has 10 to 20 per cent more muscle than a comparably sized and aged woman and since muscle burns more calories than fat does, men's metabolisms tend to be higher than women's. As a result, men can eat 5 to 10 per cent more than women without putting on any weight.

The BMR accounts for 60 per cent of your total daily energy needs, but it can go up to 75 per cent if you increase your muscle mass through resistance exercises like lifting weights, running and dancing. Since muscles are the body's calorie-burning furnace, when you build muscle, your metabolism will rise, which can cause even more calories to be burned both during and after exercise.

The metabolism, like many bodily attributes, is an inherited genetic trait – and it's hard to change biological destiny. Genetics can explain why a woman who is the same size and has the same activity level as her friend may be able to eat a lot more than her friend and still not put on any weight. But don't despair if your genes have dealt you a sluggish metabolism. You can increase your lean muscle mass and shrink your stores of body fat and, in so doing, boost your metabolism if you regularly lift weights and do a variety of weight-bearing exercises.

Maintaining Your Metabolism

Your calorie needs peak at the age of 25. After that, they start to decline by 2 per cent every 10 years. This happens because as you age, the amount of lean muscle tissue you have usually decreases while your fat stores increase. If you remain active and exercise regularly, however, your metabolism can remain strong your entire life. Remember: it doesn't matter at what age you begin exercising, because at any age, exercise will increase your metabolic rate.

Measure Your Metabolism: A Ballpark Estimate

To get an absolutely accurate measurement of your BMR, you would need to go to have it tested at a hospital or clinic specialising in weight management and metabolism. There they would use very high-tech machinery and methods and it would be a very expensive procedure. Fortunately, most people don't need to get that kind of precise measurement. Instead, you can measure your BMR yourself. While it won't be as accurate, it is free.

A crude way to estimate your BMR is to multiply your current weight in kilograms by 22 if you're a woman or 24.2 if you're a man. The body needs 22 to 24.2 calories for each kilogram it weighs to meet its very basic functional needs. So, a 64 kg (10 st) woman needs no less than 1,430 calories a day, and an 82 kg (13 st) man needs at least 1,985 calories a day. You should add 500 to that number, since the figure is based on a resting body, not an active one, and is really the fewest number of calories needed.

As I mentioned earlier, a person's calorie needs can go up or down, based on his or her individual activity levels and body shape and size. Unless you are a tiny woman, you will need at least 1,500 calories a day. If you're a taller woman, you probably need about 2,000 calories a day; if you're a man, you need about 2,500 to 3,500 calories each day, depending on your size.

If you take in more calories than you expend, it will result in your body storing fat – and you put on weight. To put on 0.5 kg (1 lb) of fat, you have to take in 3,500 calories more than you're using.

Note: This BMR formula is intended to give you a rough idea of how many calories you burn daily. I don't ever want you to count calories in your daily life, however. My clients don't count them and you shouldn't either. Base your eating plan on how your body feels, not on what your calculator tells you.

CHAPTER 6

HEALING FOODS AND HERBS

As you're developing your Real Food Life, you may want to add some healing foods or herbs to your diet to boost your energy levels, help maintain overall good health or occasionally help fight a cold. In this chapter, I'll discuss the varieties available and explain how to incorporate them safely into your Real Food Life.

Personally, I have found herbs to be helpful because they make me feel good and make me feel that I'm doing something extra to enhance my health. I don't use them daily, just when I need a boost. I also eat plenty of fruit and vegetables every day to ensure I get the medicinal properties they contain in a pure and natural form. For example, I regularly eat dandelion greens and fresh garlic to help control my blood pressure. When I feel a cold coming on, I use echinacea and drink fresh ginger tea. I love chamomile tea because it helps me relax after a long day. I also try to drink at least a cup of green tea daily because it's loaded with antioxidants.

While this chapter includes foods and herbs I've used myself and recommended to my clients, they are not intended as a cure for any health condition you may be experiencing. Rather, they should be used to enhance your health now and in the future.

Using Herbs and Other Natural Supplements

Natural food supplements and herb-based remedies have been around for centuries. Records indicate that many ancient cultures, including the Chinese, Indians, Romans and Native Americans, used a variety of herbs, plants and foods to cure illnesses. Modern medicine is rooted in herbal medicine; in fact, today around 25 per cent of pharmaceutical prescription drugs are derived from plants.

Herbs can play many roles. Certain ones, like parsley and basil, are most commonly used to enhance the taste of foods. But medicinal herbs – including the roots, bark and leaves – can be used to treat ailments or diseases and maintain good health. Natural food remedies are foods that, when eaten, have particular healthy attributes.

Medicinal herbs were once considered 'folk' or 'alternative' medicine, but they have become increasingly popular in recent years and have now started to enter the mainstream. This is a result of several factors, such as an increased awareness of the benefits of keeping fit and maintaining overall wellness, an awareness of the benefits of eating 'natural' foods and more widespread knowledge about disease prevention. Safety concerns about conventional medicines and a noted increase in the prevalence of chronic diseases have led many people to seek a natural way to maintain or improve overall health.

Many herbs have chemical properties that, when the herb is used correctly, can help protect and heal the body. But herbs always need to be used with caution. Many people in the UK self-medicate with herbs because medical doctors don't usually prescribe them. (In many other countries, particularly elsewhere in Europe and Asia, doctors regularly prescribe herbs to their patients.)

If you decide to use herbs, you need to be aware that some herbs may have negative interactions with prescription and non-prescription drugs. Natural doesn't always mean safe. If you're concerned about negative reactions or you want to learn more about herbs, you may want to visit a qualified herbalist. Look for someone with special training in herbs, a naturopathic or traditional Chinese medicine doctor, or a certified herbal practitioner through the National Institute of Medical Herbalists (see page 343), or other reputable organisation.

If you're currently taking prescription drugs, please talk to your doctor before trying any of the herbs and supplements listed below. Some of the drugs they are known to interact with are named, but not all of them.

The quality of herbal and nutritional products available commercially is highly variable. It is best to buy direct from reputable suppliers who are also used by herbal practitioners and nutritional therapists. Some recommended companies include:

▶ Baldwins: 020 7703 5550
www.baldwins.co.uk

▶ Higher Nature: 01435 882880
▶ Napier's Direct: 0131 343 6683
www.napiers.net
▶ Neal's Yard Remedies: 0161 831 7875
www.nealsyardremedies.com
▶ Organic Herb Trading Company:
01823 401205
www.organicherbtrading.com

Natural Food Supplements and Herbs

Ready to be introduced to some of the most effective healing foods and herbs? Read on.

Cayenne (Also Known as Capsicum or Chilli Pepper)

What cayenne does: Cayenne aids digestion and improves circulation. It helps to ward off colds, sinus infections and sore throats, and is good for the heart, lungs, kidneys and stomach.

Dosage: Sprinkle sparingly on savoury foods such as soups throughout the day.

Chamomile

What chamomile does: Chamomile may help promote sleep and alleviate stress and anxiety. It also acts as an anti-inflammatory for the digestive system.

Dosage: One cup of tea. Pour 300 ml (10 fl oz) of boiling water over 1 heaped teaspoon of dried flower heads (or use a tea

ball) and let infuse, covered, for 5 to 10 minutes; strain and serve. If you can't find dried flower heads, use a good-quality tea bag such as Hambledon Herbs.

Cinnamon

What cinnamon does: Cinnamon relieves diarrhoea and nausea and enhances digestion. It also helps to decongest nasal passages.

Dosage: Sprinkle on sweet foods such as porridge, or on toast.

Dandelion Greens

What dandelion greens do: Dandelion greens work as a diuretic (helping to release retained water) and relieve bloating. They're also loaded with B vitamins.

Dosage: Steam dandelion greens until soft, let cool and then add a squeeze of fresh lemon and a drizzle of extra-virgin olive oil. Toss well before eating.

Garlic

What garlic does: Garlic has anti-inflammatory, antioxidant and anti-yeast properties. It enhances the immune system and may help prevent some cancers. It may also lower blood pressure, LDL (bad) cholesterol and triglycerides, and may raise HDL (good) cholesterol. The allicin in garlic gives its characteristic odour and taste and is where most of the medicinal properties are found.

Dosage: 1 clove of fresh garlic a day

Powerful Pointers for Boosting Your Immune System

Every day, your immune system defends you from invading marauders such as viruses and bacteria. Sometimes, though, it can do with a boost. If you've noticed that you've been frequently unwell lately, help your immune system out with the following natural strategies.

- Vitamins C and E are both powerful antioxidants that increase resistance to infection and enhance the immune system. Make sure you get at least 40 milligrams of vitamin C and 3–4 milligrams of vitamin E each day.

- Try eating several antioxidant-rich foods each day. Good choices include tomatoes; sweet potatoes; carrots; peppers; broccoli; dark green, leafy vegetables; apricots; melons; citrus fruit; strawberries; wheat germ; cold-pressed vegetable oils; and nuts and seeds.

- Garlic is a great antioxidant and antibiotic that can protect against infection. It also contains phytochemicals that stop bacterial growth and may help stimulate the immune system. Make sure you eat a few cloves of raw or lightly cooked garlic regularly.

- Omega-3 fatty acids can help reduce chronic inflammation that stems from a hyperactive immune system. They also help strengthen cell membranes, which are our bodies' first defence against infection. Eat fish, nuts and seeds several times a week.

- Laughter, getting 8 hours of sleep each night, exercise and having strong emotional connections with others can help keep you healthy.

(limit the cooking time to no more than 15 minutes or the allicin becomes inactive).

Ginger

What ginger does: A powerful antioxidant and effective antimicrobial agent, ginger is useful for treating bowel disorders, circulatory problems, travel sickness, indigestion, nausea, vomiting and morning sickness. It contains shogaols, which are natural anti-inflammatory agents.

Dosage: 2.5 cm (1 in) square of candied, crystallised or fresh ginger; or one cup of ginger tea (1 to 2 tablespoons of peeled, chopped fresh ginger simmered in 300 ml/ 10 fl oz of water for about 15 minutes); or one or two 500-milligram capsules daily.

Caution: Avoid ginger supplements if

you're taking anticoagulant or blood-thinning medication.

Green Tea

What green tea does: Green tea contains an antioxidant that is 100 times more effective than vitamin C and 25 times more effective than vitamin E in protecting against cancers including oesophageal, stomach, lung, bladder, pancreatic and colon. It also promotes healthy teeth and contains polyphenols that increase HDL (good) cholesterol and decrease LDL (bad) cholesterol and can protect against heart disease.

Green tea is made from unfermented dried tea leaves, usually grown in Asia. It contains about a quarter of the caffeine of coffee and half the caffeine of regular tea; feel free to drink decaffeinated green tea if you're affected by caffeine. (Note: Milk deactivates the antioxidant properties of any tea.)

Dosage: One cup or more a day. Infuse 1 teaspoon of tea leaves (use a tea ball, if you have one) in 1 cup hot (just under boiling) water for 1 to 3 minutes, strain and drink.

Peppermint

What peppermint does: Peppermint enhances digestion and stimulates the appetite. It also alleviates chills, colic, diarrhoea, headache and indigestion.

Dosage: One cup of tea as needed. Pour 300 ml (10 fl oz) of boiling water over 1 heaped teaspoon of dried leaves (or use a tea ball) and let infuse, covered, for 5 to 10 minutes; strain and serve.

Caution: If you have gastro-oesophageal problems, such as acid reflux, do not use peppermint.

Yogurt

What yogurt does: Yogurt contains bacteria *(Lactobacillus acidophilus)* that can help maintain the gastrointestinal tract. It also helps maintain the flora of the vaginal canal and reduces the incidence of candidal vaginitis (candida yeast).

Dosage: Eat 1 to 2 small pots of low-fat natural yogurt daily.

The following herbs are ingested either in pill or liquid form (you place drops on or under your tongue or drink in water) or applied as a topical lotion, liquid or oil. You can purchase these herbs in health food shops and better chemists. You can also order them from the manufacturers over the Internet.

Echinacea

What echinacea does: Echinacea decreases the severity of cold symptoms and may lower your chance of catching the common cold. It's been approved in Germany for treating colds, influenza and upper respiratory infections. When applied topically, it enhances wound healing.

Get Relief When You're Feeling Bloated and Windy

If you're so bloated that you're wondering how your ring ever fitted on your finger, sample the following suggestions. They're guaranteed to relieve that bloated, windy feeling.

• Avoid salty foods, which can cause you to retain water and make you feel and look puffy.

• If you're eating a lot of wind-promoting foods, such as fibre-rich beans, try cutting down on your portions. Also add a few drops of Beano (an enzyme that helps digest wind-causing sugars) to your wind-producing food. Beano is available from specialist health food shops.

• Lack of vitamin E causes fluid retention as well as cramps and breast tenderness. You can increase the amount of vitamin E you get by adding some extra-virgin olive oil, nuts, seeds, brown rice or legumes to your diet. Also, take a supplement.

• Too little protein in your diet can also cause fluid retention. Make sure you have some fish, tofu, chicken or lean meat each day.

• Acidophilus can help with wind. Eat all-natural yogurt made with active cultures or take an acidophilus supplement daily.

• Fresh pineapple contains an enzyme that helps with wind and soothes the stomach.

• Fresh papaya contains enzymes that aid digestion, as does mint. Try a papaya and mint salad.

• Aniseed or fennel seeds can help soothe your stomach, decrease wind and aid digestion. Add some to your food or chew on a teaspoonful after eating.

• Drink ginger or chamomile tea. Both are age-old remedies known to help calm the stomach.

• If you get wind after eating dairy products, you may be sensitive to dairy or lactose intolerant. Try Lactaid with your milk – it's an over-the-counter lactose digestion aid.

Dosage: No more than nine 300- to 400-milligram capsules per day. It's most effective when taken at the first sign of a cold or infection; take for 8 to 10 days, then stop.

Caution: Do not use echinacea if you're allergic to closely related plants such as ragweed, asters and chrysanthemums. Do not use if you have tuberculosis or an autoimmune condition unless on the advice of an expert herbal practitioner because echinacea stimulates the immune system. Avoid this herb if you're pregnant.

Ginkgo Biloba

What ginkgo biloba does: Used to treat lack of concentration, lack of energy, dizziness, absentmindedness and confusion, ginkgo biloba increases cerebral blood flow. It may help with tinnitus (ringing in the ear) and may improve hearing.

Dosage: Three capsules of 40-milligram standardised extract a day. It takes 6 to 8 weeks before results are evident.

Caution: Do not use with aspirin or other nonsteroidal anti-inflammatory medications or blood-thinning medications such as warfarin. Do not use if you're being treated for infertility.

Kava Kava

What kava kava does: This herb helps relieve anxiety and insomnia without morning grogginess. It also relieves menopausal anxiety and may help with hot flushes. Kava kava has been used for hundreds of years by native South Pacific Islanders as a calming drink.

Dosage: No more than six 400- to 500-milligram capsules a day.

Caution: Do not take more than the recommended dose on the package. Do not take with alcohol or barbiturates. Use with caution when driving since it is a muscle relaxant. Do not use if you're taking drugs for depression. Do not take it for more than 3 months, because you can become dependent on it. Do not use if you're pregnant or breast-feeding.

(A number of cases of liver disease associated with taking standardised extracts of kava have been reported in Germany and have led to an investigation into the herb by the Medicines Control Agency in the UK. At the time of writing suppliers in the UK have been asked to voluntarily withdraw kava kava from sale. Seek advice from your doctor or herbal practitioner.)

Saw Palmetto

What saw palmetto does: This herb improves urine flow, reduces prostate gland swelling and prevents further progression of an enlarged prostate gland. It can help boost the immune system and can alleviate cystitis.

Dosage: Six 500-milligram capsules a day.

Caution: Consult your doctor for proper diagnosis and monitoring before using saw palmetto to treat an enlarged prostate gland.

Valerian Root

What valerian root does: It improves sleep without daytime drowsiness. Valerian root has been used for hundreds of years through-out Europe as a sedative, to relieve insomnia, anxiety and muscle spasms.

Dosage: For sleep only: 300 to 400 milligrams 1 hour before bed.

Caution: Do not use with sleep or mood medications because it may intensify their effects. Sensitive individuals may experience heart palpitations and nervousness; if you experience these symptoms, discontinue use.

Supplements Especially for Women

Many herbs and natural foods are particularly useful in treating women's health problems. Below I've noted a few that I've found especially beneficial.

Black Cohosh

What black cohosh does: Black cohosh controls the changes associated with menopause. It reduces the number and severity of hot flushes and increases the strength of pelvic floor muscles. Black cohosh also reduces depression, irritability, fatigue, headache, vaginal dryness and promotes sleep. It has been used in Germany since the 1950s for menopausal symptoms.

Dosage: Three 500- to 600-milligram capsules a day of the dried root. Should not be taken by women with a history of breast cancer or in pregnancy.

Dong Quai

What dong quai does: Dong quai is helpful for relieving urinary tract infections, PMS symptoms, and irregular and difficult periods with weak menstrual flow. It's used with vitex or black cohosh for menstrual and menopausal symptoms.

Dosage: Up to six 500- to 600-milligram capsules a day.

Caution: Do not use for more than 6 months. Do not use with blood-thinning or anti-platelet drugs. Avoid if you have heavy periods.

Flaxseed

What flaxseed does: A stool softener and a great source of fibre, flaxseed is a natural laxative. It's an antioxidant that can protect against breast, ovarian and prostate cancers. It's also high in omega-3 fatty acids, which may reduce LDL (bad) cholesterol. It also reduces symptoms of PMS and menopause. One of the world's oldest cultivated plants, flaxseed is currently grown for fibre (linen), seed oil (linseed oil) and seeds.

Dosage: 1 teaspoon freshly crushed seeds twice a day (sprinkled on food). Grind flaxseeds in a coffee grinder (seeds need to be crushed and eaten within 20 minutes or the medicinal properties will be destroyed) or take 1 to 4 tablespoons of flaxseed oil a day. Four tablespoons a day can increase HDL (good) cholesterol and

Say Goodbye to Constipation

Don't be embarrassed by a case of constipation. Cure it with one of the following home remedies.

- Increase your soluble fibre intake. Slowly start to include more fruit, vegetables and whole grains in your eating plan each day but avoid harsh fibre like wheat bran.
- Brown rice; dark green, leafy vegetables (such as spring greens, kale, cabbage and Brussels spouts); beans; asparagus; figs; prunes; nuts and seeds; toasted wheat germ; and berries will help fill you, flush you out and give you needed fibre.
- Rhubarb is a natural laxative. Don't eat the leaves – they're poisonous. But do cut the stalks into short pieces, add sugar or honey to taste, and cook over medium heat for about 10 minutes. Add hulled strawberries, raspberries, blackberries or blueberries (frozen are fine) and cook for another minute or so and you have a fresh, sweet-and-sour dessert that will make you 'regular'.
- Freshly ground flaxseed is a great natural laxative. Add a tablespoon or two to your cereal or salads.
- Essential fatty acids help lubricate the intestines, so add some olive oil or walnut oil to your next salad or steamed vegetable dish.
- Pour yourself a bowl of high-fibre cereal such as All-Bran, which contains 11 grams of fibre.
- Water is a great lubricant for your system. Drink at least eight 225-ml (8-fl oz) glasses a day.

decrease LDL (bad) cholesterol and triglycerides.

Caution: Do not take if you have a bowel obstruction. Take crushed seeds with at least 300 ml (10 fl oz) of water. Do not use if you have intestinal or oesophageal problems.

Phyto-oestrogens

What phyto-oestrogens do: These are oestrogen-like substances found in plants. Before the onset of menopause, they can protect against oestrogen-related cancers; after menopause occurs, they rebuild depleted levels of 'good' oestrogens and can help with symptoms of menopause.

Good sources of phyto-oestrogens include alfalfa, aniseed, basil, beans, caraway, chervil, fennel, hops, liquorice, parsley, sage and especially soya foods like tofu (try to buy organic soya food products).

Dosage: Try to have at least one good source of phyto-oestrogen-rich food daily. For example, 110 g (4 oz) beans, a herb-rich salad, or 110 g (4 oz) of tofu. Also, cook with liberal amounts of herbs.

Vitex

What vitex does: This herb is helpful in alleviating menstrual cramps and breast tenderness and regulating irregular menstrual cycles. It relieves PMS anxiety and other PMS symptoms including migraines, cramps, bloating and constipation. It stimulates milk production in lactating women. Vitex is also used to treat menopausal symptoms including hot flushes and vaginal dryness. It has been used to treat women's health problems for more than 2,000 years.

Dosage: One to two 500-milligram capsules a day.

Caution: May counteract the effectiveness of birth control pills.

PART 3

THE 8-WEEK FOOD LIFE MAKEOVER PLAN

WELCOME TO THE 8-WEEK MAKEOVER PLAN

Let's get started!

You are literally holding, in your very own hands, the power to develop your Real Food Life. I've developed this programme over years of working with all kinds of clients, from a young teenager who struggled with body consciousness to a retired businessman who needed to let go of his high-fat diet in order to save his own life. While everyone's individual circumstances are different, we all go through the same process in adopting the changes of our Real Food Lives. During these 8 weeks, you'll learn all the skills you need to define, embrace and rejoice in your very own Real Food Life.

A big part of developing your own Real Food Life is evaluating where you are now, targetting your most limiting old food life habits, sweeping them out of your life and filling in the space that remains with new, healthy, invigorating food choices. Although I can't be with you while you move through these next 2 months, I'll do my best to answer each of your questions as they arise.

In week 1, you'll become a student of your own habits, thinking about the larger issues that may have shaped your current food life. You'll set your ultimate goal and answer the question, 'What will my Real Food Life look like and how will I know when I get there?'

You'll don a white doctor's coat in week 2 to study your results and give yourself a food life diagnosis – what kind of eater are you? You'll also begin setting weekly mini-goals that will guide your choices during the week and you'll check your progress at the end with your weekly Get Real Check-in.

Week 3 is a fun one – I'll get you to do a Kitchen Makeover. We take a good, hard look at the food you've been surrounding yourself with, evaluating each item to determine if it has what it takes to remain a part of your Real Food Life. Then we'll take your show on the road, hitting the supermarket to map out a strategy for the fastest, highest-value shopping trips.

Cooking is a big part of taking responsibility for your Real Food Life and in week 4, you'll draw on everything you've learned before to enjoy the power of cooking your first Real Food Life meal.

In week 5, I'll give you fun and interesting ways to tackle the nuts and bolts of any Real Food Life week: eating a healthy, satisfying lunch and fitting in energising exercise.

By this point in your programme, you'll have made some enormous changes. During week 6, we'll take a moment to study your progress, savour your accomplishments and chart a course for the remaining 3 weeks. I've also anticipated many of your most challenging food moments, from the celebration meal at your mother's to the holiday hotel buffet brunch, and given you specific methods to deal with each one.

During week 7, we go back to the scene of your most common food life crimes – the restaurant. I'll give you targeted strategies to zoom in on the best choices on any menu, so you can relish dining out without sabotaging your Real Food Life.

Triumphant and buzzing with new possibilities, we'll launch week 8 with a talk about some hurdles that may still be holding you back (or may pop up in the future). Armed with the strength of these suggestions, you'll give any resistance to your Real Food Life the knockout punch!

In each week, I'll introduce new tasks for you to continue working on as the plan progresses. Each week builds on the next and while I might not remind you of certain ongoing tasks in the main part of the week's chapter, I've provided a handy reminder at the beginning of the week (in the checklist) and at the end of the week (in the Get Real Check-in). Along the way, I'll give you shopping lists, mental strategies, Instant Makeovers – all the powerful tools in my bag of tricks – to catapult you into your new, rich, rewarding Real Food Life. With my help and your hard work, you are about to be reborn!

CHAPTER 7

Week One:

KICK-STARTING YOUR REAL FOOD LIFE

A re those trumpets I hear? Well, if they're not playing for you, they should be. You've made a big first step – you've decided you want to get a Real Food Life. Congratulations and welcome. Now let's get started!

Just like most of the long-lasting changes we make in our lives, your Real Food Life is built from small steps that add up to big pay-offs. Each week, I'll guide you through a series of very achievable, very *satisfying* tasks that help you reach your ultimate goals. The work you do in week 1 will be the first small steps on the road to achieving significant positive changes in your food life.

Though this plan covers 2 months, there's no need to feel nervous about it. Your biggest task this week is pretty simple – just be you.

During this week, you will:

▶ Accomplish Instant Makeover 1: replace two sugared drinks per day with two glasses of water

▶ Make an appointment with your doctor for a checkup

▶ Buy a notepad or journal

▶ Fill out a quick questionnaire on the broad aspects of your food life

▶ Choose one or two ultimate goals for your plan

▶ Begin keeping your personalised food journal

▶ Complete week 1 of your Get Real Check-in

Instant Makeover 1:

Replace Two Sugared Drinks with Two Extra Glasses of Water

This week, I won't be asking you to make a single change in the way you eat, but I do want you to replace two flavoured or sugar-added drinks (such as fizzy drinks and coffee) with two glasses of water every day. Now, I ask you – isn't that a pretty low-stress way to kick-start your Real Food Life?

As the first of eight bad habits you'll cleanse yourself of over these weeks, replacing two sugared or flavoured drinks with water is the primary one for good reason. Water plays a key role in nearly every function of our bodies, including digestion, waste control, circulation and body temperature maintenance. In addition, water fills you up, so you tend to eat less. And water is instant energy when you're feeling tired. (In fact, tiredness is one of the most common signs of dehydration.) Because dehydration can leave you feeling mentally fuzzy, drinking more water can help you to think more clearly.

Now, if for some reason you never drink any sweetened drinks (coffee included), just add two glasses of water. Unless you're already drinking at least ten 225-ml (8-fl oz) glasses of water a day, you could always do with a little extra.

Imagine that you're taking a long trip. The first thing you'd probably do is buy a big map that will give you detailed information about the best roads to take. But you can't chart out your course on a map without knowing where you're starting from!

Likewise, when you begin your Real Food Life journey, you first need a plan that will 'map out' the best strategies to follow. In week 1, I'll guide you through a process that will give you an accurate view of the place you come from, food-wise. Once you establish a starting point, you can confidently point yourself towards your goal and nothing will stand between you and your Real Food Life. As you go along, these first 8 weeks will allow you to get rid of unhealthy food habits and replace them with positive, health-enhancing ones.

1. Make an Appointment with Your Doctor

OK, so let's say your road trip is a cross-country move – you're starting a new life in a whole new place. Would you just jump in your car and head out for the hills? You'd probably want to make sure your car is up to the challenge – you'd take it to the garage, get the mechanic to look under the bonnet, pump-up the tyres, change the oil.

Think of your doctor as the mechanic who can pronounce your vehicle sound for the journey. Before you start your Real Food Life, I strongly recommend making an appointment with your doctor for a checkup. If you're taking any medication, your doctor can advise you on any precautions you should take with your diet or if you have any medical conditions that might limit your ability to exercise. The chances are, your doctor will be thrilled with the positive changes you plan to make.

2. Buy a Notepad or Journal

Phobic about school supplies? I'm not going to ask you to do any homework. Your food journal is more like the notes you used to pass to your best friend in class: detailed, confessional and very educational.

Your food journal will be your constant companion, developing into a comprehensive information bank about you. In it, you'll record your goals, your emotions and everything you put in your mouth for the next 56 days.

Oh and your toilet habits. Don't forget that.

You're going to carry it around for a while, so take some time to think about what type of journal will make you feel good to write in. If you get into this kind of thing, think about colour, paper texture, size. Where will you put it – in your handbag? Trouser pocket? Briefcase? Do you prefer the flexibility of spiral bound or the soul-soothing solidity of a cloth-covered diary? Remember, you'll be looking at it every day for the next 8 weeks, so try to love it a little. Go for at least 100 pages. Slap on an inspirational sticker. Get out the glitter pen. Go mad.

3. Look at the Big Picture

I've designed the questionnaire on page 136 to help you get started thinking about your current food life. Take some time to work through it now. Answer as truthfully as possible – the outcome will help you analyse the broader issues at work in your current food life and help you develop your ultimate Real Food Life goal. (If you prefer not to write in this book, you can jot down your answers in your newly purchased journal.)

4. Determine Your Real Food Life Ultimate Goals

Now that you've thought about the big picture, it's time to home in on your ultimate goal for the next 8 weeks. Perhaps even

(continued on page 140)

Your Real Food Life Starting Point: The Questionnaire

Food touches every part of your life – and you're about to find out if that touch is a tickle or a killer punch. These questions, grouped by general category, cover many of the basic issues that affect how – and what – you eat. Underneath the jokes, these are real questions. Circle the letter of the answer that most closely describes how you feel.

Food Likes and Dislikes

1. Fruit and veggies factor into my eating with
   a. two kinds at every meal and one at every snack
   b. a salad with lunch and boiled carrots with dinner
   c. an extra scoop of tomato ketchup on my nearly daily chips

2. You will see me in the kitchen
   a. wielding courgettes and a chopping knife (I cook for myself at least 5 nights a week)
   b. tearing open a Lean Cuisine (I eat at home about 3 times a week)
   c. when hell freezes over (I never eat at home)

3. The colours of my diet
   a. look like a rainbow (with a variety of phytochemical-rich foods)
   b. look like a traffic light (two or three favourite foods)
   c. look like a 1970s beige living room (lots of refined carbs)

4. The last time I was at a fast-food restaurant
   a. I ordered a Happy Meal and played in the play area (haven't eaten it for years)
   b. I gave into a craving, but felt a little sick afterwards (eat it less than monthly)
   c. the assistant greeted me with 'Your standard order, miss/sir?' (eat it at least once a week)

5. If I'm really honest, I'd say fish is
   a. nature's irresistible power food (eat it 2+ times a week)
   b. tolerable when I'm in the mood (eat it monthly)
   c. best served crunchy (eaten deep-fried only)

Diet Mentality

1. When a new diet comes out, I
   a. don't consider following it for a minute
   b. read up on it, try it for a couple of days, then revert to my old ways
   c. make it my religion

2. If I made a chart of my weight over the past few years, it would look like
   a. the horizon (very stable)
   b. the rolling hills of Tuscany (repeatedly lost and put on the same 2 to 4.5 kg/5 to 10 lb)
   c. the Himalayas (repeatedly lost and put on 10 per cent of my body weight)

3. 'Bad' foods
   a. don't exist
   b. can feel so good
   c. make the best friends

4. I think about food
   a. when I'm hungry
   b. when I'm bored
   c. when I'm breathing

5. If I eat well during the week, by the weekend
   a. I restock with fresh foods from the greengrocer
   b. I reward myself with Friday night pizza and beer
   c. I succumb to a blur of brunch buffets and chips

Work Issues

1. Working through lunch usually means
   a. unwrapping a homemade low-fat turkey or smoked tofu sandwich on wholegrain bread
   b. taking a stab at whatever 'diet' dish the cafeteria is serving
   c. grabbing a cheeseburger and chips – and a couple of fizzy drinks to get me through the mid-afternoon slump

2. When I'm feeling overwhelmed at work
   a. I strap on my trainers and go out for a walk until my head clears
   b. I scavenge some nuts and low-fat crackers from the bottom drawer of my desk
   c. I spend wads in the vending machine

3. On the extremely rare slow day at work
   a. I catch up on paperwork and take an extra-long walk at lunchtime
   b. I linger over lunch, adding dessert and coffee to my normal meal
   c. I find myself irresistibly drawn to the receptionist's bowl of M&M's

(continued)

Your Real Food Life Starting Point: The Questionnaire (cont.)

4. When I'm angry with my boss
   a. I take a walk to clear my head and sort out my feelings
   b. I rant at my friends over lunch at the pizzeria
   c. I dive into a bag of crisps and pretend I'm crushing his head with every crunch

Home Life

1. My partner and I
   a. eat together every night, at the table
   b. eat together four times a week, twice at our favourite Chinese place
   c. eat together every night, side-by-side on the sofa

2. If I were honest about my relationship, I'd say
   a. my partner supports my efforts, often offering to make the changes along with me
   b. my partner is OK with any changes I make, as long as I don't ask him or her to change!
   c. my partner criticises my efforts and is convinced I'll fail

3. Since we got together, my weight
   a. has stayed the same
   b. has gone up or down more than 10 per cent
   c. has yo-yoed depending on life's stresses

4. I love eating alone because
   a. I cook to my taste and don't have anyone to please but myself
   b. my dinner routine is comfortable – me, the cat and the TV
   c. the fast-food restaurant bills are always under £5!

5. My flatmate and I
   a. share cooking and shopping duties and like preparing meals together
   b. bond over bags of biscuits
   c. size each other up and compete over everything

Family and Friends

1. Growing up, my mum and dad
   a. didn't worry about what or how much I ate

b. made comments, but backed off when I gave them The Look

c. hovered to the point of blocking my airspace

2. When I go home to visit, I
   a. take my own cereal, for difficult situations
   b. look forward to my favourite home-baked biscuits, but they lose their charm after the first dozen
   c. resist reacting to criticism by keeping my mouth full – the whole visit

3. When I was growing up
   a. all food was fair game, but there wasn't that much junk in the house
   b. Mum limited me to three fizzy drinks a day
   c. I spent my pocket money on bags of sweets

4. A standard evening with my best friends includes
   a. dinner and a movie
   b. dinner and a movie and a box of Maltesers
   c. dinner and a movie, a tub of caramel popcorn and a cola so large you need two hands to hold it

5. For me, standard bar fare is:
   a. a glass (or two) of wine, interspersed with mineral water
   b. a few handfuls of nuts washed down with a Rum and coke
   c. as many spicy chicken wings as the beer can extinguish

Emotions

1. When I'm feeling lonely or bored, I
   a. borrow a neighbour's dog and head for the park
   b. park myself on the sofa with a trashy novel and a low-fat snack
   c. commune with my good friends Ben and Jerry

2. When I'm angry or frustrated, I
   a. take a moment to breathe, then write in my journal about what's upsetting me
   b. call my best friend for an emergency meeting over double lattes
   c. take the phone off the hook and work my way through the biscuits that were stashed in the back of the cupboard

(continued)

Your Real Food Life Starting Point: The Questionnaire (cont.)

3. After I order a big, rich piece of cheesecake, I
   a. split it with my partner and savour every bite
   b. regret it, chastise myself and resolve to eat more healthily at my next meal
   c. order a liqueur coffee with whipped cream – when I blow it, I really blow it!

4. My food philosophy is
   a. eat to live
   b. eat now, repent later
   c. live to eat

5. When it comes to counting calories or grams of fat, I
   a. focus my efforts on checking food labels and portion sizes
   b. look only at grams of fat – calories aren't important
   c. methodically track each calorie and gram of fat as if dieting were quantum physics

Health

1. When I run to get the phone, I
   a. answer it on the first ring
   b. take a second to catch my breath and gasp out my hello
   c. why run? Screening is so much less effort

2. At 2 p.m. you're most likely to find me
   a. happily plugging away at work
   b. working steadily, but starting to think about dinner
   c. slumped at my desk, mumbling, 'must . . . stay . . . awake . . .'

before you started the questionnaire, you knew that you wanted to lose weight, acquire more energy or get your heart running more efficiently. All of those are excellent goals. While you were doing the quiz, maybe you noticed that your diet could use some more fruit and veggies or perhaps your trips to the toilet have been few and far between – in which case, fibre will be your new best friend.

Remember: as you develop possible goals, make sure each one is realistic. A goal of losing 25 kg (55 lb) in 8 weeks is unrealistic and bound to set you up for disappointment. Reducing the amount of unhealthy foods you eat, increasing your energy level, trimming your waistline by a few centimetres – these goals are not only achievable, they're probable! Getting a Real Food Life means

3. When my doctor tests my blood pressure, she
   a. puts a gold star on my chart (120/80)
   b. says it's passable, but she's not turning cartwheels (130/85)
   c. rolls out the stretcher just to be safe (140/90)

4. When it comes to my toilet business, I
   a. am so regular, you could set a watch by me
   b. am more or less regular, but sometimes need a little laxative help
   c. could write a novel in the time I spend in there

5. When I look at the hours adding up in my 'sleep bank'
   a. I feel like a billionaire (average 8+ per night)
   b. I'm living paycheque to paycheque (6 to 8 per night)
   c. I'm staring bankruptcy in the face (less than 6 per night)

Now go back and count up the number of *c* answers you've circled in each category. As you may have guessed, a *c* indicates you may be struggling with that particular food life issue. Do you notice any patterns in the way you responded? Does a particular category seem to be of special concern?

On the following lines, write down the top two categories that seem to be the biggest challenges for you.

_____

_____

_____

starting a wholesome eating programme that you can live with for the rest of your life.

For now, narrow your ultimate goals to one or two – these are your compass for the weeks ahead. Don't worry about how you're going to accomplish them just yet – we'll get to that in week 2, when we develop mini-goals, specific steps that will steadily get you towards your ultimate goal. (For instance, if your ultimate goal is to acquire more energy, your mini-goals might include drinking 2 litres (3½ pt) of water a day and replacing refined carbohydrates, such as white bread and bagels, with complex carbs, such as wholegrain bread and fruit and vegetables.) Your ultimate goal is the destination; your mini-goals are the highways and byways that will get you there.

Keep in mind that if at any time you want to change your goals or add to them, you can. For example, if you've met your ultimate goal by week 4, look back to your quiz answers and see if there's another issue you're grappling with in your food life – but first give yourself a pat on the back for achieving your first goal!

Take a look at the following list of common goals clients have shared with me over the years.

▶ *I want more energy!* Do you need stamina? Do you want to find foods that make you feel revved up and keep illness at bay?

▶ *I want to re-educate myself about food!* Do you want to become your own nutritionist so you can better understand food and make sensible food choices?

▶ *I want to lose weight!* Do you want to find an eating plan loaded with foods lower in calories and fat that satisfy you and fill you up?

▶ *I simply want to find foods I like that are good for me!* Do you want to find an eating plan that you can live with, that's enjoyable, tasty and easy, with a variety of foods that are emotionally and physically satisfying?

▶ *I want to eat more healthily!* Do you want to find foods that lower your cholesterol and reduce your risk of heart disease, diabetes and cancers?

▶ *I want to stop the food obsessions once and for all!* Do you want to find a place with your food where you simply feel calmer and more relaxed?

Open your journal and write your ultimate goals on the first page. The physical act of putting them on paper will strengthen your resolve and help solidify them in your mind. Then flip to the last page and write down an ultimate reward you'll give yourself when you complete the plan. Of course, the achievement of your goal is a tremendous gift in and of itself, but how will you mark the occasion of your success – with a new dress? A fancy night out on the town with just the two of you? That new cappuccino maker you've had your eye on? Make it something you'd consider too extravagant for every day – you really want this to feel like getting a gold medal.

Once you've made this contract with yourself, you have your destination. Now you just have to gather information for the journey.

5. Start Your Food Journal

Now that you've set your ultimate goals, the next step in getting a Real Food Life is to start keeping a food journal. I get all my clients to do it and you need to do it, too. It may seem like a drag at first, but in fact it's

WEEK: _____	DAY: _____	
Time	**Food** (include amount)	**Comments** (include the situation or activity, how you felt before and after eating, etc.)

the most valuable tool you have. Keeping a food journal not only makes you accountable for what you eat, but it will also help you to see your eating patterns and understand just how much (or how little) you eat, when you eat and why you eat.

Start your food journal on the next blank page of your notebook. Look at the template above. I recommend copying this simple chart into your notebook. It will help you to remember to include all the informa-

tion that will be so vital when you begin your analysis of your journal. After noting that this is week 1, day 1, use the journal to record absolutely everything you eat and drink during the day. (This may seem daunting at first, but once it becomes a habit, my clients tell me it keeps them accountable for what they eat, is very gratifying and helps them feel in control.)

The first column will not only help you to keep track of the times when you ate but

(continued on page 146)

LIVING A REAL FOOD LIFE

Nancy's New Food Life Has Her Sailing through the Menopause

Name: Nancy
Real Food Life Issues: Experiencing symptoms of menopause, craving carbohydrates

When I met Nancy, she was a 51-year-old school teacher and mother of three (two at college and one teenager still at home). She was going through the menopause and had many common symptoms, including hot flushes, weight gain around her waist, mild depression and exhaustion. She had never before had a sweet tooth, but for the first time in her life, she craved (and indulged in) biscuits and sweets. On top of this, she always felt bloated – like she was retaining water all the time. Here's where I found her:

3 November

Stevie Johnson caught me today. I was reaching into my desk, trying to get a sweet while the children had their heads down. I almost had the sweet unwrapped, inwardly cursing the loud plastic crinkling, when I nearly jumped out of my skin. Stevie shouted, 'Mrs M, how come you're allowed to eat sweets and we're not?'

Instantly, every child's head shot up and they all started half-whimpering about how 'it's not fair' and 'teachers are always. . . .' It was humiliating. I had to stand up and eat some humble pie, which was not the flavour I was craving. I told Stevie he was right. I even apologised. I took the bag of sweets out of my drawer and very dramatically dumped it in the bin.

Of course, I fished it out at break time.

In analysing Nancy's food journal, I saw that she ate a lot of high-sugar foods and very little protein. The first thing I asked her to do was cut back on those high-sugar foods. This would help stabilise her mood, reduce her depression and cut down on the hot flushes. I also got her to significantly cut her intake of refined carbohydrates, such as wheat pastas like macaroni and spaghetti, and replace them with whole grains including quinoa and brown rice for lunches and dinners and high-fibre cereal for breakfasts and snacks.

Nancy had avoided protein because she thought it was too 'fatty' and would contribute to her weight gain. I explained that the body needs protein to release water and repair muscles. I also noted that it would improve her concentration and would help curb her sweet cravings. She gradually added some to her eating plan. She especially liked fish and began eating it several times a week. Not only was it a great source of low-fat protein, but it was also a great source of omega-3 fatty acids. To get even more healthy essential fatty acids, she added pumpkin seeds to her salads and dressed her vegetables with olive oil. On my recommendation, she also started to take the nutritional herb black cohosh each day to help with her hot flushes.

For years, Nancy had avoided breakfast. She thought it took too much time and she didn't feel hungry in the morning. But this neglect caused her to have severe blood sugar swings and contributed to her afternoon sweet binges. Together, we found quick and light breakfasts she could enjoy. Fruit smoothies were a good choice for her. When she felt a little more hungry, she would opt for a hard-boiled egg with wholemeal toast and a piece of fruit. She quickly realised that eating breakfast gave her the energy she needed to last until lunch.

Nancy also began taking lunch with her to school, instead of foraging around the cafeteria or grabbing something quick and usually nutritionally unsound, at a fast-food restaurant near the school. Her packed lunches now always included some high-quality protein, such as a grilled chicken breast or prawns, along with a lot of vegetables and some wholegrain leftovers like brown rice or barley. Nancy recognised that having a hearty lunch really helped her to maintain her energy level through the afternoon – and almost completely squashed her desire for a 3 p.m. sweet fix. We made sure, however, that she had a snack if she wanted it, but instead of a packet of biscuits, she would reach for a soya yogurt with wheat germ and walnuts, or an apple with a little bit of peanut butter.

By the end of 8 weeks, Nancy was pleased to find that she had lost 4.5 kg (10 lb). Her body had released the excess water that made her feel puffy. Nancy was finally able to put on her rings and take them off easily and that was a boost to her mood. She was excited that her new food life fitted into her lifestyle with little effort. She was especially excited that the hot flushes had virtually disappeared and her cravings for sweets were no longer a constant issue. Overall, Nancy felt happier and more energised than she had since the onset of her menopause.

also how frequently you ate (perhaps you'll discover that you feel best when you're grazing on mini-meals throughout the day, for example). In the second column, record the approximate amount of food you ate. In the final column, write down all other relevant information, including what you were doing before eating; whether or not you were alone or with others; and how you felt both physically and emotionally before, during and after eating.

Finally, in a tiny, discreet area, reserve a bit of space in your journal to record your toilet visits. You could use a personalised system, but why not go for the old standards number 1 and number 2? While this may feel slightly strange at first, I assure you that this will help you to monitor how your system is functioning. If you have a bowel movement only every 2 days, that's an indication that you aren't eating enough fruit, vegetables and whole grain, fibre-rich foods (and maybe one of your goals should be to get regular!).

Don't forget to include a weekend in your food journal, so it reflects 7 consecutive days. After all, everyone knows weekend eating is an entirely different animal than the regimen of weekday meals. Remember: the only difference in what goes into your mouth this week is more water. Don't change anything about the way you eat this week. We need this time to see patterns in the way you eat and to identify the areas of your food life

that need to change. For example, maybe you'll discover that you eat differently on weekends, that family dynamics trigger 'food reactions' in you, that boredom causes you to eat a lot at night or that damaging thoughts about yourself influence what you eat.

The cardinal rule of getting a Real Food Life: be honest. About what you eat, how much, how often and, most important, how it feels. If you aren't honest, this whole process will be an exercise in futility. There's a compelling reason why you picked up this book and being honest is how you'll find out what's behind it. This isn't a diet. There is no such thing as 'cheating' or 'being bad'. By honestly and accurately recording what you eat, you'll give yourself the information you need to make positive changes and ultimately feel better about yourself in relation to food.

To get started, look at some sample entries from a few of my clients. Because they included detailed information about their motives for eating, how they were feeling at the time and the activities they were doing prior to eating, they were able to gain important insights into their eating patterns.

Your food journal is a powerful magnifying glass; with it, you'll get a much clearer picture of what you put into your body and how it makes you feel. Busy lives and a lack of basic knowledge about eating well have caused many of us to block the signals that pass between our bodies and minds. We

Time	Food	Comments
1:00 P.M.	1 chicken roll	Feeling like I totally messed up lunch. It was late and I was starving. Went to see a movie with the kids and HAD to get something before then. Had the chicken roll from a pizzeria next door instead of having popcorn, but it wasn't great.

Time	Food	Comments
3:00pm	Small Crab Salad w/ touch of mayo, lettuce and tomato.	Was in the fridge. I really wasn't hungry but it was there... I was helping my husband put away groceries.

Time	Food	Comments
Around 10:30 P.M.	Handful of M&M's two handfuls of potato crisps	Had a craving for chocolate, which I haven't eaten in a long time. Had some M&M's while I watched TV, but then I craved salt, so I had crisps.

don't know how to acknowledge different levels of hunger or to recognise if we're eating to fill emotional hunger or actual physical hunger. As you work to develop a Real Food Life, you will start eating in an aware way; you will recognise true hunger signals; and you will start hearing what your body really needs and wants and know how to satisfy it.

Finally, take special note of meals that are dominated by carbohydrates or protein. Then, note how you feel just before you eat your next meal. Say, for example, you eat some black bean soup for lunch, which is high in fibre and protein. Then, you notice that it's 6 p.m. before you're even thinking about food again and you've skipped your typical 3 p.m. trip to the vending machine (which was one of your goals!). You need to record that you had a positive response to proteins. Conversely, maybe you had a muffin for breakfast, which is mainly carbs, and you notice that you're ready for lunch at 11 a.m. instead of 1 p.m., which is when you usually start considering lunch. Note then that pure carbs don't sustain you as long as other foods (in fact, they're quickly emptied from the stomach when eaten alone). This awareness of how your body responds to different food groups will help you in the weeks

6. Complete Your First Get Real Check-in

When you're on a trip, doesn't it feel good to stop occasionally and check the map to reassure yourself you're on the right path? At the end of your Real Food week, maybe on a Sunday afternoon, take your food journal to your favourite chair, settle in with a cup of ginger or green tea and assess your progress.

Checking off the boxes in your Get Real Check-in will give you a well-deserved sense of accomplishment. Take time to record your feelings in your journal. Consider them notes to the new you, the one who will exist in the future, after you've achieved your goals. When you look back, you'll see how far you've come and how much you have to be proud of.

You'll notice that there's also a checkbox for a weekly reward. This might be a quick lunch-hour manicure, a longer-than-average soak in the bath, a CD you've had your eye on. Too many of us rush by our smaller successes, keeping our eyes on the big prize – losing 10 kg (20 lb), cutting down our cholesterol, exercising four times a week. But each completed step is its own finish line and deserves to be heralded as the victory it is – after all, you're not just drinking more water or becoming aware of what you're putting in your mouth, you are taking control of your food life.

Get Real Check-in

Assess your progress by checking off each of the following items you achieved during week 1.

❏ Instant Makeover 1: I replaced 2 sugared drinks with 2 glasses of water.

❏ I made an appointment with my doctor, to tell her of my plans for a new food life.

❏ I purchased a notebook or journal and personalised it.

❏ I completed the 'Real Food Life Starting Point' questionnaire and thought about the broad aspects of my food life.

❏ I selected one or two ultimate goals for the next 7 weeks.

❏ I kept my food journal each day.

❏ I rewarded myself for my intentions and my efforts.

Weekly Words: On a blank page in your journal, write a couple of paragraphs about what it feels like to keep your food journal. Has it been empowering? Annoying? Educational? Discuss how you think keeping a food journal will help you reach your goal.

CHAPTER 8

Week Two:

ANALYSING YOUR CURRENT FOOD LIFE

How do your arms feel right now? They should feel good and stretched out from all the pats on the back you ought to be giving yourself! By completing week 1, you've taken a very important step in beginning your Real Food Life.

Put on your lab coat – it's time to get down to some serious analysis. All the great research you did in week 1 feeds directly into week 2's main purpose: to analyse your current food life and create a new eating plan that will be the core of your Real Food Life. The work you do now will benefit you for ever. Don't worry – I'll take you through it step-by-step.

During this week, you will:

- ▶ Accomplish Instant Makeover 2: replace your current breakfast with high-fibre cereal
- ▶ Add one extra glass of water (aim for at least 6)
- ▶ Keep week 2 of your food journal
- ▶ Analyse the results of your week 1 food journal
- ▶ Determine if you're a protein-based or carb-based eater
- ▶ Determine whether you prefer grazing or traditional meals
- ▶ Try out sample menus
- ▶ Set 'mini-goals' as a way to achieve the ultimate goals you set in week 1
- ▶ Complete week 2 of your Get Real Check-in

Instant Makeover 2:

Replace Your Current Breakfast with a High-Fibre Cereal

If you don't currently eat breakfast, this is like a double whammy to your Real Food Life. The body needs breakfast to kick its metabolism into gear for the day – if you don't eat breakfast, you could be slowing your metabolism down by up to 5 per cent. Furthermore, by not eating in the morning, you set yourself up for energy drain, mental fuzziness and lunchtime bingeing.

Fibre is a key to your Real Food Life

for so many reasons: it fills you up, keeps your blood sugar stable, helps relieve constipation and helps cut down on how much fat you eat. Fibre itself has no calories and is found only in plant-based foods, so when you're eating a high-fibre meal, you're automatically increasing your intake of the healthiest stuff.

High-fibre cereal sticks with you, digesting more slowly than a bagel, to keep you satisfied longer. And never fear, today's high-fibre cereals are not the prunes-and-wheat-germ fare of our parents' generation – many are so tasty you'll find yourself looking forward to your morning meal.

1. Do a Complete Analysis of Your Week 1 Food Journal

When I work with clients, I get them to submit their food journals to me after 7 days and I analyse what they've written. By studying their journals, I'll see their main source of calories and fats and note their nutritional deficiencies. The timing of their food choices is amazingly telling – I can immediately recognise when they eat mindlessly and when they're actually hungry. I notice what foods they like and eat all the time and the foods they don't include. Since I can't be with you

in person, I'll show you how to analyse your journal for yourself.

Nutritional Analysis

Take your food journal from week 1 and count the number of servings of foods and food groups you ate from throughout each day. Using the Food Journal Analysis Chart (see page 154), tally up your portions. You might want to make several photocopies of this chart or duplicate it in your journal so you can use it not only for this week, but for the weeks to come as well.

In part 2 of this book, I discussed in

detail the food components of a Real Food Life. As you work through the following journal analysis, turn back to the previous section whenever you feel you need a refresher on this information.

After you've filled out the chart, turn to a fresh page in your journal to answer the questions below. The Real Food Life Targets that appear after each section will help you see where you need to increase certain food intakes and decrease others.

Carbohydrates

▶ Complex carbohydrates are found in foods such as breads, grains and cereals. How many servings of complex carbs did you have this week?

▶ Where are your complex carbohydrates coming from?

▶ Is your total number of servings more or less than you thought?

▶ Are the carbs you eat mostly in the form of refined white flour such as bagels, white bread and white rice? These refined carbohydrates are probably responsible for a great deal of your hunger after meals. Replace refined carbs with complex and you'll definitely feel a difference.

▶ Are you eating any whole grains or wholegrain products? Whole grains provide extra fibre and balance blood sugar.

Real Food Life Target: You need 3 to 10

servings of complex carbohydrates each day (where you fall in the range depends on your individual penchant for carbohydrates).

Fruit and Vegetables

▶ Fruit is nature's healthy snack, providing antioxidants, phytochemicals and fibre. How many servings of fruit did you have this week?

▶ What kinds of fruit did you choose?

▶ Is your total number of servings more or less than you thought?

▶ As much as we might wish it, apple pie, rhubarb crumble and fruit chews do not count as fruit servings. If you drink 100 per cent pure fruit juice, count one 225-ml (8-fl oz) glass as only half a serving of fruit when it comes to health benefits since fruit juice has none of the fibre and only some of the phytochemicals of whole fruit. Furthermore, fruit juice has a lot more calories than whole fruit.

▶ Vegetables will soon become the foundation of your Real Food Life. How many servings of vegetables did you have this week?

▶ What kinds of vegetables did you choose?

▶ Is your total number of servings more or less than you thought?

▶ Are you counting white potatoes – especially when French-fried – as a vegetable? While that may technically be true, that

(continued on page 156)

The Food Journal Analysis Chart

For each of the 7 days that you kept your food journal last week, record the number of servings that you ate of each of the following foods. Then count up the number of servings that you ate from each group, such as carbohydrates, fruit, vegetables and so on.

Servings

Food	Day 1	Day 2	Day 3	Day 4	Day 5	Day 6	Day 7
CARBOHYDRATES White bread							
Wholemeal bread							
Muffins							
Bagels							
White rice							
Brown rice							
Grains							
Whole grains							
Cereal							
Wholegrain cereal							
Pasta							
Other							
TOTAL							
FRUIT Fresh, tinned, or frozen fruit							
100 per cent fruit juice							
Dried fruit							
TOTAL							
VEGETABLES Fresh vegetables							
Cooked vegetables							
TOTAL							
PROTEINS Chicken (without skin)							
Chicken (with skin)							
Eggs							

Servings

Food	Day 1	Day 2	Day 3	Day 4	Day 5	Day 6	Day 7
Turkey (without skin)							
Turkey (with skin)							
Fish							
Beef (lean)							
Beef (fatty)							
Pork							
Lamb							
Cold meats							
Sausages							
Beans/legumes							
Soya food							
Other							
TOTAL							
DAIRY FOODS							
Whole milk							
Semi-skimmed milk							
Skimmed milk							
Full-fat cheese							
Reduced-fat cheese							
Yogurt							
Other							
TOTAL							
FATS							
Butter							
Margarine							
Vegetable fat							
Groundnut oil							
Lard							
Corn oil							
Bacon							
Other							
TOTAL SATURATED/ HYDROGENATED FAT							

(continued)

The Food Journal Analysis Chart (cont.)

Servings

Food	Day 1	Day 2	Day 3	Day 4	Day 5	Day 6	Day 7
Avocados							
Nuts and seeds							
Olive oil							
Rapeseed, sunflower, or safflower oil							
Other							
TOTAL MONOUNSATURATED OR POLY-UNSATURATED FATS							
BEVERAGES Water							
Green tea							
TOTAL WATER							
Fizzy drinks							
Diet fizzy drinks							
Fruit juice drink							
Coffee (hot or iced)							
Black tea (hot or iced)							
Herbal tea							
Other							
TOTAL SOFT DRINKS/ JUICE/COFFEE/TEA							

bland monotone white translates to very little nutritional value and tons of carbs. Try eating sweet potatoes instead, a power food packed with phytochemicals.

▶ Do you eat any dark-coloured vegetables such as broccoli, spinach, peppers, asparagus, sweet potatoes, carrots, spring greens or kale? Expand your vegetable repertoire to include a wide spectrum of colours. Look at my recipes beginning on page 259 for some ideas, then try one new recipe every week to expand your vegetable diet.

Servings

Food	Day 1	Day 2	Day 3	Day 4	Day 5	Day 6	Day 7
Beer							
Wine							
Alco-pops							
Mixed drinks							
Other							
TOTAL ALCOHOLIC BEVERAGES							
SNACK FOODS/ FAST FOODS							
Biscuits							
Cake							
Crisps							
Pretzels							
Sweets							
Ice cream							
Pizza							
Burgers							
Chips							
Fried chicken (or fried chicken sandwich)							
Other							
TOTAL							

Real Food Life Target: We're told to 'Strive for 5' portions of fruit and vegetables but I recommend you aim higher – at least 4 servings of vegetables and 3 to 4 servings of fruit each day – they're filled with vitamins, minerals, phytochemicals and fibre.

Protein

▶ Protein builds muscle and helps our brains function well – it's also one of the most satisfying food groups we can eat. How many servings of protein did you have this week?

What's a Serving?

This handy chart shows you at a glance what constitutes a serving of each type of food.

Complex carbohydrates: One slice of bread; 25 g (1 oz) ready-to-eat cereal; 75 g (3 oz) cooked cereal, rice or pasta; or one medium sweet or regular potato

Fruit: A medium apple, banana or orange; 110 g (4 oz) cooked or fruit tinned in its own juice, chopped; 75 g (3 oz) berries; 175 ml (6 fl oz) fruit juice; or 40 g (1½ oz) dried fruit

Vegetables: 25 g (1 oz) of raw leafy greens; 50–75 g (2–3 oz) of other types of veggies that are cooked or raw and chopped; 175 ml (6 fl oz) low-sodium vegetable juice; or 7 to 8 carrot sticks

Protein: 50–75 g (2–3 oz) cooked lean meat, fish, poultry or tofu; 1 egg; or 110 g (4 oz) cooked dry beans

Dairy: 225 ml (8 fl oz) skimmed cow's milk, soya milk or yogurt; 50 g (2 oz) processed cheese or soya cheese; or 40 g (1½ oz) natural cheese

Fats: 1 tablespoon of olive or rapeseed oils; 10 g (½ oz) of butter; 2 tablespoons of low-fat mayonnaise or 1 tablespoon of mayonnaise-like salad dressing; 2 tablespoons of sunflower or pumpkin seeds; 4 to 6 walnuts; 10 g (½ oz) of nut butter; 3 to 4 tablespoons of hummus; or one-quarter of an avocado

Water: 225 ml (8 fl oz)

▶ What kinds of protein did you choose?

▶ Is your total number of servings more or less than you thought?

▶ Is your protein mainly from animals or plants? If it's mainly from meat, are you making lean choices (chicken, turkey, fish or lean beef) or fatty ones (burgers, fried foods, cold meats, hot dogs)? The saturated fats in the second group are deadly business.

▶ Are you eating any protein from soya foods such as soyabeans, soya nuts or tofu? Your supermarket is full of tasty options.

▶ Do you get most of your protein from processed meat such as bacon, salami, corned beef, pastrami and ham? Processed foods add high levels of sodium that can aggravate high blood pressure.

▶ Are you incorporating beans and legumes into your diet or do you avoid them because they upset your stomach? Beano can help digest fibre-rich foods such as beans and other vegetables. (See page 72 for preparation instructions that can also help.)

▶ Is there any fish in your diet? You

should eat fish at least twice a week; more often is even better because fish is so rich in omega-3 fatty acids, which can reduce your risk of heart disease.

▶ How often do you eat eggs? Eggs are a good source of high-quality protein; just make sure they are prepared with a minimum of butter and other fats. If you have diabetes or high cholesterol or are overweight, you can eat up to four eggs a week. Otherwise, you can eat up to seven a week.

Real Food Life Target: You should eat 175 to 225 g (6 to 8 oz) of lean protein daily.

Dairy

▶ Calcium is essential to everyone's diet, to keep bones strong and cells functioning well. How many servings of calcium-rich foods did you have this week?

▶ What kinds of calcium-rich foods did you choose?

▶ Is your total number of servings more or less than you thought?

▶ Are you lactose-intolerant and avoid milk because of discomfort? If so, try the lactose-free options or even calcium-fortified soya milk – many of my clients like vanilla flavoured. You can also try Lactaid when you eat dairy foods. It's an over-the-counter product that helps you digest lactose.

▶ Do you eat yogurt on a regular basis? One small pot of natural yogurt can give you about 30 per cent of your daily requirement for calcium and a solid boost of protein – try it with berries, cereal or even in dips.

Real Food Life Target: Depending on your age, you should be taking in at least 700 to 1,000 milligrams of calcium each day. If you're 50 or older, I recommend you should aim for 1,200 milligrams a day, which amounts to three servings of calcium-rich foods daily.

Fat

▶ Believe me, not all fats are bad – the brain and hormones require fat to operate effectively. How many kinds of foods with fat did you have this week?

▶ What kinds of fat did you choose?

▶ Is your total number of servings more or less than you thought?

▶ Do you know where your fat is coming from? Is it saturated or unsaturated? Read food labels to see what kinds of fats you're consuming (see page 48 for a primer on deciphering food labels). Most of your dietary fat should come from a variety of omega-3 fatty acids or monounsaturated fatty acids.

▶ Are you eating any foods that contain omega-3 fatty acids (such as eggs, cold-water fish, walnuts, Brazil nuts, flaxseeds or flaxseed oil, rapeseed oil, sunflower seeds or pumpkin seeds)? Are you eating any monounsaturated fats (such as avocados, olive oil, olives, high oleic sunflower and safflower oils, and almonds)? If you answered no to these questions, try to gradually change your fat sources to those listed, which are good fats.

▶ Are you using margarine or butter in your cooking? Do you eat at fast-food restaurants a few times a week? Do you try to eat fat-free? Do you eat a very low-fat diet all day but then binge on ice cream or biscuits at night? Do you use full-fat salad dressing? If any of these pertain to you, you are probably not getting enough essential fatty acids and may be getting too much saturated and hydrogenated fats.

Real Food Life Target: You need 1 to 2 servings in total of essential fatty acids and monounsaturated fats each day. Always avoid saturated and hydrogenated fats.

Beverages

▶ Remember, water is essential to a Real Food Life. It helps in every aspect, from keeping food moving through your system to helping you determine if you're hungry or not. How many beverage servings did you have this week?

▶ What kinds of drinks did you choose?

▶ Is your total number of servings more or less than you thought?

▶ Have you noticed how much water you drink each day? This includes soda water, mineral water and tap water. Try to drink at least eight 225-ml (8-fl oz) glasses of water each day.

▶ Take note of the number of caffeinated drinks you consume each day. Are you drinking mostly fizzy drinks? Is coffee your idea of water? Do you crave sugary fizzy drinks to keep you going? If you answered yes to any of these questions, revisit your Instant Makeover from week 1 and replace two flavoured drinks with water.

▶ Have you included green tea? How about peppermint or ginger tea? Green tea contains antioxidants and may protect against cancers and high cholesterol. Ginger and peppermint teas aid digestion and are available at the supermarket or your local coffee shop. Don't drink peppermint tea if you have problems with acid reflux, however.

▶ Do you drink a number of glasses of beer, wine or other alcoholic drinks each day? Alcohol is a diuretic, so for every alcoholic beverage you consume, you should drink a comparable amount of water. Alcohol is also very high in calories.

▶ Is your urine darker than straw? Do you need to urinate only a few times a day? If so, you need to drink more fluids. Your extra toilet breaks will be balanced out with more energy and less snacking.

Real Food Life Target: You should drink at least eight 225-ml (8 fl oz) glasses of water each day and even more if you drink coffee or other caffeinated beverages.

Physical Analysis

Now that you know exactly what you ate last week, take a minute to work out how your body felt about those foods. We are all individuals – everyone's body reacts in its own way to different meals. Once you make the connections between your foods and feelings, you'll automatically start choosing food that makes you feel healthy, energised, balanced and satisfied but not stuffed.

In week 1's quiz, 'Your Real Food Life Starting Point', you looked at the big picture of your body's reactions to foods. Now we're getting down to the nitty-gritty. To assess your physical reactions to food, turn to the next page in your journal and write down your answers to the following questions.

Energy: Did some meals give you a lot of quick energy but then make you crash out? Did some meals give you energy for hours?

From your week 1 food journal, take note of which foods caused you to get energised and stay that way. Those foods – which are different for everyone – should become the mainstay of your new food life. As often as you can, avoid foods that make you crash and burn.

Toilet business: Are your bowel movements regular? Do you suffer from constipation? You should have at least one bowel movement a day. If you 'go' less than once a day, chances are you're constipated. Drink more water and eat more high-fibre foods including fruit, vegetables and whole grains.

Bloat factor: After you eat a salty dinner, do your face and hands swell the next day and do you feel uncomfortable and puffy?

If so, you're probably sensitive to sodium and need to cut back on your salt intake. Don't add salt when you cook – most foods contain ample amounts of natural sodium. When you eat out, don't hesitate to request that your meal should be prepared with very little added salt. If you can't avoid eating a salty meal, drink lots of water both during and after the meal. And the next day, eat plenty of foods that have a high water content, such as fruit and vegetables, to flush out your system. (See 'High-water Foods' on page 66 for a list of specific foods.)

Sugar cravings: When you have a craving for sweet things, do you eat an entire packet of biscuits in a sitting? And then do you feel really guilty for eating all of them?

Refer to the lists of snacks on pages 23, 25 and 30 and choose two that appeal to your tastebuds. Have the first when you're craving something sweet. If that doesn't do the trick, have the second snack. By sticking to healthy snacks like these, you'll be able to get through your craving without the guilt.

Complex carbohydrates: How did you feel after eating a meal high in complex carbohydrates (such as pasta or pizza)? Did you get sleepy or more energetic?

▶ If you got sleepy, then you should eat this type of meal less often or only at night.

Or have just a small portion along with some lean protein.

▶ If you felt energised, you'll probably want to keep that meal as part of your Real Food Life.

Meat: Do you like the taste of meat or do you avoid it because you think it's too fatty and unhealthy?

▶ If you like the taste of meat, you can dine on it, but stick to small portions of leaner cuts, which are kinder on your system and won't make you feel as sluggish. Lean meats, like roast turkey, are a great source of high-quality protein, vitamins and minerals.

▶ If you're vegetarian or don't have a taste for meat, you can get high-quality protein and nutrients from other sources such as soya foods, beans and legumes, or fish and shellfish.

Dairy: How did you feel after you ate a meal with a lot of dairy products? Some people's bodies can tolerate dairy foods; other people's bodies can't digest it at all.

▶ If you have no problem eating dairy foods, great! They're a great source of calcium and protein – feel free to enjoy two or three servings daily.

▶ If you don't feel well after consuming dairy foods, avoid them, but make sure you're getting your calcium from other sources, such as leafy green vegetables, tinned sardines and a supplement.

You may never have noticed that feeling bloated or sluggish is a result of the foods you eat until you started keeping your food journal. If a food makes you feel bad, you should probably avoid it. But beware – eliminating an entire food group from your diet will lead to food obsessions and can also lead to nutritional deficiencies. If you love a food and absolutely must have it, eat it only occasionally, realising you'll have to deal with the consequences. You may notice that when you cut back on foods like this, you actually love them less when you do have them. You may also discover new favourites to substitute that actually make you feel fantastic.

Emotional Analysis

We eat for many reasons – physical hunger, emotional pain, chronic stress. (Sometimes we're more likely not to eat when we're under stress.) Part of discovering your eating patterns and adjusting them, if necessary, requires you to examine all the emotional components of your eating patterns.

After keeping your food journal and analysing it, you will probably notice that emotions affect your eating patterns. We touched on some of these issues in week 1's quiz, but here are a few more targetted questions.

▶ When you've had a particularly tough day, do you find yourself eating a large meal, then lying on the sofa to unwind?

▶ After a confrontation with your boss, colleague, friend, spouse or child, do you find solace in whatever food makes you 'happy'?

▶ Do you find that binge-eating when you're frustrated or upset gives you comfort and relief (at least until reality sets in)?

▶ When you've finally accomplished a long, hard project, do you treat yourself by buying favourite foods and then eating until you fall into a food coma?

▶ When you're alone at night, do you find yourself eating uncontrollably?

▶ Do you feel guilty after having a large dinner complete with a rich dessert?

▶ Does drinking too much coffee or cola make you feel jittery and cranky?

▶ When you eat a fast-food meal, do you feel sluggish and depressed?

▶ Does eating a big dinner prevent you from sleeping well and then the lack of sleep affects your whole next day?

While there's no way to completely separate food from feelings, you need to recognise your emotional reactions to food and minimise their significance. Refer to chapter 2 for strategies for handling specific food/emotion issues. It's critical to remember that food's purpose is to nourish your body and make you feel good, not torture you or make you feel guilty. Learning what your emotional eating triggers are and how to master them is a cornerstone of a Real Food Life.

2. Diagnose Your Type: Protein-based or Carbohydrate-based Eater?

In my practice, I've found that I can group people's eating habits and tendencies into two basic categories, either protein-based or carb-based. If you find you respond well to either carbs or protein, you need to make sure you include a serving of your favoured nutrient in each of your meals. Also, protein- or carb-rich snacks will be more satisfying to you. Using your food journal and the descriptions below, discover which group you best fit into.

Protein-based Eater

Many of my clients find that protein keeps them more satisfied, more energetic and less hungry all day long. Does this sound like you?

When you eat more protein, you seem to think about food less often and don't feel the need to constantly forage for other foods to satisfy you. You find that eating a decent portion of protein, such as lean meat, fish, soya foods, dairy or even beans, with each meal and snack helps prevent mood swings while helping to curb cravings – especially sugar cravings. You feel 'bloated' when you eat a lot of carbs at one time. (Note: Even if you're a vegetarian, you could be a protein-based eater if you find you feel best when you've eaten veggie-based protein like soya foods and beans.)

Here's the key: just because you might feel better eating a protein-based plan doesn't mean you don't still need your fruit, vegetables and complex carbohydrates every day. The fibre, nutrients and energy-power of carb-based foods are an integral part of a Real Food Life.

Carbohydrate-based Eater

On the flip side, many others among my clients prefer a carbohydrate-rich diet. Are you like them?

Carbs fill you up without making you feel overstuffed. You love the way carbohydrates give you stamina that lasts all day. You feel that eating more carbs helps you to think better and helps stabilise your mood – you feel calmer, more relaxed and less moody. For you, eating carb-rich foods with every meal and snack helps curb your 'sweet/salty/junk food tooth' in the afternoon. You don't feel your meal is 'complete' unless you have a serving of pasta, rice, potatoes or wholemeal bread. If you're more athletic, you like to eat carbohydrates before and after your workouts because you find it improves your strength during the workouts and helps refuel your body afterwards. If you're vegetarian, you find this option easy to adopt, as carbohydrates come mainly from plant-based foods.

One thing to keep in mind if you determine that you are a carb-based eater is that eating a little bit of protein is necessary. Protein not only helps repair muscles and is necessary for the good functioning of the body, but eating a little protein with each meal will also keep cravings, hunger and binges at bay.

3. Diagnose Your Style: Are You a Grazer or a Traditional Three Square Meals Eater?

Once you work out whether you tend towards eating protein-based foods or carbohydrate-based foods, another focus of your eating plan is whether to graze or eat more structured meals. Some people prefer grazing, eating five to six small, light 'meals' throughout the day; others prefer to eat more conventionally, with three 'big' meals and a light snack or two. Again, your body will tell you what's right for you – you just have to listen!

Grazing

Your parents were probably always after you with admonitions like, 'Don't eat that! You'll spoil your appetite!' Well, this time mum was wrong – as long as you don't eat more calories than you would with three regular meals.

Many of my clients love grazing – eating up to six small, low-calorie, balanced meals each day – because it makes them feel like they're eating all day long. Grazing greatly reduces cravings and helps you feel in control of your food life because you decide when it's time to eat, not the clock. By eating every 2 to

3 hours, you never get too hungry, so you're less likely to binge. You may also find that you're good at listening to your body and can tell when your appetite first gears up, signalling that you should eat. If you've experienced this sensation, you're probably a grazer.

Biologically, grazing helps to maintain blood sugar levels, which prevents mood swings and that 'starving' feeling that comes from low blood sugar. Small meals tell the body to release less of the hormone insulin, so more calories are burned.

Personally, I love grazing. It helps me keep my Food Life in check. When I eat six small meals a day, I feel really good, energetic and balanced all day long.

Three Square Meals Eating Style

Still, some of my clients prefer eating in a more conventional structure of three main meals. Eating three square meals with a light snack or two fits into their lifestyle better than planning several mini-meals. You may find that grazing feels a little out of control, because you may *think* you're eating too often.

You can get a Real Food Life and still enjoy bigger meals – the two are not mutually exclusive. If you choose to eat larger meals, however, I still recommend eating a light snack, such as a yogurt and fruit, between meals to maintain blood sugar levels, prevent 'crashing', and prevent that starving feeling that often leads to overeating at subsequent meals.

Once you know your basic eating style, we'll move on to creating your eating plan.

4. Experiment with Sample Menus

The best thing about getting a Real Food Life is that you get to make it your very own. In the upcoming weeks, you will be changing and fine-tuning your plan and you'll definitely notice a change in how you feel.

To get you started, I've designed the sample eating plans beginning on page 166. I've included options that will give you maximum energy. Use these menus as a guideline in designing your own meals and snacks. Whether you select a protein-based or carbohydrate-based, grazing or meal-oriented plan, feel free to sample from any of the other plans. Just cut down your portions at mealtimes if you're a grazer. If you're going down the meal-eating route, have much smaller snacks.

Notice that many of the sample meals are vegetarian – proof positive that you can still get a Real Food Life despite any special dietary concerns you might have.

If you start out on one plan but aren't satisfied after a few days, tinker and tweak. Maybe you want protein in the morning and carbs in the afternoon or vice versa. Remember, it's *your* plan. Having a Real Food Life is all about balance, variety, feeling good and finding out what works for you.

Protein-based Sample Menus

Breakfast

1 glass water

Three Square Meals Style

A. Tomato and Cheese Omelette: 1 whole egg and 4 egg whites, 2 teaspoons grated Parmesan cheese or 2 tablespoons reduced-fat Cheddar cheese, 1 sliced tomato and 1 teaspoon olive oil to coat the pan

150 g (5 oz) melon

B. Protein Smoothie: 225 ml (8 fl oz) fat-free natural or soya yogurt, handful of ice cubes, 150 g (5oz) blueberries (or other fruit), 1 teaspoon vanilla (optional) and 50 g (2 oz) plain tofu (optional) mixed in a blender

C. 2 slices low-fat cheese or low-fat soya cheese (50 g/2 oz)

1 or 2 soya breakfast sausages or soya hot dogs

1 leftover Baked Apple (see page 321) topped with 2 tablespoons chopped walnuts or pumpkin seeds or 1 raw apple

Grazing Style

A. Egg, Cheese and Veggie Scramble: 1 scrambled egg, 25 g (1 oz) grated low-fat

> *Protein-based daily food intake at a glance:*
> - 2 to 4 servings carbohydrates
> - 225 g (8 oz) protein
> - 3 servings fruit
> - 4 to 6 servings vegetables
> - 2 to 4 servings fat
> - 2 to 3 servings calcium-rich food

cheese, 1 sliced tomato, 1 spring onion, 1 tablespoon chopped parsley or basil and 1 teaspoon olive oil to coat the pan

B. 25 g (1 oz) high-fibre, low-sugar, low-salt cereal

4 walnuts, crushed

225 ml (8 fl oz) skimmed milk or low-fat soya milk

½ banana or 75 g (3 oz) blueberries

C. 225 ml (8 fl oz) low-fat yogurt

1 boiled egg

25 g (1 oz) cheese

Midmorning snack

1 cup green tea and 1 glass water

Three Square Meals Style

A. 2 wholewheat crackers with 2 slices (50 g/ 2 oz) roast turkey breast and mustard

B. 2 wholegrain crackers with 110 g (4 oz)

cottage cheese and 2 tablespoons salsa

C. 1 bowl (225–300 ml/8–10 fl oz) Creamy Carrot Soup (see page 277)

1 piece fruit

Grazing Style

A. 10 baked tortilla chips

110 g (4 oz) low-fat bean dip

Unlimited baby carrots

B. 1 small apple

1 tablespoon all-natural nut butter (peanut, almond or walnut) or a small handful of nuts or seeds

C. 1 low-fat fruit yogurt or low-fat soya yogurt

2 tablespoons wheat germ and 4 crushed walnuts

Lunch

2 glasses water

Three Square Meals Style

A. 1 or 2 Turkey Burgers (see page 297), each with 1 small wholemeal pitta, lettuce and sliced tomato, 2 teaspoons tomato ketchup and 1 tablespoon low-fat mayonnaise

1 serving (110 g/4 oz) Aubergine Caponata (see page 270)

B. Tossed salad: 50 g (2 oz) lettuce (salad

in a bag), unlimited tomatoes and carrots, 75 g (3 oz) sliced roast turkey breast, 110 g (4 oz) tinned beans (rinsed well), 1 slice low-fat soya cheese, ¼ avocado, 1 tablespoon extra-virgin olive oil and unlimited vinegar or lemon juice

C. Chopped vegetable salad: 150 g (5 oz) vegetables (carrots, tomatoes, peppers, red onions, broccoli and cauliflower), 1 small tin (75 g/3 oz) drained tuna, 1 hard-boiled egg, 110 g (4 oz) red kidney beans and 2 tablespoons Blue Cheese Dressing (see page 263)

Grazing Style

A. Mixed salad: 75 g (3 oz) salad, 2 tablespoons Caesar dressing (see page 262), 75 g (3 oz) lean roast beef and 110 g (4 oz) cooked beans

B. 1 bowl (225–300 ml/8–10 fl oz) Chicken Soup (see page 275)

2 to 3 wholewheat crackers

C. 2 veggie burgers, each with 1 slice wholemeal bread, 1 slice (25 g/1 oz) low-fat soya cheese, 2 teaspoons tomato ketchup and 1 tablespoon low-fat mayonnaise

1 pear

D. 2 servings Lentil Salad with Lemon and Feta (see page 284)

1 small wholemeal pitta

75 g (3 oz) smoked tofu

1 grapefruit

Afternoon snack

1 glass water

Three Square Meals Style

A. 1 slice (25 g/1 oz) low-fat soya cheese

1 piece fruit

B. 3 tablespoons Lemony Hummus (see page 284)

Unlimited baby carrots

C. 110 g (4 oz) tinned, rinsed beans

1 small handful of nuts or seeds

Grazing Style

A. ½ raw apple

2 tablespoons low-fat vanilla yogurt or soya yogurt

1 tablespoon chopped nuts or seeds

B. 50 g (2 oz) leftover meat, fish, chicken or tofu

2 servings Roasted Vegetables (see page 267)

C. 2 wholegrain crackers topped with 110 g (4 oz) low-fat cottage cheese and either a chopped pear or 1 teaspoon mango chutney

Dinner

2 glasses water

Three Square Meals Style

A. 110 g (4 oz) Tuna with Green-Herb Pesto (see page 308)

200 g (7 oz) mixed vegetables (spinach, mushrooms and broccoli) sautéed in 1 teaspoon sesame oil and 2 teaspoons olive oil, with 2 teaspoons low-sodium soy sauce

1 sliced beefsteak tomato with 1 tablespoon Caesar Dressing (see page 262)

B. 1 bowl (225–300 ml/8–10 fl oz) French Onion Soup (see page 274)

110 g (4 oz) Fillet Steak with Mushrooms (see page 316)

1 small baked sweet potato or 1 serving Puréed Sweet Potatoes (see page 271)

50 g (2 oz) mixed salad with 1 tablespoon extra-virgin olive oil and unlimited balsamic vinegar or lemon juice

C. 1 slice (150 g/5 oz) Mama's Meat Loaf (see page 309)

1 serving Herby Tomato Salad (see page 260)

1 serving Layered Potato and Courgette Pie (see page 268)

Grazing Style

A. Chinese takeaway: steamed mixed vegetables (unlimited); 110 g (4 oz) steamed chicken, tofu or prawns; 75 g

(3 oz) brown rice; and 2 tablespoons brown, black bean or garlic sauce

B. 1 piece (110 g/4 oz) Oven-baked Crispy Sole (see page 307)

2 servings Sautéed Broccoli and Garlic (see page 272)

1 small baked sweet potato

C. 1 tin vegetarian chilli

75 g (3 oz) brown rice

225 g (8 oz) broccoli and courgettes sautéed in 2 teaspoons olive oil and 1 teaspoon sesame oil, with 2 teaspoons low-sodium soy sauce, 1 clove crushed garlic, lemon and ½ teaspoon sesame seeds

D. Unlimited Roasted Vegetables (see page 267)

1 serving Quinoa with Fried Onions (see page 290) mixed with 110 g (4 oz) tinned, rinsed kidney beans and 1 tablespoon grated Parmesan cheese

Nighttime snack

1 glass water

Three Square Meals Style

A. 1 slice (50 g/2 oz) Very Creamy Cheesecake (see page 325)

1 cup chamomile tea

Grazing Style

A. 1 small pot vanilla yogurt with 5 crushed almonds and a sprinkle of cinnamon

Carbohydrate-based Sample Menus

Breakfast

1 glass water

Three Square Meals Style

A. 2 slices wholemeal toast

1 tablespoon low-fat cream cheese

1 tablespoon jam or all-fruit spread

1 medium banana

B. 1 Muffin Galore (see page 319)

2 teaspoons nut butter

2 teaspoons jam or all-fruit spread

Carbohydrate-based daily food intake at a glance:

- 6 to 10 servings carbohydrates
- 175 g (6 oz) protein
- 3 to 4 servings fruit
- 4 to 6 servings vegetables
- 2 to 4 servings fat
- 2 to 3 servings calcium-rich food

1 Baked Apple (see page 321)

C. 1 bowl (40–50 g/1½–2 oz) high-fibre, low-sugar, low-sodium cereal

225 ml (8 fl oz) skimmed soya or cow's milk

150 g (5 oz) berries or 1 medium banana

2 tablespoons chopped walnuts or pumpkin seeds

Grazing Style

A. 1 honey wholemeal or oat bran muffin

1 tablespoon nut butter

1 tablespoon jam or all-fruit spread

B. 25 g (1 oz) high-fibre cereal

1 small pot low-fat or soya yogurt

75 g (3 oz) berries

C. 1 bowl porridge (50 g/2 oz uncooked oats) made with 225 ml (8 fl oz) skimmed milk or soya milk

1 small box (25 g/1 oz) raisins

Sprinkle of cinnamon

1 piece fresh fruit (optional)

D. 1 or 2 slices wholemeal toast

2 teaspoons all-natural peanut butter or 1 tablespoon low-fat cream cheese

2 teaspoons jam or all-fruit spread

225 g (8 oz) fruit salad or 1 piece fruit

Midmorning snack

1 cup green tea or ginger tea and 1 glass water

Three Square Meals Style

A. 2 wholewheat crackers

1 slice low-fat cheese

B. 1 slice wholemeal bread

2 tablespoons Lemony Hummus (see page 284)

Grazing Style

A. 225 g (8 oz) mixed fruit

1 tablespoon toasted wheat germ

2 tablespoons low-fat cottage cheese

B. 2 wholewheat crackers

2 tablespoons Roasted Garlic and White Bean Spread (see page 283)

C. 4 wholewheat crackers

2 tablespoons Lemony Hummus (see page 284)

1 sliced tomato

Lunch

2 glasses water

Three Square Meals Style

A. 2 rolls sushi (tuna, salmon, crab, prawn – your choice)

50 g (2 oz) green salad with 1 table-spoon vinaigrette dressing

110 g (4 oz) tinned, rinsed black beans

B. 2 servings Middle Eastern Tabbouleh Salad (see page 291)

1 small (75 g/3 oz) tin tuna or salmon

2 tablespoons low-fat mayonnaise

1 medium wholemeal roll

C. 1 serving Pasta Primavera (see page 295)

4 tablespoons Roasted Garlic and White Bean Spread (see page 283)

4 wholewheat crackers

Grazing Style

A. 1 Vegetarian Asian Tofu Sandwich (see page 299)

25 g (1 oz) salad with 2 teaspoons olive oil and lemon

B. 2 slices wholemeal bread with ½ avocado, mashed; 1 slice (25 g/1 oz) low-fat cheese; sliced tomatoes and lettuce; and 1 tablespoon low-fat mayonnaise

1 apple

Afternoon snack

1 glass water

Three Square Meals Style

A. 1 tablespoon all-natural peanut butter

1 slice wholemeal bread

1 apple

B. 1 small pot low-fat fruit yogurt or low-fat fruit soya yogurt

1 chopped pear

25 g (1 oz) high-fibre cereal

Grazing Style

A. Unlimited fresh vegetables

2 tablespoons Blue Cheese Dressing (see page 263)

1 piece fruit

B. Fruit Smoothie: 1 small pot fat-free natural yogurt, 150 g (5 oz) frozen blueberries, 2 tablespoons wheat germ and handful of crushed ice

C. 1 small low-fat bran muffin

2 teaspoons all-natural peanut butter

D. 1 bowl (225–300 ml/8–10 fl oz) Chunky Mixed Vegetable Soup (see page 281)

E. 1 small bowl (25 to 30) Twiglets and 1 piece fruit

Dinner

2 glasses water

Three Square Meals Style

A. 1 bowl (225–300 ml/8–10 fl oz) Texas Black Bean Soup (see page 279)

1 serving Macaroni Cheese (see page 294)

350 g (12 oz) spinach sautéed in 1 tablespoon extra-virgin olive oil with 1 clove chopped garlic

B. 1 tin vegetarian chilli

1 medium baked sweet potato

BESTBITES

Top 5 Foods to Eat for Energy before the Big Meeting

Before your next big meeting, snack on one of the foods below. Then go into your meeting with confidence, knowing that you'll still have plenty of energy when the last agenda item is wrapped up.

- 1 or 2 slices of wholemeal bread with nut butter and jam or low-fat cheese
- Large mixed fruit salad with low-fat regular or soya yogurt and wheat germ
- Chopped salad with olive oil and lemon and grilled chicken or smoked tofu with a small wholemeal roll
- A bowl of high-fibre cereal with skimmed or soya milk, a banana and a small handful of chopped walnuts
- 1 whole egg and 3 egg whites, scrambled, with wholemeal bread and a piece of fruit

50–75 g (2–3 oz) salad with ¼ avocado, 1 tablespoon olive oil and lemon juice or vinegar

C. 110 g (4 oz) Salmon Teriyaki (see page 306)

1½ servings Mexican Rice and Beans (see page 286)

350 g (12 oz) mixed vegetables or broccoli sautéed with chopped garlic, 1 teaspoon sesame oil, 2 teaspoons rapeseed oil and 2 teaspoons low-sodium soy sauce

Grazing Style

A. 1 serving (100–150 g/4–5 oz) Aubergine Parmesan (see page 303)

75 g (3 oz) mixed salad with 1 tablespoon olive oil and lemon

1 whole Incredibly Tasty Mediterranean Roasted Pepper (see page 265)

B. 1 serving Spinach and Cheese Pie (see page 305)

175 g (6 oz) cooked brown rice

300 g (10½ oz) mixed vegetables sautéed in 1 tablespoon olive oil

50 g (2 oz) mixed salad with 1 tablespoon olive oil and lemon

Nighttime snack

1 glass water

Three Square Meals Style

A. 1 slice (50 g/2 oz) Banana-Date Cake (see page 323)

1 cup ginger tea

Grazing Style

  A. 1 piece fruit

    1 slice (5 cm/2 in wide) Blueberry Angel Food Cake (see page 322)

  B. 1 piece fruit

    Small piece dark chocolate (10 g/½ oz)

5. Set Mini-goals

You've already taken great leaps and bounds in your Real Food Life – so why shouldn't you give yourself credit for them? Mini-goals are a fun, easy way to stay on course to achieve your ultimate goal, but they also give you something to celebrate in the here and now and boost your motivation every day.

You've done a lot of investigative work this week. Look back over the week's findings and see where you'd like to make changes, then turn to the first page of your journal and just meditate on your ultimate goal for a second. What changes could you make that would make your ultimate goal a reality? Don't forget to think about your bigger-picture issues from week 1's quiz.

When setting mini-goals, think 'quantifiable, measurable and achievable'. For example, 'I will eat one serving of green vegetables (quantifiable) six times (measurable) this week (achievable).'

Shoot for at least one nutritional goal and one emotional goal for each week. Note them at the top of your food diary page every morning. I'll remind you to put them in the checklist that begins each chapter – and to congratulate yourself on achieving them in the Get Real Check-in at the end of each chapter.

Get Real Check-in

Assess your progress by checking off each of the following items you achieved during week 2.

❏ Instant Makeover 2: I replaced a low-fibre breakfast with a high-fibre cereal.

❏ I added an extra glass of water. I'm now drinking at least six glasses per day.

❏ I did a complete analysis of my findings from week 1.

❏ I determined whether I am a protein-based or carb-based eater.

❏ I determined if I'm a grazer or a traditional meal eater.

❏ I tried at least one sample menu.

❏ I set week 3 mini-goals that will help me achieve my ultimate goals.

❏ I kept my food journal each day.

❏ I rewarded myself for my intentions and my efforts.

Weekly Words: Write a couple of paragraphs in your journal about the biggest surprise you felt when you looked at your food analysis. Discuss the way you think your mini-goals will help you achieve your ultimate goal.

CHAPTER 9

Week Three:

DOING THE REAL FOOD LIFE KITCHEN MAKEOVER

Your Real Food Life is about to hit home – your home. Week 3 of the Food Life Makeover Plan is all about remaking your home and your shopping habits so they'll support you, not sabotage you.

First, you'll do the Real Food Life Kitchen Makeover. You'll sweep out those items that can hamstring your efforts, clearing the way for the nutrition-packed all-stars that will easily, seamlessly take their place. While this makeover won't feature a manicure or a foot massage, I promise it will be equally invigorating!

Then we'll take our show on the road and visit the supermarket, where you'll learn how to size up the shop at a glance and devise a strategy to get the best foods in the least amount of time. The skills you learn

now will help you automatically gravitate towards the best foods for you, so you can restock with solid nutritional staples every time you go shopping.

> **During this week, you will:**
>
> ▶ Accomplish Instant Makeover 3: replace a half-hour of TV-watching with sleep
> ▶ Add one extra glass of water (aim for at least 7)
> ▶ Follow your week 3 mini-goals
> ▶ Keep week 3 of your food journal
> ▶ Give your kitchen a Real Food Life Makeover
> ▶ Go food shopping
> ▶ Complete week 3 of your Get Real Check-in

Instant Makeover 3:

Replace the Nightly News with Some Extra Snooze Time

While sleep and food don't appear to go hand in hand, getting more sleep is a major step towards a healthier lifestyle. I regularly see that sleep deprivation exacerbates many of my clients' food issues. When you are overtired, you may have noticed feeling hungrier – that's because your body is crying out for more energy! Still, you have to get through the day and, as your energy plummets, so does your mood – another prime risk factor for snacking and bingeing.

Instead of staying up late watching an extra half-hour of primetime shows or news that probably has little impact on your life, get some extra sleep. When you wake up feeling refreshed, you will be better equipped to make good food choices and resist the temptations that would sound so appealing to a sleep-deprived mind. You won't be groggy in the afternoon – and you won't need a sugar-loaded snack or fizzy drink for a lift. Plus, you'll feel more in tune with your body and what it really needs – often just a tall glass of water! – instead of just quickly turning to food to fill all of your needs.

1. Give Your Kitchen a Real Food Life Makeover

When you tried out your tailor-made menu plan in week 2, did you need to make a special trip to the supermarket? Part of the idea behind the Kitchen Makeover is to ensure that you'll have smart, nourishing choices on hand all the time.

Try to plan your Kitchen Makeover for a time when you have several hours to spend. Or, if you have a tough week at work and can't spare any time, split up the following tasks over a series of nights. Monday, the cupboards. Tuesday, the refrigerator. And so on. Each segment of the makeover should take less than 30 minutes. If you're really stuck for time, try the 10-Step Kitchen Makeover (see page 180), distilled down to the most powerful changes.

The kitchen makeover is one of my favourite things to do with clients because it's so liberating! You make a fresh start, physically removing the vestiges of your old food life to reinforce the positive choices you've made for your Real Food Life. Whether you cook a lot or rarely, filling your kitchen with

Simple Ways to Improve Your Slumber

Having trouble getting your Zzzs? Sleep tight tonight with these slumber-inducing strategies.

- Avoid spicy or fatty dinners, both of which can cause indigestion that may keep you awake at night.

- People who eat too few calories during the day often wake up hungry during the night or very early in the morning, so make sure you get enough food. It's a good idea to eat some protein with your dinner. Because it stays in your stomach longer than some other foods, it will keep you from waking because of hunger.

- Watch what you're eating: foods such as cabbage, broccoli, peppers and cauliflower can cause bloating and wind, and may cause restless nights.

- Eat a carbohydrate-rich snack after dinner. Carbs help release serotonin, a brain chemical that makes you feel calm and relaxed. A few wholewheat crackers with a teaspoon of nut butter might do the trick.

- Cut down on or completely eliminate caffeine. This includes coffee, black tea, cola and chocolate. (It's best to do this gradually, since cutting caffeine out of your diet quickly can lead to headaches and fatigue.) Though it contains much less than black tea or coffee, green tea does have some caffeine, so drink it only before 2 p.m. if caffeine affects your sleep. Another option is to buy decaffeinated green tea.

a variety of fresh fruit and vegetables, healthy choices for snacks and quick meals and even no-fuss frozen and convenience foods will keep you and your Food Life on track.

These five suggestions will help you make a smooth start.

1. Tackle the cupboards/larder and the refrigerator/freezer separately.

2. Systematically read the ingredient label of every product you have, keeping this question in mind: 'Will this food be part of my Real Food Life?'

3. Keep a pad of paper and a pen nearby, so you can keep a running shopping list of new foods you will need.

4. Keep rubbish bags handy. They will be used to hold the food you will throw away or give away.

5. Be patient. Your Kitchen Makeover may take an investment of time, but the dividends are worth it!

Cupboards

Start your kitchen makeover with your cupboards. Take everything out of your cupboards and place it on your kitchen table. If you have too much stuff to put there at one time, work in segments: above the stove, below the counter and so on. As you read the label to evaluate each food product, ask yourself, 'Does this help or hinder my progress to my Real Food Life ultimate goal?' (See page 48 for information on how to read labels.) Put the 'no's' immediately to the side to be thrown away. If you're on the fence about an item, remember my motto: when in doubt, throw it out.

Some of my clients feel wasteful throwing 'perfectly good' food away. My answer? I would not ask you to throw 'perfectly good' food away. I'm asking you to release the burden of food that does not support your goals. If being 'wasteful' still makes you uncomfortable, pack up unopened boxes and tins to donate to a food shelter or give away. Then, throw away anything already opened that directly sabotages your goals for getting a Real Food Life. Keeping items around that aren't good for you isn't doing yourself any favours.

The foods below often pop up in my new clients' homes. I'll suggest certain items to add or subtract from your cupboards, but remember – the choice is always yours. This is your new food life.

High-sugar cereals. Do you have several boxes of sugary cereals? Do you have any whole grain, low-sugar and low-salt cereals (hot or cold)?

Consider throwing away any cereals that contain 12 grams of sugar or more per serving. If you really love sugary cereal as an occasional treat for you or your children, consider buying the small snack packs – you'll get variety and controlled portions. Otherwise, get rid of it. If you don't have any wholegrain cereal, add it to your shopping list.

Processed foods. Do you have a lot of tinned or packaged foods that are high in sodium, saturated fat, hydrogenated oils and preservatives?

Give these foods to a friend or throw them out. If you're afraid your family will feel deprived without these foods they love, remember that by getting rid of processed foods, you are saving your family's health.

Vegetable oils. Is most of the oil in your cupboard sunflower or corn oil? Do you have white vegetable fat? Do you have olive oil?

Throw out vegetable fat immediately – it's cement for your arteries. You should also get rid of the regular sunflower and corn oil. Replace them with olive oil and rapeseed oil (also available in cooking sprays). Consider trying walnut oil, flaxseed oil or high oleic sunflower oil.

Refined grain products. Are the only grains you have egg noodles and white rice? Do you have any semolina or wholewheat pasta? Do you have any grains such as quinoa, barley, buckwheat, bulgar wheat or brown rice?

Whole grains and wholewheat pastas are a must – add them to your list. Save the white rice and egg noodles for occasional use.

Tinned goods. Do you have tins of processed meat like ham or corned beef? Pork and beans? Tuna packed in oil? Any sardines? Are your soups creamy chowders and high-fat instant noodle soups or are they low-fat, high-fibre and filled with vegetables? Do you have plain tinned beans and chopped tomatoes?

The tinned meat, pork and beans and vegetable oil-packed tuna should be given away. Keep tuna packed in olive oil. If you have none on hand, add low-fat tinned soups and tuna packed in water to your shopping list. Tinned beans, tinned salmon and chopped tomatoes make excellent, versatile staples.

Snack foods. Do you have boxes or bags of sweets or biscuits that contain 'partially hydrogenated oil' as a major ingredient? What about crackers – do they contain any fibre at all? Do you have potato crisps, corn crisps or tortilla chips? Are they in big bags that make it difficult to stop eating?

Throw out the sweets and biscuits and replace them with high-quality dark chocolate and dried fruit (such as raisins and apricots), which will satisfy the sweet cravings. Get rid of the white-flour, no-fibre crackers and add wholegrain crackers to your list. Low-fat bean dip and salsa can make an excellent addition, if they sound good to you. (Try them with baby carrots instead of crisps.) Tortilla chips can stay, if you can limit yourself. If you can't resist them, toss them out.

Root vegetables. Do you buy large bags of white potatoes? A net bag of onions? Fresh garlic or ginger?

Unless you have a large family, get in the habit of buying potatoes in smaller bags or even individually, so you're more conscious of how often you eat them. Consider acquiring a taste for sweet potatoes – they're more nutritious than white. Buy only as much garlic as you need for each week, thereby ensuring freshness. On the flip side, buy onions in bulk and use them often. Store fresh ginger and garlic in the fridge after you cut it.

Breads. What varieties do you have? Do you have any dark or wholemeal breads?

Toss the marshmallowy white bread to make room for wholemeal breads – they're more filling, satisfying and fibre-filled than white breads.

Tea and coffee. Do you have jars of coffee and only black (regular) tea? Do you have

The 10-step Kitchen Makeover

The last thing I want is for the time commitment required for the Kitchen Makeover to be an obstacle that hinders you from getting a Real Food Life. If time's short but your intentions are good, these 10 easy switches will get you a lot closer to your goals.

1. Replace vegetable fat with olive oil.
2. Replace 'marshmallowy' refined white bread with wholemeal bread.
3. Replace fatty cold cuts of meat with tinned tuna or sliced turkey breast or lean roast beef.
4. Replace processed peanut butter, which contains hydrogenated oil and added sugar, with natural nut butter (such as peanut, almond, walnut or soya).
5. Replace full-fat mayonnaise with low-fat mayonnaise.
6. Replace whole milk with skimmed milk or low-fat soya milk.
7. Replace crisps with nuts and seeds.
8. Replace cola and coffee with water and green or herbal tea.
9. Replace instant, dehydrated soups with good-quality, organic tinned soups.
10. Replace sweetened sugary cereals with wholegrain cereals.

any herbal tea at all? Any green tea?

If you don't have any, add herbal tea and green tea to your shopping list. You might also want to try chicory-based beverages. Coffee and black tea are fine in moderation, but a great habit to get into is drinking more green and herbal tea.

Cooking staples. Do you have any flour other than bleached, like wholemeal? What about sugar? Honey? Saccharine or aspartame? Hot sauces? Spices and herbs?

Wholemeal flour can be a satisfying supplement to your white flour. (In baking, sub-

stitute up to half of the amount of white flour called for with wholemeal flour for very satisfactory results.) Use sugar and honey sparingly, but throw away all products containing saccharine or aspartame. (They promote a 'sweet tooth', the bane of many food lives. And we still have little definitive proof of their long-term effects.) As for the herbs, spices and hot sauces, use them to your heart's content.

Refrigerator

When you go through your refrigerator, do it a shelf at a time. Ask yourself the same question as you did when you went through your cupboards: will this item help me towards my goals or keep me from achieving them? The goal is to make room for lots of fresh vegetables, fruit and refreshing waters.

Water. Do you have bottles of water, a container or a filter jug? Do you keep mineral water on hand? What about fizzy drinks?

The top shelf of your fridge should be dominated by water in any and all forms. Keep your water jug or bottle towards the front and pour a glass whenever you open the fridge. Soda water counts. Fizzy drinks don't. They should be a special-treat beverage, not a staple. If you simply can't resist the daily fizzy drink, you should get rid of it.

Fruit. How many pieces of fruit are in your fridge, if any? What about fresh vegetables?

You should have enough fruit and veggies to last you at least a few days or the whole week (depending on how often you shop). Opening the door to your fridge should reveal a rainbow of colour – prepared salads, carrots, roasted red peppers, spinach, broccoli, rocket, asparagus, celery, carrots, squashes, peas.

Dairy. Do you have any full-fat dairy products? Any low-fat yogurts, milk and cheeses?

Many people lose their taste for full-fat milk when they go down to semi-skimmed, then skimmed – even if you don't like fat-free milk, these modest changes can make a big difference. Stock up with other low-fat dairy items like low-fat cottage cheese and yogurt.

Processed meats. Do you have sandwich meat? Meat and breakfast meat products? Do you have any soya food products in your fridge?

Throw away salami, bacon, sausages and other processed meats. Replace them with fresh turkey breast and lean roast beef. All-natural chicken sausages or soya hot dogs can be used instead of pork sausages. If you haven't already, consider buying soya foods such as smoked tofu (it tastes like smoked cheese), pre-sliced soya cheese or regular tofu (which comes in a variety of flavours); all of these are great as part of a snack or meal.

Eggs. Do you have eggs? Keep them (check their expiry date), since they're a fast and nourishing meal or snack. Consider hard-boiling a few for quick, convenient snacks.

Fats. Do you have any margarine or butter? What about nut butters, and nuts and seeds?

Throw out the overprocessed margarine, but keep the butter to use in very small amounts. (I like mashed avocado as a bread-spread – with or without a little low-fat mayonnaise. It's a much healthier fat than butter.)

(continued on page 184)

LIVING A REAL FOOD LIFE

A Kitchen Makeover Got Nadine Back On Track

Name: Nadine

Real Food Life Issues: Overstressed, fast-food diet, no time to cook

Nadine is a busy mother at home with two small children. When she left the workforce to take care of her first baby 6 years ago, she was excited to have more time to make a nice home, bring up her child and even have some time for herself. But several years and another child later, she still didn't have the time to keep her house as nice as she wanted. And forget about exercise or quality time for herself. Time was always about the children and Nadine felt worn out, stressed out, bloated and awful. Here's where I found her:

20 May

After breakfast this morning, Ethan started screaming about getting one of those action figure toys at the fast-food place. I'd been up all night with Samantha's croup and my last nerve was shot by 10 a.m. He can really make a fuss when he wants something! Finally, I gave in and we all piled into the car. He got the toy and went to play on the jungle gym and I finally had peace. I savoured the moment with a milk shake and large fries. I was actually starting to feel human again when I saw that nosey school governor. I'm sure she looked down on my tracksuit and stained T-shirt before she put on a fake smile and asked me to make biscuits for the school fair. I said yes, of course, while inwardly seething. I probably would have punched her if I could have summoned the energy.

After I analysed her first week's food journal, I saw lots of nutritional black holes. Nadine ate hardly any fruit, vegetables, fish or whole grains, so it was no wonder to me that she felt bloated much of the time. The majority of her diet was refined carbohydrates in the form of muffins, bagels and pastries, and very high saturated fat and high-sodium fast food. I wasn't surprised that she had been unsuccessful in her efforts to lose the weight she had put on during her second pregnancy.

Before long, I got Nadine to break her fast-food habit (the children came later).

When I explained that the only good thing about this food is that it is fast – and that's no reason to eat it – and that it's almost completely devoid of any vitamins and minerals, Nadine re-evaluated its convenience. I also explained that her diet of refined carbs and fast food contributed not only to her inability to lose weight, but more important, to her feelings of being worn out, stressed and bloated. Together, we created a wholesome eating plan she could stick with, filled with foods she liked and could prepare quickly and with minimal fuss. I also got her to start drinking at least 4 glasses of water a day, which quickly turned into 8 glasses a day.

Next, Nadine and I gave her kitchen a makeover. I showed her how to read food labels and explained what to look for – and avoid – in packaged foods. We threw out most of the unhealthy foods in her larder, especially those with hydrogenated fats, refined white flour and too much sugar. We then went grocery shopping and stocked her cabinets, refrigerator and freezer with an assortment of healthy and fast foods including soya foods, frozen and fresh vegetables, dried and fresh fruit, nuts and seeds, olive oil, lean beef, chicken and fish.

Replacing foods high in saturated fats with those high in essential fatty acids was hard for Nadine to get used to, but she was determined to improve her diet for herself and her children. She started eating a handful of nuts and seeds each day and used olive oil on her salads and when cooking vegetables. I introduced her to smoked tofu, which she loved and continues to eat almost every day in a sandwich or on a salad. She realised that it was a delicious and wholesome snack both she and her children could happily and healthily devour.

Within 2 weeks, Nadine felt much less bloated, her energy levels increased and her excess water weight came off. She continued to go food shopping at least once a week, armed with a shopping list loaded with wholesome foods for quick and balanced meals and snacks. Soon, she began making and packing lunch for herself and her children (when necessary). Making lunch helped her stay on track with her food life, plus it saved her quite a bit of money.

By week 5, Nadine recognised that she needed to find time for exercise, so she started doing workout videos a few times a week while the children napped. Exercise made her feel great and gave her even more energy. She also lost 7 kg (16 lb) and felt much happier and more satisfied with her life than she had in years.

High in protein and good fat, nuts and seeds should definitely be in your Real Food Life, but keep them in the refrigerator so they won't turn rancid. Peanut butters with hydrogenated oils and added sugar should go, but they should be quickly replaced by all-natural peanut butter (stir it when the oil separates). Keep cashew butter, almond butter or soya nut butter in the refrigerator, too.

Random stuff. Everybody's fridge is full of random stuff, but what's the best for your Real Food Life? Here are a few tips.

▶ Sugar-added jams are truly pointless when there are so many delicious all-fruit spreads out there. Buy the best-quality items you can find and use them sparingly – the flavour will really come through.

▶ Hummus, a delicious, nutrient-rich chickpea and garlic spread, is a great sandwich food or dip (with crackers or vegetables). Consider making this a new food staple – try the recipe on page 284.

▶ Throw out low-fat dressings that are loaded with additives and sugar; they also often contain the wrong types of fats. (I suggest alternatives in the shopping list on page 186.) Check out the recipe chapter for homemade dressing ideas.

▶ Throw out full-fat mayonnaise; keep low-fat mayonnaise, low-sodium chutneys, mustards, tomato ketchup and relishes.

Freezer

The freezer is a marvellous tool for your Real Food Life. You can stock it with homemade meals that keep you on track and healthy convenience products for satisfying, quick meals-at-the-ready. As with the cupboards and refrigerator, ask yourself, 'Will this help me towards my goals or keep me from achieving them?' Then, decide what to keep and what to throw out.

Frozen meals. Do you see many frozen ready-meals? Are they extremely high in bad fats, sodium and preservatives that you can't even pronounce?

Unless you're an expert label reader, it's sometimes hard to determine how healthy a pre-prepared dinner is. One good rule of thumb: if a product contains hydrogenated oils, artificial colours, artificial flavours and more than 10 grams of fat per serving, you should get rid of it. Refer to the shopping list for frozen meals and side dishes that are lower in fat and sodium and taste great.

Frozen veggies and fruit. How many different kinds of frozen vegetables or fruit are in your freezer?

Frozen fruit and vegetables are great to keep on hand. They're loaded with vitamins and minerals and they're super-convenient. Toss frozen berries into a smoothie or a bowl of yogurt; nuke frozen spinach with a sprinkle of garlic salt.

Frozen meat. Do you have any frozen meats? Sausages?

With the exception of ham, typical breakfast items such as sausages and bacon are extremely high in saturated fat. Toss them. Also get rid of frozen meat pies and pasties. Keep the frozen chicken, frozen fish and lean meats for handy meals, soups or stews. Frozen veggie burgers and veggie hot dogs are also great for fast and easy meals.

Frozen desserts. How many different ice creams, ice cream products and frozen desserts do you have? Are they full of fat?

We all need a special treat, but do we really need it in every flavour? If you can limit yourself to serving sizes, keep a maximum of one full-fat, extra-rich ice cream on hand as a super-special treat. Otherwise, throw out all the extra-rich iced desserts and replace them with sorbet, sorbet bars, frozen low-fat yogurt and soya milk desserts.

2. Go Food Shopping

When I work with clients, part of my consultation includes a fun, educational trip to the shops. Typically, we'll go to their local supermarket or health food shop and spend some time browsing through the aisles, reading labels and choosing tasty foods that will pave the way to their Real Food Life.

Don't think that just because you don't cook at home, you won't benefit from the shopping trip. Part of being responsible to your Real Food Life goals is to give yourself the tools to achieve them. I'm not insisting that you cook, but you should take at least one trip to the supermarket to stock your larder with healthy, quick meals and snacks.

From your work on the kitchen makeover, you should now have a list of items you need to replace (for example, a bottle of olive oil to replace unhealthy corn oil). If you're already in the habit of cooking at home, you probably have a decent number of staples – particularly items like onions, pastas, seasonings and tinned goods – even after doing the kitchen makeover.

Or perhaps you're like many of my clients, left with a bottle of mineral water and a jar of pickles. In that case, this first food shop may be very big. Staples last, so if you buy a lot now, you won't need to buy them again for quite some time.

Sadly, I won't be there to accompany you on your shopping trip, but below I've detailed a strategy that will help you navigate through the different areas of your shop. Actually, a good maxim of food selection is Shop the Walls – that's where the fresh produce, dairy and meat sections are. Everything in the middle of the shop has been processed in some way.

Take along a copy of my shopping list and feel free to adjust it to your tastes. It includes a number of different brands that may be available in your shop.

(continued on page 188)

185

The Get a Real Food Life Shopping List

Use this handy list as a reminder of your shopping strategies while you're in the supermarket. If your shop doesn't stock the items recommended, speak to an assistant – often they'll be happy to add different foods if they think customers are interested.

Fruit and Vegetables

Prewashed salads
Baby carrots
Cherry tomatoes
Garlic, onions, ginger
Dark green vegetables (kale, spring greens, spinach, broccoli)
Cauliflower, asparagus, green beans
Bananas, apples (make sure they're hard), oranges, other seasonal fruits
Lemons, limes
Fresh herbs

Bread, Crackers and Bread Products

Wholemeal muffins (the toasting variety)
Crackers and rice cakes (Finn Crisp, Ryvita)
Wholegrain bread (Hovis, Allinsons, Kingsmill)
Fruit-filled breakfast pastries or cereal bars (look for organic, low-fat brands)

Dressings and Sauces

Salad dressing (Simply Delicious or other all-natural, low-fat, low-sugar, low-sodium brands)
Barbecue sauce (Newman's Own or other all-natural brand)
Tinned tomatoes (all-natural, low-sodium brand)
Passata (organic or all-natural brands)
Salsa (all-natural brand)

Cereals

Honey Puffed Kashi, Kashi Good Friends, Kashi Go Lean
All-Bran
Bran Flakes
Weetabix
Shredded Wheat

Porridge oats
Toasted wheat germ

Staples, Condiments and Grocery Items

Low-fat mayonnaise (Hellmann's)
Tomato ketchup (low-salt)
Bragg Liquid Aminos (to flavour just about anything)
Mustard (Dijon)
Worcestershire sauce
Vinegar (red wine, balsamic, cider, rice wine)
Hot pepper sauce (Tabasco or another all-natural hot pepper sauce)
Tinned tuna in spring water or olive oil
Tinned salmon
Tinned sardines (with bones)
Fat-free tinned chilli (organic or all-natural brand)
Tinned low-sodium soup (Seeds of Change, Heinz Organic, Amy's or another organic or all-natural brand)
Tinned beans (low-sodium or sodium-free brand)
Rice (brown, Arborio, jasmine)
Spices, herbs and seasonings, including black pepper, cayenne pepper, cinnamon, cumin, garlic powder, kosher or sea salt, oregano, paprika, pure vanilla extract and rosemary
All-natural nut butter
Jam or all-fruit spread (St Dalfour, Duchy Originals, Whole Earth or other all-fruit or mostly fruit brands)
Mineral water
Green tea, chamomile tea
Swiss water process decaffeinated coffee

Snack Foods

Dried fruit (apricots and raisins)
Pretzels (fat-free, all-natural variety)
Small bags of oven-baked or reduced-fat crisps

The Get a Real Food Life Shopping List (cont.)

Twiglets
Nuts or seeds (walnuts, Brazil nuts, sunflower seeds, pumpkin seeds)

Dairy and Refrigerated Foods
Skimmed milk
Fat-free natural yogurt (organic tastes best, including Yeo Valley and Rachel's bio-live, fat-free versions)
Low-fat cottage cheese
Parmesan Reggiano (a small chunk of real Parmesan is worth the money)
Quark cheese or low-fat fromage frais
Low-fat cream cheese
Nondairy cheese singles
Soya cheese slices
Low-fat Swiss, Jarlsberg, Gouda or Edam cheese
Eggs
Hummus (or try recipe on page 284)
Wholewheat tortillas (low-fat, if available)

Start your shopping trolleys!

Produce Aisle

Most supermarkets open on to the fruit and veg section – what a lucky break! Whichever eating plan you're embarking on, fruit and vegetables are a mainstay.

Fruit. Buy enough to get three servings a day for the week. While you'll have the best selection in spring and summer, there are fresh, tasty fruits available throughout the year. Also consider frozen fruit and fruit tinned in its own juices.

❯ Apples, bananas and oranges are especially transportable, making them great for snacks on the run.

❯ Consider precut melon and pineapple – what could be easier?

❯ Tropical fruits, like mango and papaya, are available all year round. Let them ripen until they're soft to the touch, peel, remove the seed and serve.

❯ Fragile berries should be eaten

Soya Foods

Veggie/soya sausages and hot dogs
Plain, flavoured or smoked tofu
Soya milk
Provamel and other soya products (organic brands to look out for include Cauldron Foods, Dragonfly, Oasis and Taifun)

Frozen Foods

Soya/veggie burgers
Vegetable-based organic frozen dinners (choose organic brands such as Tivall, Amy's, Good Life, Respect or similar)
Frozen prawns or lobster (plain)
Wholegrain waffles
Frozen dessert (Häagen-Dazs sorbet, frozen low-fat yogurt)
Frozen fish sticks (breaded with wholegrain crumbs)
Frozen chicken nuggets or soya 'chicken' nuggets (organic brands)
Frozen fruits and vegetables (organic is best; otherwise plain, no sauce)
Frozen organic oven chips

within a day or two of purchasing. Wash them just before using or they'll rot.

▶ A squeeze of fresh lemon or lime brightens the flavour of drinks, salads and other foods.

Vegetables. With the large number of prewashed and precut vegetables on the market, getting your five servings a day should be a doddle. If the vegetables don't look fresh, remember that frozen ones and plain tinned ones can be just as nutritious.

▶ Choose sturdy vegetables that cook quickly and make tasty leftovers, such as broccoli, cauliflower, green beans or a hardy green such as kale, pak choi or Swiss chard. Steam, microwave or sauté it with a little olive oil and a clove or two of crushed garlic.

▶ Choose prewashed salads and spinach.

▶ Celery, cucumbers and baby carrots are proven child-pleasers.

▶ Buy veggies that lend themselves to snacking, like baby carrots, precut celery stalks and cherry tomatoes.

▶ Stock up on staples such as onions and fresh ginger. They last for weeks in your refrigerator.

▶ Fresh herbs add flavour and freshness to sandwiches, soups, omelettes and even prepared dishes. If you're not sure which you like, start with basil and add it to spaghetti sauce, then branch out into parsley or coriander next week.

Bread Aisle

If none of the wholegrain breads included on the shopping list are sold at your local super-market, choose a product that lists whole-meal or another wholegrain flour as one of the key ingredients.

▶ Try breads that have sunflower seeds, pumpkin seeds, sesame seeds or flaxseeds in them for added fibre and vitamin E.

▶ If you prefer eating a carbohydrate-based meal plan, you might consider more than one variety of bread.

Grains, Beans and Tinned Goods Aisle

Don't be afraid to stock up here. Rices, grains and pasta last for years on the shelf – and unopened tins line the shelves of supermar-kets for months.

▶ Try some wholewheat pasta. While the taste is different to semolina-flour pasta, each serving yields a potent fibre dose.

▶ Any brown rice variety, including the quick-cooking type, is better than white rice, but for some dishes, such as risotto, you'll need (white) Italian Arborio rice.

▶ Stock up on several tins of beans – chickpeas, kidney, black, white – choosing lower-sodium or salt-free varieties whenever possible.

▶ Stock up also on low-fat soups (check the label if you're not sure of the fat content) and tinned tomatoes.

Condiments Aisle

Most condiments – except mayo – have a very long shelf life, even after opening. Condiments are flavour boosters that enhance cooked foods, homemade dress-ings, and salads and sandwiches. Buy prod-ucts with all-natural ingredients whenever possible.

▶ If you're replacing your oil or stocking your kitchen for the first time, consider buy-ing a bottle each of extra-virgin olive oil, rapeseed oil and toasted sesame oil.

▶ Instead of the big cylinder of table salt, look for sea salt, kosher salt or reduced-sodium salt.

▶ Vinegar adds a sharp, tart flavour to salads and cooked foods with no fat and very few calories. Buy many different kinds – they last for ever.

▶ All-fruit spreads last for a year or two in the fridge after opening.

Dairy Aisle

Fresh dairy foods like milk and yogurt are perishable, so don't feel compelled to buy a lot of them. Always look at the expiry date and choose the latest one. (As an alternative, consider long-life cow's milk or calcium-added soya milk.) If you store cheese well-wrapped in the fridge, it'll last for weeks.

▶ You should always have some milk on hand to drink or use on cereal – choose skimmed, semi-skimmed or soya (with calcium added).

▶ Opt for natural, low-fat or fat-free yogurt and avoid those with artificial sweeteners. Organic yogurt tastes especially good.

▶ Buy a whole chunk of Parmesan cheese – the flavour is so superior to the pre-grated kind, it will really impress you. To make it last a year, wrap it first in a slightly damp paper towel and then tightly in foil.

▶ Make sure you buy a carton of eggs. Hardboiled eggs make a great snack on the go.

▶ Quark and fromage blanc (French for 'white cheese') are both low-fat or fat-free soft spreadable cheeses; buy them as an exotic replacement for cream cheese. They're particularly tasty on toast with a little jam.

▶ The dairy aisle also features most of the fresh soya items. Packaged tofu and soya products have expiry dates, so read and heed them.

Meat and Fish Aisle

Meat freezes well, especially in big freezers. Avoid grey or 'dead'-looking meat and if it's prewrapped, make sure it's not sitting in a pool of its own liquid. If you're buying fish, plan on cooking it that same night – otherwise, freeze it or buy prefrozen.

▶ Skinless chicken breasts, parts or whole birds are extremely versatile and lower in fat than most other meat.

▶ For beef, opt for sirloin steak (I love it marinated in barbecue sauce and then grilled) or fillet steak or minced sirloin – all are lower in fat. Better yet, get the butcher to mince the sirloin to order. It'll taste fresher and you'll know it's the cut you want.

▶ Try minced turkey or chicken breast as a beef substitute.

▶ If you buy whole fish, like trout or sea bass, look for clear, sparkling eyes – grey, cloudy eyes mean the fish is old.

Frozen Food Aisle

If you're lucky enough to be blessed with a large freezer, go mad! Frozen foods are designed for convenience and last up to a year.

▶ Frozen soya foods like veggie burgers and hot dogs cook in under 10 minutes – some varieties of veggie burger can even go in the toaster!

▶ Frozen veggies and fruits can substitute for fresh when the produce aisle is looking less than up-to-scratch.

▶ Frozen prawns are as good as fresh; in fact, most of the 'fresh' prawns you bought in your life were actually defrosted before they were sold to you.

▶ Avoid frozen ready-meals as much as possible. They're processed to death and usually filled with fat and salt. If you need a quick meal, look for organic or vegetarian meals. Always scan the label to avoid hydrogenated and saturated fats and excess sodium (less than 0.1 gram of sodium is good).

As you're putting away your groceries, take a moment to see how your shelves and fridge look now – do you see more colour? More shapes and varieties of food? You should feel good – you've accomplished another giant step on the road to getting a Real Food Life.

Get Real Check-in

Assess your progress by checking off each of the following items you achieved during week 3.

❏ Instant Makeover 3: I replaced a half-hour of TV-watching with extra sleep time.
❏ I added an extra glass of water – I'm up to 7.
❏ I achieved my week 3 mini-goals.
❏ I set my week 4 mini-goals.

❏ I gave my kitchen the Real Food Life Makeover (the long or short version).
❏ I went food shopping.
❏ I kept my food journal each day.
❏ I rewarded myself for my intentions and my efforts.

Weekly Words: Write a couple of paragraphs in your journal about how you felt throwing away food – was it difficult, liberating, a little of both? Discuss how your new kitchen will help you achieve your ultimate goal.

CHAPTER 10

Week Four:

COOKING FOR YOUR REAL FOOD LIFE

For some people, cooking is a passion they can't live without.

And then there are most of my clients. Many of them are intimidated by cooking – they weren't taught how to do it, don't own cookbooks and don't feel comfortable cooking for themselves. As a result, they eat out often, relying on other people to prepare their meals and ultimately feeling disconnected from their food.

Cooking is a great way to learn exactly what you're putting into your mouth. When you cook, you learn a key Real Food Life skill without even thinking about it: portion control. Because you measure so often when you're cooking, you learn to develop an 'eye' for portions. You'll have a mental picture of what they look like from your travels as a cook.

> ### During this week, you will:
>
> ▶ Accomplish Instant Makeover 4: replace corn oil with olive or rapeseed oil
>
> ▶ Add one extra glass of water (reach 8 glasses a day)
>
> ▶ Follow your week 4 mini-goals
>
> ▶ Keep week 4 of your food journal
>
> ▶ Refine your eating plan
>
> ▶ Cook your first Real Food Life meal
>
> ▶ Learn how to plan for future Real Food Life meals
>
> ▶ Complete week 4 of your Get Real Check-in

Cooking comes down to control. You decide whether to use corn or olive oil. You decide to lightly sprinkle salt as opposed to

Instant Makeover 4:

Replace Corn Oil with Olive or Rapeseed Oil

Forget all those years of brainwashing – fat can be healthy! The trick is, you have to favour the good kinds of fats (and it won't hurt to avoid the bad ones altogether).

Replacing corn oil with olive or rapeseed oil stacks the good fat odds in your favour. Monounsaturated fats, like those found in olive and rapeseed oils, lower the 'bad' cholesterol in your blood. The polyunsaturated fats in corn oil do, too, but they also lower your 'good' cholesterol. (Saturated fats – those found in animal products and fried foods – raise your total cholesterol and increase your risk of heart disease.) When eaten in excess, polyunsaturated fats may promote cancer; monounsaturated fats protect against it.

Eating a lot of food with corn oil also increases the proportion of certain fatty acids in your body. If you eat too much corn oil, you can cancel out all the good you're doing by eating foods rich in omega-3 fatty acids, such as salmon, sardines and flaxseed.

If you're not a fan of olive oil's distinctive flavour, try rapeseed oil, which offers a very versatile flavour that many can't distinguish from corn oil. Buy it and try it today!

pouring it on. You decide to select the leanest cuts of chicken and you probably won't dip it in butter (as they do in restaurants). Your food is literally in your own hands, putting you in the driver's seat of your Real Food Life.

Before we get to cooking, take a moment at this halfway point to assess where you are with your Real Food Life. Reflect on the changes you've made by asking yourself the questions that follow – the answers will guide you through the second half of your Real Food Life Plan.

1. Refine Your Eating Plan

By now, keeping your journal has become a fully entrenched habit. You've probably grown to be an eager student of your own eating habits. Isn't it empowering to draw the direct connection between what you put in your mouth and how it makes you feel?

Let's take some time here in week 4 to revisit your food journal in more depth. Reflecting on where you are now, the compelling changes you've made and how different your Food Life feels now can bolster your dedication to reaching your ultimate goals.

Turn to a fresh page in your journal, ask yourself the following questions and note the answer that sounds most like how you feel.

Am I hungry throughout the day? If the answer is yes, try one of these suggestions:

▶ *You may have cut out too many complex carbohydrates from your diet.* Try increasing your complex carbohydrate intake by 1 or 2 servings for a few days (noting how you feel in your journal). If you feel 'fuller' by eating more carbohydrates, continue with that amount of carbs in your diet.

▶ *You may not have enough fibre in your meals.* Pick up a box of low-sugar/high-fibre cereal. Have a bowl for breakfast or eat it as a snack with some low-fat yogurt.

▶ *You may have lowered your fat intake too much.* Since fat slows the emptying of the stomach, a fat-free or low-fat meal will cause you to feel hungry quicker. Two servings of fat a day might not be enough, so add another and see how you feel after a few days.

▶ *You may not be drinking enough water.* Dehydration can cause false hunger and make you feel tired and lethargic. You might be reaching for food instead of the needed glass of water.

Am I feeling tired much of the time? If the answer is yes, try one of these suggestions:

▶ *You may not be taking in enough calories.* Carefully examine your food journal to see if you're falling short in any category or several. Add a snack to boost your caloric intake. If that doesn't help, try increasing your food plan by one serving in each food group to boost your caloric level.

▶ *You may be on the three square meals plan.* If you're not already doing the grazing plan, try eating six mini-meals each day. Many of my clients love this way of eating because it makes them feel like they're eating all day long and they feel they have more energy.

▶ *You may not be eating enough protein.* Protein helps slow down the emptying of the stomach, yielding sustained energy that lasts all afternoon. If you don't eat at least a little bit of protein with your carbohydrates, you'll feel hungry and tired quickly thereafter.

▶ *You may not be eating enough complex carbohydrates.* Complex carbs are the main source of energy for all bodily functions. A lack of complex carbohydrate will make you lethargic and probably constipated (because of lack of fibre), which can also slow you down.

▶ *You may not be eating balanced meals.* Salads with lean meats and grains are great for getting a balance of complex carbs and proteins. Or skip the meats and try adding a soya alternative.

Am I emotionally unsatisfied with what I'm eating? If the answer is yes, try one of these suggestions:

LIVING A REAL FOOD LIFE

Carly Bade Farewell to Her Binges

Name: Carly
Real Food Life Issues: Bingeing, always hungry

When I met Carly, she was a college student. She had no concentration at college. She told me that she felt she had too little energy. Plus, she was chronically constipated. Carly always felt hungry – as many teenagers do – but she could never enjoy the food she ate because eating to the point of fullness made her feel guilty. The pressure to be thin, to fit in, and to wear the latest belly-revealing outfits caused her to shun food – at least in public. She admitted to me that, in private, she regularly binged on biscuits, sweets, crisps and fast foods. She would alternate these binges with starving herself. Here's where I found her:

18 September

I did it again. I always think I'm going to be able to stop myself, but then I get in the middle of a packet of biscuits and I just think, 'Why bother stopping? I'm already a fat pig.' And then I just eat and eat and eat until I've worked through my whole stash and I feel like I'm going to explode. Then all I want to do is lie around with my jeans unbuttoned and moan. It's like that Christmas feeling, but at least then, everyone's doing it!

It's always so much more fun when we all eat together, especially at Heather's house. Her mum doesn't think twice about all the food that disappears, she just buys more! My mum's always hanging around, bugging us, embarrassing me - I can tell she's afraid I'll put on weight. I just don't understand how Heather and Lisa can eat everything I do - sometimes so much MORE - and still look like

▶ *You may be stuck in the 'diet' mentality.* If you're constantly pining for your old food life or 'foraging' for food, not satisfied with your meals, you need to change your eating plan. Getting a Real Food Life should empower you and help you get rid of the soul-draining diet mentality that is hazardous to your emotional relationship with food.

little twigs? Lisa told me her mum uses laxatives when she needs to fit into a cocktail dress for a party - I wonder if she's doing the same thing...? That would be a revolting way to lose weight... but who knows? Maybe I'll try it...

After Carly told me about her starving and bingeing, I explained the health risks associated with those behaviours. I explained that bingeing and starving interfered with her body chemicals and contributed to the symptoms she wanted to relieve. We worked together to set up a nourishing eating plan with enough calories so she didn't feel constantly hungry. This kept her from bingeing, which would have started the whole bingeing/starving cycle all over again. Her eating plan consisted of a variety of complex carbohydrates (she especially loved porridge for breakfast), lean proteins (turkey sandwiches for lunch and seafood dinners), fruit, vegetables and essential fatty acids (she adored sunflower seeds and loved avocados).

To start with I got her to drink 8 glasses of water each day. We also made sure she ate plenty of fruit and vegetables every day and, much to her relief, by week 2 she no longer suffered from constipation. By week 3, Carly realised she no longer felt constantly hungry and she had much more energy. She started to recognise that the punishing cycle of starving and then bingeing on unhealthy foods really did play a part in her symptoms.

I also gave Carly some cooking ideas she could use at college. I taught her how to make simple and fast foods like poached salmon, Veggie Trio (see page 269) and Middle Eastern Tabbouleh Salad (see page 291), all of which can be done in the microwave. I also shared strategies for ordering sensible foods at restaurants and at the college cafeteria.

In the first 8 weeks that we worked together, Carly noticed dramatic improvements. For the first time since her adolescence began, she was able to recognise what 'full' felt like and she knew that it was normal to feel that way. Her attention span improved dramatically and resulted in better grades. But most important, Carly realised that she hadn't binged once since she began working with me and that felt really good to her.

▶ *You may be more of an emotional eater than you thought.* Your Real Food Life should not make you feel deprived. You can eat and should eat plenty of the foods that make you feel good. But remind yourself that if you listen to your body more and recognise that you have many food choices, your food life can become much more emotionally satisfying.

▶ *You may not be experimenting enough.* Experiment with the different food options I've recommended in the various eating plans. If you're eating a meal and feel something is missing, if something isn't tasty enough or it's not satisfying to you, engage your food awareness, review your food journal, analyse what's going on and remedy it.

▶ *You may not be getting enough essential fatty acids.* Fat feeds your brain, so if your diet is too low in fat, it can make you feel emotionally unsatisfied. Try eating more deep-sea, cold-water fish, like salmon, herring and mackerel.

▶ *You may not be satisfying your cravings.* First, identify the craving. Remember, you can have any food you want in your Real Food Life, but limit less wholesome choices to small quantities. Or try a 'healthier' version of your craving – a turkey burger instead of a hamburger, chocolate sorbet instead of chocolate ice cream. You'll satisfy your craving and support your Real Food Life at the same time!

Am I bloated? If the answer is yes, try one of these suggestions:

▶ *You may have eaten pasta.* Pasta is a common culprit in bloating. Next time you eat it, take note of how you feel a few hours afterwards and the next day. If it's causing discomfort and bloating, eat it as a treat instead of a staple.

▶ *You may have eaten a lot of high-fibre foods.* High-fibre foods, such as beans, whole grains and lots of vegetables, can take a while for your body to get used to and until then, they can cause discomfort. If you find you're experiencing a lot of wind after high-fibre meals, cut back and add them in more slowly. Until your body gets used to them, try just a small portion of beans on top of your salad or as a side dish. Also, rinse beans well, which eliminates some of the enzymes that cause wind and bloating or use Beano (a bottled enzyme) on cooked vegetable and bean dishes.

Am I finding the plan inconvenient? If the answer is yes, try one of these suggestions:

▶ *Your plan is too time consuming or hard to follow.* If so, you need to start adapting it until you find what works for you and your lifestyle. A successful Real Food Life can change and vary depending on your situation, the season, your inclination and your mood.

▶ *You don't like doing one shop a week.* Try doing a big shop every other week, with smaller trips to the local market for fresh items as needed.

▶ *You dine out often and find it hard to stick to your plan.* Almost every restaurant has healthy options, if you know what you're looking for. Take time to consider the dining-out information on page 228.

Drawing from the suggestions that seemed to resonate with you, use this information to inform the decisions you make in the next step: cooking!

2. Cook Your First Real Food Life Meal

At its essence, your Real Food Life is all about eating nourishing foods that you love. Once you embrace your Real Food Life fully, cooking to support that love won't feel like a labour. Even if you're a die-hard dining-out junkie, trust me – there will come a time when you'll want to prepare your favourite foods for yourself, just the way you like them, rather than relying on restaurants or take-away menus.

Whether you're a beginner or an experienced cook, being comfortable in the kitchen will help you support your healthy eating habits for years to come. I have helped clients who literally didn't know how to boil water have success in the kitchen, so I know you can have success, too. The best way to settle in is to roll up your sleeves and experiment with some of the recipes in this book (starting on page 259).

To counter your kitchen fear, I've noted some steps to lessen your anxiety. Follow the Top Ten Tips I've included below, which will make sure every experience in the kitchen is a successful one.

1. As with all worthwhile pursuits, preparation is key. Read the recipe all the way through to see if you have all the ingredients on hand; if not, write the missing ingredients on your shopping list. A read-through also gets you familiar with the recipe, gives you an idea of how long it will take to make and lets you know if you need special equipment.

2. Go shopping for ingredients you need to make the recipe.

3. Read the recipe all the way through once again, so you'll understand the methods and steps involved.

4. Place all the ingredients on the work top. This visual is a great double check to make sure you have enough of the ingredients you'll need, including the ones you may have assumed you had on hand.

5. Collect all necessary kitchen equipment – cutting board, sharp knives, pots, pans and so on.

6. Wash, dry, chop, cut, dice, preheat – set the stage for the main event. Just as your favourite TV chefs measure and place their ingredients in various bowls before beginning, you will be able to cook quickly, smartly and efficiently if you follow this method. This way, you can motor through your recipe without having to stop and prepare another ingredient.

7. Commence cooking. As you go, follow the recipe step-by-step. Nothing should

come as a surprise to you now since you've already read it twice.

8. Mini-sermon: be safe. Never leave a cooking pot unattended. You don't have to watch it like a hawk, but don't leave the house when something is cooking in the oven or on the hob.

9. Adjust the recipe, if necessary. If you prefer your vegetables al dente, feel free to cook them for less time than called for in the recipe. Likewise, if you want something cooked more, increase the cooking time by a minute or two.

10. Try to embrace cooking as fun and therapeutic. I find that cooking helps me calm down and it gives me enormous pleasure to see my family enjoying something I have made for them. As a bonus, cooking helps me take care of my Real Food Life because I prepare the foods that fit into the programme I've made for myself.

Are you a beginner? If so, start with soup. It's easy to make, hard to burn and requires minimal technique, yet you still get to practise your cooking skills. And since soup is a dish that really cooks itself, you don't have to worry about 'messing it up'.

Soup is also a great way to get in more of the vegetables you may be missing out on in your Real Food Life. For example, if you want to eat more yellow and orange vegetables, preparing Roasted Acorn Squash Soup (see page 280) is a great way to accomplish that. Squash is very high in beta-carotene and cooks up very creamy and smooth, but it's still very low in calories. A big bowlful is a winning starter or great side dish.

Are you lacking in confidence? If you aren't that comfortable in the kitchen, there's nothing like some practice to build up your confidence. Try making at least one or two meals during week 4 and build from there. Take a trip to a local kitchen shop and buy a few new gadgets to reinforce your commitment to cook. Consider getting a garlic press, a steamer basket and maybe a new knife. You will be amazed at how easy cooking can be if you have the right tools.

Are you an experienced cook? Aim to make at least three meals for yourself during week 4. This is a great way to incorporate new foods into your Real Food Life (such as soya products, fresh fish and more vegetables). The more you cook for yourself, the more you reinforce your new good food habits.

Regardless of your skill level, you're sure to reap health benefits from taking the time to cook. Please try many of the tasty recipes I've included, starting on page 259. These recipes are the same ones I make for my family and I guarantee they taste great. Choose some to try and don't be afraid to experiment with some new flavours. Each recipe will be wholesome and tasty and will help you get the most out of your Real Food Life.

Cheat a Cold or Flu

Stuffed up? Feeling achy? Show your cold or flu who's boss with these powerful strategies that will have you feeling better faster than you can say 'achoo'.

- Cayenne and other hot peppers (dried and fresh) keep mucus flowing and help with congestion and headaches. So turn up the heat in your next meal.
- Garlic helps stimulate the immune system and inhibits the growth of bacteria. If you don't mind garlic breath, eat several raw cloves a day until your symptoms subside. (They're very tasty added to soups and salads.) If bad breath is a concern, take enteric-coated garlic capsules in 300-milligram dosages three times a day for as long as your cold symptoms last.
- Ginger combats inflammation, so drink ginger tea, add fresh ginger to your food or eat a few pieces of crystallised ginger.
- Drink lots of fluids: water, tea, soup. They will keep you hydrated, help mucus to flow and flush out your body.
- Eat plenty of fruit and vegetables, including those rich in beta-carotene, such as apricots, sweet potatoes, carrots and broccoli. Beta-carotene helps maintain mucous linings in the nose and lungs.
- Vitamin C in its many forms will help. It lowers levels of histamine, a chemical that's responsible for the stuffiness associated with colds and flu. It also appears to strengthen white blood cells, which are essential for fighting infection. Load up your plate with citrus fruits, berries and tomatoes. Also take a supplement of 500 to 1,000 milligrams.
- Getting at least 8 hours of sleep a night can help your body fight off infection.
- Chicken soup really helps! It clears mucous membranes and contains loads of nutrients that boost the immune system. Check out my recipe on page 275.

3. Planning Your Future Real Food Life Meals

For all cooks, time is often the biggest obstacle to making home-cooked meals. Cooking's biggest trick is to find shortcuts and time-savers. For me, two of the best all-around timesaving tools are two things you already own: a refrigerator and freezer. With those and a little planning, you can really save time and energy when you're short on both but still want to enjoy wholesome home-cooked foods. When you plan your meals in advance, you enable yourself to prepare a meal in a minute, just by defrosting it and reheating it.

Here are some great ways I've found to use your refrigerator and freezer to their fullest, most timesaving capacity.

Cook ahead. Double your recipes and freeze the extra for another day. If you have some extra time, make a batch of spaghetti sauce or dishes that freeze well, like stews, soups or casseroles such as lasagne or Aubergine Parmesan (see page 303).

Pre-portion. Immediately after cooking, place the food in individual serving containers – sealable freezer bags work well. If you plan on eating them within a few days, stick them in the fridge; otherwise, they'll keep in the freezer for up to 6 weeks (longer for soup).

Prepare extra basics. Whenever I cook my own burgers from minced turkey breast, I always make and freeze a few extra. With a vegetable or two and a grain or starch, this is a yummy, fast meal.

Freeze soup. I always double the quantity of a soup recipe and freeze individual- or double-size portions to have as a meal or part of a meal later on. Be aware, though, that not all soups freeze well. Don't freeze soups with potatoes in them – they get mealy and don't reheat well.

Pre-bake muffins. Muffins freeze well, so split a batch – keep some out for the next few days and freeze the rest. These muffins can be part of a breakfast on the run, a snack in the afternoon or a dessert in the evening. (See the recipe on page 319.)

Get Real Check-in

Assess your progress by checking off each of the following items you achieved during week 4.

- ❏ Instant Makeover 4: I replaced the corn oil I had been using with olive or rape-seed oil.
- ❏ I added one extra glass of water – I'm at my goal of 8!
- ❏ I achieved my week 4 mini-goals.
- ❏ I set my week 5 mini-goals.

- ❏ I re-analysed my Food Plan and made appropriate adjustments.
- ❏ I cooked my first Real Food Life meal.
- ❏ I learned how to plan for future meals.
- ❏ I kept my food journal each day.
- ❏ I rewarded myself for my intentions and my efforts.

Weekly Words: Write a couple of paragraphs in your journal about what it felt like to cook your first Real Food Life meal. Did you like it more than you thought you would? Discuss how making this a habit will help you reach your ultimate goal.

CHAPTER 11

Week Five:

FINE-TUNING YOUR REAL FOOD LIFE

'Let's do lunch!'
Who doesn't love to hear that sentence? Lunch offers a wonderful opportunity to catch up with your friends. Breaking bread bonds us to each other in a way few other activities can.

Just like other meals, lunch offers you a great opportunity to practise the principles of your Real Food Life. Packing your lunch helps you stay in control. In week 5 of your Real Food Life plan, I'll offer you numerous tips on how to lunch intelligently.

By this point, you should be eating better and finding that your new habits are feeling more familiar and comfortable. You're shopping wisely and making more sensible eating choices with your newfound knowledge and strategies. Your body should also be adapting

> **During this week, you will:**
>
> ▸ Accomplish Instant Makeover 5: replace white bread with 100 per cent wholemeal bread
> ▸ Follow your week 5 mini-goals
> ▸ Keep week 5 of your food journal
> ▸ Pack your own lunch
> ▸ Diversify your diet
> ▸ Add exercise to your Real Food Life
> ▸ Complete week 5 of your Get Real Check-in

to the better food you're giving it. You should be feeling more energetic and healthy. Celebrate the fact that you're well on your way to getting a Real Food Life!

Instant Makeover 5:

Replace White Bread with 100 Per Cent Wholemeal Bread

Many of my new clients share the same uncomfortable malady: constipation. But within a few weeks, they're feeling regular and less bloated. Why? They've simply started eating more fibre-rich whole grains.

If you didn't already do so in your Kitchen Makeover, throw out that squishy, lifeless white bread. To your body, the refined carbohydrates in white bread act like pure sugar. Replace it with 100 per cent wholemeal bread, which is packed with constipation-relieving fibre. Wholemeal bread also does a better job of filling you up and satisfying your hunger. Plus, it's higher in the vitamins and minerals that keep your body young and healthy.

Since you have been gradually increasing your intake of high-fibre foods for the past several weeks, your body should be used to the fibre by now. If not, try Beano to prevent intestinal distress. It really helps.

I hope that you've also grown more adventurous in your food selections and are feeling more confident about your choices. With some well-placed inspiration and a little bit of creativity, there's no reason why your Real Food Life should ever be boring. In week 5, I'll talk about a number of ways you can diversify your diet. The world of wholesome food is a never-ending garden of riches – there is no end point, no 'perfect' diet. Continue to experiment with new foods and keep your tastebuds guessing!

Finally, we'll talk about exercise. While this book focuses primarily on foods, exercise is a huge part of your Real Food Life. Food is fuel, simple as that. Ideally, the amount of energy you take in is equal to the amount of energy you expend. On the flip side, the more energy you expend, the more choices you'll have for your Real Food Life.

In addition to burning calories, exercise has a million other immediate benefits – it drains stress from your body, makes your clothes fit better, gives you an inner buzz that's better than any drug or drink. Exercise in some form should be part of your daily life and I'll give you lots of suggestions on how to incorporate more movement into your daily routine. Challenge yourself to find some way to move your body every second you're not sleeping, even if it's just fidgeting in your chair!

1. Pack Your Own Lunch

If there's a common element that most of us share regarding lunch, it's that we usually eat it every day. What's different is where we eat it. We might eat it in cafeterias, restaurants, fast-food places, takeaways or simply wherever we can grab a bite.

Lunch can be a challenge if you're always relying on someone else, whether it be a restaurant or cafeteria, to keep your food needs in mind. Remember that portions at restaurants are usually much larger than what you actually need to eat – often they could take the place of two or three meals. Restaurants also ladle on sauces, dressings and unhealthy fats that you wouldn't dream of using in your own cooking. Fast food and takeaways may fit into any lunchtime break, but you can easily eat much more than you need to or will feel good about later.

Hitting the lunch circuit with friends and colleagues can also cause overeating because in our minds, socialising often equals indulgence. Friends or colleagues may unwittingly sabotage your efforts to eat healthily. You might feel peer pressure to order or share a 'bad' meal or dessert with your friends.

Making a packed lunch helps you avoid these scenarios. If it has been years since you've packed a lunch for yourself, it's time to give it a try. Ideally, you should try to take your own lunch 4 days a week.

This doesn't mean that you have to eat solo, like Cinderella stuck inside eating gruel while her sisters are out having a ball. Plan lunch dates with your friends and encourage them to order a takeaway, and you can all eat outside in a park. Or, in a cafeteria, you can certainly share the table with friends who have bought their lunches. When your friends see how tasty and fulfilling bringing a lunch can be, more than likely they'll start making packed lunches for themselves.

Need more convincing? Think how full and contented your purse will be. Making your own lunch can save you a lot of money. Save money, gain energy – seems like a good deal to me!

Keep these tips in mind to make your lunches fun and healthy.

Sandwiches. Sandwiches are generally the best and most portable lunch item you can make.

❯ During your weekly shop, buy a loaf of wholemeal bread, some deli-sliced turkey breast or roast beef, a cos lettuce and a few ripe tomatoes. There are your sandwich fillings for the week. (Pack the sliced tomatoes separately to keep your sandwiches dry during the day.)

❯ Keep a jar of all-natural peanut butter and low-sugar jam or fruit spread on hand. A bonus: PB&J sandwiches don't need to be refrigerated.

(continued on page 208)

Lunch Lists

A greasy cheeseburger and fries from the fast-food joint down the street. Questionable beef curry from the cafeteria. Take heart! You don't need to be tied down to unhealthy lunch choices like these any more. Read on for a plethora of nutritious lunch options – whether you're making a packed lunch, dining in a cafeteria, grabbing something at a fast-food place, or ordering a takeaway. There are even choices for afternoons when you want extra energy.

What to Take

If you take lunch every day instead of going out or ordering a takeaway, you'll save at least 100 calories a day (which translates to 4.5 kg/10 lb a year) and a significant amount of money. Try packing some of the following healthy lunch options.

- Turkey or roast beef sandwich on wholemeal bread, with lettuce, slices of tomato and 1 tablespoon low-fat mayonnaise and/or mustard
- Egg salad sandwich (1 whole hard-boiled egg with 3 hard-boiled egg whites, with chopped apple and low-fat mayonnaise on a small wholegrain roll)
- Salad with 1 scoop of either egg salad, curried tuna salad or chicken salad made with low-fat mayonnaise
- Leftovers, such as roasted chicken (110 g/4 oz) and a vegetable
- Peanut butter and jam on 2 slices of wholemeal bread
- 4 tablespoons hummus inside 1 wholemeal pitta bread with baby carrots and lettuce
- 1 low-fat yogurt and one low-fat blueberry muffin (or see muffin recipe on page 319)
- 600 ml (1 pt) vegetable soup (see recipe on page 281) with a wholegrain roll or a salad or both
- Frozen ready-meals that contain fewer than 300 calories

To accompany your packed lunch, try one of these tasty options: a handful of Twiglets, 1 small bag of oven-baked, low-fat crisps, 1 small box of raisins, 2 jaffa cakes or 1 piece of fruit

What to Eat at a Cafeteria

Most cafeterias offer at least some healthy lunch options – you may just need to seek them out. Here are some ideas to get you started.

- Salad bar salad (heavy on the raw and steamed veggies), with a drizzle of olive oil or 1 tablespoon vinaigrette dressing; with half a grilled chicken breast (about 110–150 g/4–5 oz) or a medium-size piece of roasted chicken (110–150 g/4–5 oz) or 75–110 g (3–4 oz) tuna or a large spoonful of beans (not drenched in oil)

• 1 medium baked potato with a sprinkle of cheese and a green salad drizzled with olive oil and vinegar

• 2 servings vegetarian chilli with 4 wholegrain crackers

• Small portion of hot roast beef (75 g/3 oz) with two vegetables

• Roast beef or turkey sandwich on wholemeal bread with lettuce, tomato and mustard

• 1 veggie burger on a small wholegrain roll, with lettuce, tomato and a small pack of tomato ketchup; a salad with a drizzle of olive oil or 1 tablespoon vinaigrette dressing

• 1 piece grilled or roasted chicken with 75 g/3 oz cooked brown rice (or 1 slice wholemeal bread); a salad with a drizzle of olive oil or 1 tablespoon vinaigrette dressing

Fast-food Picks

Fast-food restaurants are starting to get the message that many of their customers want healthier options. Check out the following list, which includes items offered at many fast-food establishments.

• Grilled chicken sandwich with mustard (no mayonnaise)

• Roast beef sandwich (no butter and no mayonnaise or low-fat mayonnaise only) with lettuce, tomato and mustard

• Baked potato with 2 tablespoons of cheese (no butter)

• Green salad with a drizzle of low-fat dressing

• Veggie burger

• 2 slices thin-crust pizza (take off half the cheese and add veggies if they're available) and a salad with a drizzle of low-fat dressing

• Salad with grilled chicken and a drizzle of low-fat dressing

• For your drink choice, choose water or semi-skimmed or skimmed milk

Safe Bets to Order from Takeaways and Home-delivery Services

Just because food is being delivered to your doorstep doesn't mean that it has to be unhealthy. When you ring to place your order, explore what healthy alternatives might be available that aren't listed on the menu. Many restaurants will be happy to prepare something special – you just need to request it.

(continued)

Lunch Lists (cont.)

Safe Bets to Order from Takeaways (cont.)

• Steamed mixed veggies with tofu, chicken or prawns and a sprinkle of black bean sauce or garlic sauce; small portion (75–175 g/3–6 oz) brown rice

• 2 sushi rolls (12 pieces) (maki) with green salad and a cup of miso soup

• Tandoori chicken, fish or vegetables; small portion (75–175 g/3–6 oz) pilau rice

• Pasta e fagioli (pasta and bean soup) with a green salad dressed with a little olive oil and lemon or vinegar and a small wholegrain roll

• Grilled chicken fajita made with 2 small tortillas (just a dab of sour cream or omit it altogether) with 1 tablespoon guacamole, lettuce and tomatoes

• 2 slices thin-crust pizza (with half the cheese removed) and a mixed salad

Lunches to Energise

These lunches are low in complex carbs and high in protein, so they won't make you feel sleepy after eating them.

• 225 g/8 oz (the size of 2 packs of playing cards) grilled fish (salmon and tuna are especially good choices); sautéed vegetables

• 1 Unfried Chicken Breast (see page 311) with steamed veggies and tzatziki (garlic and herb yogurt) dressing

• 1 Turkey Burger (see page 297) in a small wholemeal pitta with a green salad

• 1 serving chicken and walnut salad (with 1 tablespoon low-fat mayonnaise) on lettuce with 4 wholegrain crackers

• 1 serving Roasted Vegetables (see page 267) with leftover barbecued sirloin steak (about 75 g/3 oz) with a slice of wholegrain toast

• 1 tin vegetarian chilli and a green salad

Salads. Salads offer a great way to get in several of your vegetable servings at one time.

▶ Prepackaged lettuce is simple for instant-gratification salads.

▶ Toss in some baby carrots, slices of cucumber and some cherry tomatoes. Then add tofu, leftover chicken or tinned tuna.

▶ Rinsed, tinned beans, like kidney beans or chickpeas, give salads staying power.

▶ Add a wholemeal roll for a perfect balance of carbohydrates that will keep you going strong all afternoon.

Leftovers. Often what was just OK the

night before will be a treat for lunch the next day.

▶ Keep that leftover pasta. Any addition of vegetables and high-quality protein, such as chicken, meat sauce or baked tofu, will make it filling and delicious. You can even eat it cold!

▶ Make a large pan of soup at the weekend and take it with you to warm up in the microwave for lunch throughout the following week.

▶ When you make dinner, make extra for yourself for the next day's lunch. That goes for vegetable dishes as well as main courses.

Convenience foods. Instead of relying on the vending machines or takeaway shops, make your own fridge a convenience shop.

▶ Add easy-to-pack lunchtime foods to your shopping list: freshly sliced turkey, cooked chicken, precut carrots, hummus, single-serving packs of nuts, fruits and vegetables are always great to bring along.

▶ Reusable microwave- and freezer-safe plastic containers are the lunch-packer's best friend. Use these to carry your food with no fear of spilling and reheat it in the same container.

▶ Buy yogurt and cottage cheese in individual serving sizes to take with you.

▶ Fruit is the perfect fat-free lunch dessert. It's wrapped in its own natural packaging, generally comes in a single-serving size and is sweet enough to use as a pudding.

Packing tips. A little preparation is the key to making your packed lunch appealing at any hour.

▶ Pack your lunch the night before and put it in the fridge. You'll spare yourself one extra task during your morning rush.

▶ Wash and cut up a mound of different raw vegetables and store them in the refrigerator. When you're packing lunch, place a few handfuls in a sealable plastic bag (with low-fat salad dressing, hummus or a fat-free dip in a small sealable container) and you have an easy, healthy snack or lunch side dish.

▶ If you have access to a microwave, try out healthy varieties of frozen organic or vegetarian dinners. All you have to do is heat and eat, giving you extra time for a walk or to do a bit of shopping over lunch.

▶ The night before, cook one or two soya or vegetable burgers or hot dogs and take them in the next day with crackers. Or, if you have access to a freezer and microwave at work, just pack the frozen burgers or hot dogs and cook them right before eating.

2. Diversify Your Diet

Eating a rich assortment of healthy foods is the fun and pleasurable cornerstone of any Real Food Life.

Because you're adjusting your eating habits, a natural instinct is to start limiting yourself to a few reliable foods that fit your programme and are easy to make. But if you don't explore your possibilities, you put yourself at risk of getting into an eating rut. And if you get into a rut, you're more likely to be tempted by a high-calorie food because you feel you owe yourself some pleasure for all the drudgery you've endured.

In addition, every food has its own set of nutrients, so eating many different types of foods will ensure you're getting the widest possible variety of vitamins and minerals. So if you find yourself looking at the same meals day after day, mix it up. Here's how:

Experiment! Take a food that you enjoy and try a new recipe for preparing it. Start with some of the recipes beginning on page 259. If you always gravitate towards grilled chicken, for example, try your chicken roasted, baked or sliced into a salad.

Include fish in at least two meals a week. If you have difficulty preparing fish for yourself order it each time you eat out and see which varieties you enjoy the most. Then, try variations on these themes at home. Fish tastes great when it's prepared simply and it cooks quickly, so it's the perfect food for your Real Food Life.

Add zing with different spices and flavourings. For a whole new taste sensation, add different spices, herbs or flavourings to your usual dishes. Curry powder, five-spice powder, paprika, cumin, hot pepper sauce and low-sodium soy sauce are some of my favourite flavour boosters. Adding curry powder to tinned tuna along with low-fat mayonnaise, apples and raisins creates an entirely new, zesty type of tuna salad. Look through your cookbooks to find new recipes using new flavours that still fit into your Food Life.

Add new greens. If you've never had dandelion greens or kale, give them a try. Wash the leaves and cut off tough stems, chop the leaves and then steam until wilted. Place in a bowl and season with lemon juice, a drizzle of olive oil and a dusting of black pepper. Then toss well. Greens are delicious and brimming with nutrients.

Satisfy your sweet tooth with kiwifruit. Not only is kiwifruit sweet and tangy, but this fuzzy green fruit has more vitamin C than an orange. Or how about a mango, a very sweet and filling tropical fruit? You can even try new fruit combinations blended into smoothies. Strawberry-banana or blueberry-peach are two great combinations.

Go international! Have you ever eaten hummus? I love this Middle Eastern chickpea dip. (You may have noticed I can't stop talking about it!) It's usually available in the refrigerated section of most supermarkets, near the cheese and other dairy foods. Or try my recipe on page 284. Sample some with sliced tomato and wholewheat crackers for a tasty, satisfying snack or light lunch.

Spruce up your salads. Add chopped

walnuts, raisins, pears or apples. They'll add a new dimension in taste and texture to your usual bowl of lettuce. Also, try a different dressing (see the recipes on pages 262 and 263 for some ideas).

3. Add Exercise to Your Real Food Life

Your body was meant to operate. Your legs are there so you can walk or run. Your arms aren't just attachments dangling from your body – they're to help you swim and lift weights. If you want your arms, legs, heart and lungs to last for a long lifetime, you have to give them work to do.

Regular exercise also relieves stress, helps you sleep better and longer and makes you feel better about yourself. After any workout, even a 20-minute walk, I always feel better and feel like I have accomplished something important on my own that no one can take away from me.

You'll find that exercise also goes a long way towards keeping you on track with sensible eating. Once you've made the connection between what you put into your mouth and how much energy it takes to burn it up, you'll realise that a 300-calorie fizzy drink would require you to run several miles to shed those calories.

When you exercise, you also increase your lean muscle mass. This, in turn, increases your metabolism and makes you burn more calories even when you're at rest. So this week, I want you to start moving your body any way possible, as often as possible. Simply try to incorporate as much movement into your everyday routine as you can. If you have never exercised before, check with your doctor to make sure she agrees you're ready to start doing some physical activity.

Any movement, even a 5-minute walk, is better than sitting still. Exercise helps you live longer, feel healthier and have more energy than any other single activity you could do, including several of the huge changes you've made in your eating plan. Do it today.

Here are some creative ways to slip some exercise into your routine.

▶ Walk everywhere that's less than a mile away, provided it's a safe, well-lit route.

▶ If walking all the way isn't possible, park your car before you get to your destination and walk at least 10 minutes from your car and 10 minutes back.

▶ Get up into the attic, down into the basement or out to the garage and give it the cleaning you keep meaning to do. It's not work now – it's exercise!

▶ Similarly, get out in the garden and pull up weeds, prune or do any other gardening activity.

Kitchen CURES

Ease Sore Muscles with These Simple Strategies

Whether you overdid it at the gym, spent the day rearranging furniture or got involved in any other activity that made your muscles ache, check out the pointers below. They'll ease the ache and help you to prevent soreness in the future.

- Sore muscles mean that your muscle fibres have torn. This is a natural and desirable state that prompts muscles to repair themselves and become stronger. Overly sore muscles aren't good, however. Working out to the point where your muscles are achingly sore actually slows down the healing process and, of course, prevents you from continuing your exercise regimen.

- Work out different muscle groups on different days, so that each group gets a day of rest between workouts.

- Protein helps repair muscles and aids in the healing process, so eat a little extra protein when your muscles feel sore.

- Treat yourself to some fresh pineapple. Bromelain, an enzyme found in pineapple, can help the healing process.

- Calcium and magnesium help repair connective tissue and the skeletal system. Make sure you eat foods that contain both of these nutrients. Try low-fat or fat-free dairy foods, seafood, soya foods and nuts and seeds.

- Antioxidant-rich foods can help speed up the muscle-healing process, so have some dark green, leafy vegetables; legumes; porridge; asparagus; avocados; mangoes; or tomatoes.

- On days you work out, drink an additional 4 to 5 glasses of water (yes, that means 12 to 13 total glasses); it may help relieve soreness later.

- Don't forget to stretch your muscles. Stretching helps to maintain flexibility and relieve soreness.

▶ Always use the stairs instead of the escalator or lift. If you're really adventurous, try doing the steps two at a time – it will help build muscle.

▶ Carry your baby instead of using the pushchair.

▶ Go dancing. Hit a club and step out to your favourite tunes from the 1970s and 1980s. Or go in the opposite direction and try a ballroom dancing class.

▶ Go roller-skating or swimming. If it has been years since you've tried either of these, you might have forgotten how much fun they are. Be sure to wear protective gear when you pull on those skates, though.

▶ Hop on your bike instead of getting into the car if you're going relatively short distances. Again, put on a helmet.

▶ Try yoga. This ancient exercise method combines meditation, breathing and stretching in ways you never imagined before.

▶ Join a gym and hire a trainer to develop a personalised programme for you. This way, you'll get personalised instruction on how to use the equipment and the trainer

can teach you fun routines you might never have discovered otherwise.

▶ If you already have a gym membership, simply experiment with a new machine or piece of equipment on your own each week. Read the directions first or get help from a staff member.

▶ Follow an exercise video. This is an easy way to sweat off some weight in the comfort of your own home. You can choose step aerobics, martial-arts routines, abdominal exercises or countless other styles. Use it at least three times a week.

▶ Find an exercise partner. Draft a friend, colleague or family member to join you in your quest for fitness. Having someone expecting your company can motivate you when you're feeling sluggish and having a friend there will make the time speed by.

Get Real Check-in

Assess your progress by checking off each of the following items you achieved during week 5.

❏ Instant Makeover 5: I replaced white bread with 100 per cent wholemeal bread.
❏ I achieved my week 5 mini-goals.
❏ I set my week 6 mini-goals.
❏ I packed my own lunch.

❏ I diversified my diet.
❏ I added exercise to my Real Food Life.
❏ I kept my food journal each day.
❏ I rewarded myself for my intentions and my efforts.

Weekly Words: Write a couple of paragraphs in your journal about how your reassessment of your goals last week affected your behaviour this week. Do you feel reinvigorated? Discuss how looking regularly at your mini-goals will help you reach your ultimate goal.

CHAPTER 12

Week Six:

REFINING YOUR REAL FOOD LIFE

If eating were a sport, you'd be about to turn professional.

That doesn't mean you're eating a lot or even that quickly. Just like an athlete, you've developed highly sensitive techniques to make the most of the natural power of your body. By the time you enter week 6 of your Real Food Life, you've mastered most of the skills we nutritionists (or coaches!) hope our clients will embrace. If certain hurdles have stood in your way in the past – cravings, binges, unhealthy choices – you've since sailed over them with ease, once and for all.

You have more energy, your skin and hair feel and look better, you're more alert and you have a better overall sense of well-being. You know that accepting responsibility for your food choices increases your ability to

During this week, you will:

▶ Accomplish Instant Makeover 6: replace one cup of coffee with one cup of green tea
▶ Follow your week 6 mini-goals
▶ Keep week 6 of your food journal
▶ Compare your food journal from weeks 1, 3 and 5
▶ Review your ultimate goals
▶ Eat more!
▶ Look at your daily food issues
▶ Do at least 10 minutes of exercise on 3 separate days
▶ Complete week 6 of your Get Real Check-in

Instant Makeover 6:

Replace One Cup of Coffee with One Cup of Green Tea

Even if you're the biggest Java junkie and green tea isn't one of the brews you would normally choose, you owe it to yourself to give it a try. If you're currently drinking a lot of coffee – or fizzy soft drinks – each day, replace just one of those servings with a cup of green tea.

This drink, made from the unfermented leaves of the tea plant, is milder and less bitter than black tea. It has half the caffeine of coffee and drinking a cup or two per day may reduce your risk of cancer. In fact, a cup of green tea offers you as many health-enhancing antioxidants as one or two servings of vegetables.

Keep a stash of green tea bags handy and walk past the steaming coffee pot or money-hungry soft drinks machine. At the end of the day, you'll have taken in less nerve-jangling caffeine and reinforced your protection against disease.

make other changes you desire. You may not realise this about yourself, though.

That's the purpose of week 6 – to review your plan thus far, remind yourself of how far you've come and regroup for the future. First, let's look at the history of your food journal.

1. Compare Your Food Journal from Weeks 1, 3 and 5

For a humble little notebook, your food journal is really a powerhouse of information. As your constant companion for the past 5 weeks, your journal has helped you learn about your cravings and energy dips, understand the importance of portion control, even out the imbalances in your diet and achieve more control and energy in your Real Food Life.

Let's review three key weeks in your journal, so you can see how far you've come, realise how much you've learned and readjust your programme for the next 3 weeks. (You can either just think about these questions or write your answers to them in your journal.)

Week 1: Remember that during week 1, you were just observing your former food life, your personal eating style and any shortfalls in nutrition. Normally my clients are amazed by the difference a mere 5 weeks makes. Prepare yourself – it could be a bit surprising.

❙ What kinds of breakfasts were you eating? Were they loaded with sugar? Were you eating breakfast at all?

❙ What kinds of lunches were you eating? Did you *ever* take your own lunch? Did you frequent the fast food restaurant or the deli?

❙ What happened during the afternoons? Were you snacking on chocolate or quaffing loads of coffee?

❙ What did dinners look like? Huge wads of calories, drenched in heavy fat sauce? Not a trace of fresh vegetables or quality protein?

Week 3: By week 3, you'd started implementing changes into your plan. You did your Kitchen Makeover and went food shopping. Perhaps your journal already reflected some changes, large and small.

❙ How often did you eat out in week 3?

❙ Were your meals after the Kitchen Makeover different from the ones before it?

❙ Had you already begun eating more balanced meals (for example, more lean proteins if you were a carbohydrate-based eater or more high-quality carbohydrates if you were a protein-based eater)?

❙ Had you settled into a loose schedule that felt good for your type (three square meals style or grazing style)?

❙ Had you begun setting (and keeping) mini-goals?

Week 5: Now look at your journal from this past week – do you notice a big difference?

❙ What foods had you eaten before that are now entirely absent? Why?

❙ What foods have been showing up a lot more often? Why?

❙ How many meals did you prepare for yourself in week 5 versus week 3? Versus week 1? What do you notice about the nutritional quality of those meals versus the takeaway or restaurant food that used to take its place?

❙ Have you noticed a difference in your energy level? Your toilet habits? Your cravings?

❙ Have your mini-goals affected your eating habits since week 2?

❙ Are you making progress towards your ultimate goal?

The biggest change my clients typically notice at this point is how many of the foods they used to eat regularly have been replaced with more wholesome, nutritious and balanced foods. Congratulate yourself on this accomplishment because it's a big step towards achieving your Real Food Life. Changing your Food Life takes energy and thought and you should know that you are well on the way to feeling even better and more alive and making choices with positive health benefits.

2. Review Your Ultimate Goal

Sometimes my clients are real overachievers – they find halfway through their Food Life Plans that they've already achieved their ultimate goals.

I'm joking, of course. There's nothing 'over' about this – in fact, there's nothing stopping you from making and achieving hundreds of ultimate goals. In fact, continual goal-setting is a good principle to take with you beyond the Real Food Life plan. Goal-setting, in eating and in the rest of life, keeps us in touch with what we really want. It's a great way to help us measure current choices, feel accomplished and remain enthusiastic about healthy habits. Instead of 'giving up' decadences that may taste or feel good in the moment, you're gaining all the personal power – and energy and vitality – that comes from controlling your own Real Food Life.

When my clients achieve their first goal, I counsel them to immediately create a new goal, one that will keep them motivated until the end of the programme and beyond. Look back to week 1's quiz and see if there are other issues you'd like to tackle. Perhaps you started out wanting more energy, but now you want to get serious about weight loss. Perhaps you've already lost a bit of weight and now you want to tackle your sugar addiction.

Don't worry – you still get 'credit' for your first goal! Turn to the first page of your journal. Next to the ultimate goal, write 'ACHIEVED'. Draw a star or smiley face next to it – something to denote that you set a goal and achieved it. And most important, *give yourself your reward*. Whatever you planned at the beginning, make sure you do it now. (This is a critical, often-skipped step in the programme, but I urge you to do it. Nothing reinforces good habits like promises kept to yourself.)

Underneath your first goal, write down your next ultimate goal and pick a new, completely different but equally enjoyable reward for this one. You can continue doing this kind of goal-setting motivation with yourself for the rest of your Real Food Life. Think of this as your body's extra credit – with no limits!

3. Eat More – Strategically

This one sounds easy, doesn't it?

As I recommend to all my clients at this point in the food programme, I want you to start adding a little more food to your eating plan. If you have experienced some weight loss in the first few weeks, at this point you may reach a weight plateau. However, even if you haven't been trying to lose weight, now is the time to increase the number of calories you consume.

Many of us were brought up with a diet

mentality that told us if fewer calories were good for weight loss, almost none would be better. Nothing could be further from the truth. Remember, when you eat too few calories, your body wants to conserve energy and so slows everything down – especially your metabolism. You don't want your body to conserve energy. You want your body to know there is a constant supply of energy coming in so it will always burn calories efficiently.

Note: If you're comfortable with your food amounts and don't want to add extra food, this isn't a required component of getting a Real Food Life. My experience, however, is that people enjoy additional food – surprise, surprise! – especially when it leads to additional energy and no weight gain.

Start with favourites. Choose a food group you love and can't get enough of, like complex carbohydrates. Take this opportunity to try something you've been neglecting because you didn't want to use your precious allotment of servings – perhaps a new whole grain like bulgar wheat.

Branch out. If you started out as a primarily carbohydrate- or protein-based eater, try branching out into the other side. Many people who start off in one camp find their tastes changing as their bodies do.

Enjoy your weekends. If you eat a mostly balanced and wholesome diet during the week, your body has learned to efficiently process the food. Eating just slightly more – no more than 200 extra calories – at weekends will tell your body to work extra hard to burn those extra calories.

On page 158, we discussed what a serving of carbohydrates or protein is, so remember: adding one more serving daily to your food intake isn't a licence to overeat.

4. Look at Daily Food Issues

As you continue on with your Real Food Life, you might come up against some challenging eating situations. Brimming with tempting nibbles, crisps or fountains of cocktails, social gatherings are often food-centric, full of staples of your old food life that no longer fit in your plan.

For those key moments when you find yourself dealing with more of these challenges than you'd like, I've collected some surefire strategies to keep your plan on track. Two tricks that work no matter what the occasion: before you go, review your goals, visualise the situation you're about to walk into and mentally practise what to eat to stay within your plan. Second, by all means, don't 'save your appetite' for the party – in fact, do the opposite. Have a snack. Arriving full and satisfied will make those cheese puffs a lot less appealing.

Remember, your Food Life is your own. By week 6, you have a very clear picture of

(continued on page 222)

LIVING A REAL FOOD LIFE

John Exercised – and Ate – His Way Back to Health

Name: John
Real Food Life Issues: Weight gain, exhaustion, indigestion

John is a workaholic financial executive in his mid-thirties. His competitive industry dictated his 14-hour workdays. Like many workaholics, he regularly used food as a stress-reliever and coffee as a stimulant. He ate when he felt tense, he ate at meetings, he ate when the stock market went up or down, and he ate and drank when he went out with his friends or business associates, which was at least three times a week. Here's where I found him:

25 August

I am so glad my office is air conditioned. Just the walk from my car to the office is so disgusting when it's hot - I sweat, my legs rub together, I feel like I'm going to pass out. To make matters more humiliating, my trousers hardly fit me any more. I had to slip out of a meeting sideways a few days ago because I was afraid the seam in the seat was about to give.

I don't know what my problem is. It's not as though I'm doing anything differ-ently. I might not have been addicted to chocolate back at college, but I drank a lot more beer! I'm dreading the reunion. I know people are going to come up to me and say things like, 'Looks like you're not starving in finance!' Well, screw 'em. I work hard, I play hard. That's the way the system works. You don't get to where I am by spending your whole day at the gym.

When I met him, John was used to eating whatever was around or whatever was fast – and a lot of it, at that. Since his life revolved around work, he no longer found the time to go running, to go to the gym or to play tennis with his friends. Between the volatile finan-cial market, no time to eat properly and long hours sitting in an office, John put on 9 kg (20 lb) in the few months before he came to see me. His weight gain caused his blood pres-sure to go up, decreased his energy levels and exacerbated his chronic indigestion.

When he showed his food journal to me, I noticed that John was a serious coffee junkie and he drank hardly any water – both of which contributed to his indigestion and promoted dehydration. The dehydration, in turn, resulted in a lack of energy. John's first Real Food Life change was to cut back on coffee to no more than 2 cups a day and to increase his water consumption to at least 8 glasses a day, with a cup or two of green or ginger tea to help with his indigestion. Two weeks later, his chronic indigestion was practically eliminated.

Then John focused on cutting out the kebabs, pizza and other fast foods that tempted him around his office and on his way home from work late at night. He replaced his usual snacks with a few pieces of fresh fruit and a handful of nuts, which satisfied his hunger but also gave his body vital nutrients without loading up on bad fats.

Since snacking was a major part of John's life that he wasn't willing to give up, we devised a selection of healthy, energy-producing snacks that he could reach for in times of hunger (and, occasionally, when particularly stressed). His snack list included hummus with wholewheat crackers and baby carrots, tinned low-fat soup and leftover chicken and vegetables (which he really loved). All of these filled his stomach, gave him energy to keep going and kept him satisfied.

To also help with his energy levels, especially in the morning, I suggested that John eat breakfast. So for the first time in years, he ate a morning meal, usually in the form of a low-fat yogurt, fresh fruit and a piece of wholemeal toast with jam and a little low-fat cream cheese. He quickly recognised that breakfast did give him energy all morning long.

He also came to realise that stress at work and lack of sleep were major factors in his overeating and tiredness. First he left 15 minutes earlier, then half an hour earlier and then an hour or so. He also started sleeping 6 to 7 hours a night instead of his usual 4 to 5. Plus, he began exercising. He had a weekly tennis game with a friend and also started running once a week. He then added a weekly workout at the gym. The exercise not only helped him sleep better but also relieved much of his anxiety.

Within 4 weeks of starting his new food life, John had more stamina, experienced less stress and wasn't constantly eating. By the end of 8 weeks, he had lost 7.5 kg (17 lb), his blood pressure was almost back to normal, his indigestion was gone and he had energy to spare.

how good you feel when you eat wholesome foods. Use that feeling to motor your body past those cheese puffs.

Meals at a Friend's or Family Member's House

Good times, good friends, good food – they all seem to go together. When the gang's all here, there can be enormous pressure to fit in and eat what everyone else is eating. Here are some strategies to help you stay in control.

▶ Whatever the menu is, be prepared and plan your food intentions. For example, tell yourself, 'I'm going to have only cut-up veggies with a little dip and a glass of wine before dinner. At dinner, I will eat very small portions of the healthiest items being served. I'll stop eating when I'm comfortably full.'

▶ Don't let anyone bully you into eating something you don't want. If someone puts food on your plate that you didn't want, leave it. If they get annoyed, tell them you're trying to stick to an eating plan and that you'd love it if they could support and respect that.

▶ Compliments go a long way – begin them early and continue often. Talk about how great the food smells, rave about the first few bites and slow down when you've had enough. If someone comments on what's left on your plate, simply say, 'I wish I could eat more!' Let them assume you mean you're absolutely stuffed.

Christmas Celebrations

The Christmas season need not result in an all-or-nothing feeding frenzy. A little mental preparation will keep you on course.

▶ Remember that no food is taboo. You can eat any food you want as long as you keep yourself accountable by writing in your food journal what, when and why you ate it, and as long as the portion sizes remain in keeping with your Real Food Life eating plan.

▶ Create a plan of action before you go to celebration meals. If celebration meals whip you up into a food frenzy, before you get there write down your food intentions and the strategies you will use to combat the eating situations.

▶ Overhaul your favourite recipes to make them fit into your food life. Many old favourite recipes can easily be 'retooled' to fit into your new style of eating. If you can't redo it yourself, look at the December issues of the women's or food magazines – the story of cutting fat from Christmas favourites turns up every year.

▶ The best defence is a good offence – prepare your counterstrike by taking food with you to homes or parties you know will not offer any options that fit in with your plan. You can try the other dishes, but eat your own food in abundance and without compromise.

Natural Fixes for Diarrhoea

Diarrhoea has been the topic of more than its share of jokes, but when you have a bad case of it, it's no laughing matter. Check out the following strategies for all-natural relief.

- Brown rice is binding, so it reforms stools and can calm the stomach. It can also help replenish your stores of B vitamins, which can get lost through diarrhoea. Eat small portions throughout the day.
- Take an acidophilus supplement to help rebuild good bacteria in your intestines.
- Diarrhoea is dehydrating, so be sure to drink at least 10 glasses of water and a few cups of green tea throughout the day.
- Chicken soup will rehydrate your body and calm your stomach.
- Ginger tea is excellent for relieving cramps and abdominal pains. Drink this soothing beverage all day long.
- Bananas will help as well.
- Avoid dairy foods for a few days because they can aggravate loose stools.

Travelling for Business

You don't have to remain a prisoner of the mini-bar or restaurant pudding trolley. Prepare for your Real Food Life the way you'd prepare for your trip – plan ahead and pack well.

▶ Before you go, buy some wholesome foods you can take with you on the plane, train, car or bus. Portable snacks such as crackers, nuts and seeds, a sandwich and dried or fresh fruit can fit into everyone's food life.

▶ Pack a meal as if you're taking lunch to work. Any food you take along will be much better than the food available on the train or plane. Or ring ahead to ask for a vegetarian or heart-healthy meal, if available.

▶ Avoid the mini-bar in your hotel room because it's there to tempt you (and make you spend too much on small indulgences). If you can't resist, give the key back to the main desk. Or ring ahead or ask the receptionist to get the mini-bar emptied out for you. Then fill up the empty space with healthy snacks such as yogurt, low-fat cheese, mineral water and fruit.

▶ If the buffet is too tempting, stick to room service – especially at breakfast.

▶ Make fish your automatic selection when you eat out. Not only is it filling and nutritious but, if you're eating out a lot, you'll get to try a number of different types and preparation methods. Order vegetables along with your meal, which will also keep you satisfied.

Holidays

Holidays are all about fun. But how much fun will it be to arrive back with a spare tyre or rebound sugar cravings? Your Real Food Life should be flexible enough to let you enjoy just about any location. Enjoy yourself, but always be on the lookout for healthy choices.

▶ Foods you have successfully eliminated in your Real Food Life may feature large on holiday. Eating a small amount of these foods is fine, but be warned: your body may not be used to them and they may actually make you feel sick. People who have cut back on rich foods or red meats can get stomach aches or diarrhoea when they eat a lot of them again.

▶ Don't go mad with alcohol – it dehydrates you, fills you with empty calories and weakens your resolve. If you've cut down your drinking recently, the effects will be swift and overwhelming. At the very least, make sure you drink one 225-ml (8-fl oz) glass of water for every alcoholic drink you have – and exercise the following day to sweat it out.

▶ Shun ideas such as 'Come on, you're on holiday, eat what you want!' Remember, you will eat all your Real Food Life choices – you just don't have to eat unhealthy foods.

A Word on Unexpected Friend or Family Hostility

As you progress with your new food life and start to feel and look great, some people – even people who love you – may become jealous or threatened. They'll show it in unexpected ways, like encouraging you to eat foods you don't include in your Real Food Life. Perhaps they will become critical of your appearance and try to sabotage your efforts at getting a Real Food Life.

Over the years, I've regularly heard variations on 'My wife thinks I look too thin', 'My mother doesn't understand why I need to eat before dinner', or 'My boyfriend always asks me if I should be eating from my food plan'.

Remember, first and foremost, this is not your issue – it's theirs. Maybe they also want to eat better and are jealous that you have been successful; maybe they think once you become healthier, you won't need them any more. These are not rational feelings, but they are honest feelings. Lost in the confusion of these feelings, they may not even be aware that their actions are undermining your efforts.

Keeping these thoughts in mind, try not to lash out at them. Realise they are just dealing with their own 'stuff', and it's not your job to help them feel better – they have to do it for themselves.

Share with them your food intentions and explain to them that their behaviour isn't helping you achieve your goals. It's your responsibility to yourself to speak up and tell them what your needs are. After advising many clients, I've discovered most friends and family members aren't conscious of their sabotage. After talking it through, sabotage turns into support.

Friends and family members may get upset or frustrated with you, but this is a time when you need to assert what you want. You are taking care of yourself, your health and your food life – those who love you will eventually come round. They may even join you.

Get Real Check-in

Assess your progress by checking off each of the following items you achieved during week 6.

❏ Instant Makeover 6: Each day, I replaced a cup of coffee or a fizzy drink with a cup of green tea.

❏ I achieved my week 6 mini-goals.

❏ I set my week 7 mini-goals.

❏ I compared my food journal from weeks 1, 3 and 5.

❏ I reviewed my original goals and realised what I've accomplished. I rewrote my goals as necessary.

❏ I devised a plan for eating more.

❏ I examined some food issues.

❏ I kept my food journal each day.

❏ I exercised for at least 10 minutes on 3 separate days.

❏ I rewarded myself for my intentions and my efforts.

Weekly Words: Write a couple of paragraphs in your journal about what it felt like to look at some key friend and family food issues. Were there any situations that really popped up? Discuss how being honest and assertive with your close friends and family will help you achieve your ultimate goal.

CHAPTER 13

Week Seven:

DINING OUT IN YOUR REAL FOOD LIFE

When we first see each other, many of my clients confess an over-dependence, even an addiction, to restaurant food. And, really, who doesn't love to eat out? You sit down and people literally serve you. No wonder everyone who's stressed on a regular basis – from mums at home to busy executives – loves the indulgence of dining out.

Yet, once you've spent a couple of weeks on the Real Food Life plan, you may be justifiably wary about straying back into restaurants again. 'They're full of fat!' I hear you saying. 'Think of the portions!'

Of course you should think of all that. But your Real Food Life is just that – a life. You still have to get out there and live it.

That's why we're focusing this week on

During this week, you will:

- ▶ Accomplish Instant Makeover 7: replace your afternoon coffee or sweet treat with a walk and a healthy snack
- ▶ Follow your week 7 mini-goals
- ▶ Keep week 7 of your food journal
- ▶ Devise a dining-out strategy
- ▶ Read guidelines for ordering at restaurants
- ▶ Devise your own junk food strategy
- ▶ Add a food you've been afraid of to your eating plan
- ▶ Exercise for at least 15 minutes on 3 separate days
- ▶ Complete week 7 of your Get Real Check-in

Instant Makeover 7:

Replace Your Afternoon Coffee or Sweet Treat with a 10-Minute Walk and a Healthy Snack

Why exactly are you eating that midafternoon chunk of cake or piece of chocolate? Perhaps it gives you a nice treat to sweeten a dragging afternoon and maybe it gives you a bit of energy to see you through until dinnertime. But it's not contributing to a Real Food Life.

Instead, take yourself in a different direction by heading out of the door for a 10-minute walk. The exercise will firm your legs and backside and strengthen your heart and lungs.

Breathing some fresh air and getting blood pumping through your body during your jaunt down the street or around the park is almost guaranteed to perk you up more than that sugary snack would have done.

When you return from your walk, have a healthy snack such as half a cantaloupe, half a small honeydew melon or a low-fat bran muffin with some almond butter. The combination of a 10-minute walk and a nutritious snack will help you sail through the rest of the afternoon.

how to handle the curves and steep cliffs of even the trickiest menus and the most tempting junk food. It's all a question of balance and choices. Every menu has at least one thing that fits in with your plan. Below you'll discover the treasure map to finding it.

1. Dine Out Using Real Food Life Strategies

By week 7, I'm sure you've already gone into restaurants. Maybe you scoured the menu, trying to find something that would fit into your plan. Maybe you thought you'd nailed it and then your skinless breast of chicken appeared in a bath of butter.

Never fear – you have many weapons in your arsenal. Your power as a restaurant patron lies in your order. Take time to do it well. Try a few of these tricks for getting exactly the foods you want in restaurants.

Prepare Your Plan of Attack

It's amazing how much trouble you can get into even before your meal hits the table. Take a proactive stance against the unhealthy food assault catapulting in from all sides.

Spoil your appetite. Before you leave for dinner, eat something substantial like a bowl of soup, a piece of leftover chicken, a piece of toast with low-fat cheese and leftover vegetables, or a yogurt with fruit and nuts. If you're following your Real Food Life at home, no matter what you eat, it will never be equivalent in calories and fat to an indulgent restaurant starter.

Know where you're going. Become familiar with the dining guidelines for different kinds of restaurants (see page 230) and try to know what you're going to eat before you even walk in the door. Don't let the menu sway you. If you've been to the restaurant before and you can resist the temptation, don't even open the menu. Order what you'd like and let the waiter sort it out. It's your meal – have it your way.

Avoid the bread basket. The bread basket is one of the leading culprits of overeating at restaurants. I almost always send it back, because out of sight is out of mind. If that sounds horrible to you, take one slice of bread and enjoy it with your meal. Just keep in mind that bread can add on an additional 500 calories, not even including the butter or olive oil that usually accompanies it.

Limit yourself to one alcoholic drink. Alcohol, whether in the form of cocktails, wine or beer, can weaken your resolve for exercising thoughtful moderation with your food. Plus, it dehydrates you and doesn't give

you any nutritional benefit. So, when you go out, try to limit yourself to just one drink – or order a bottle of fancy water instead.

Drink water. Bet you've never heard this from me before. (Ha!) I know I'm sounding like a broken record, but drink water before, during and after every meal, regardless if it's at a restaurant, at home or anywhere else.

Place Your Order with Confidence

Many of my clients start out by being intimidated by waiters. They worry that they're holding the waiter up with their questions and requests. Don't be shy about questioning the waiter. And don't worry about wasting his time – it's his job.

Be constantly aware of portion sizes. Trust me: you won't need a starter *and* a main course in many restaurants today. Some restaurants have been known to serve up to seven times the normal serving size for a meal.

Aim to leave food on your plate – or get the waiter to wrap up half of the portion before your serving even comes to the table. Starters are generally more realistic portion sizes. Look for your favourite and order it as a meal with a side salad or order two starters – one that is more vegetable-based.

Ask, ask, ask. And continue asking. Is it fried? What kind of sauce comes with it? What side dishes are served with each order? Can I have brown rice instead of white?

Always request sauces and dressings on the side. When you do this, you'll realise how little sauce and dressing you really need on your food.

Don't order something new when you're very hungry. If you do, you'll probably order too much food, you'll probably overeat and you'll regret it later. If you're starving order a standby that you know is good for you (see the list below).

Order plenty of vegetables. Get a large mixed salad or order vegetables sautéed in a little bit of olive oil or steamed with sauce on the side (so you can lightly dip them in the sauce).

Sip some soup. Soup is a good high-volume food that will fill you up. Look for vegetable, broth-based and bean soups. Avoid cream-based soups and chowders.

Finish with a Flourish

Don't put down your guard after the waiter scurries off to the kitchen with your order. You'll still need to exercise some caution when your perfectly ordered meal arrives in front of you.

Stay alert. It's easy to get caught up in an engaging conversation and eat everything on your plate without even thinking about it. So stay alert. After you've eaten your allotted amount, get the waiter to wrap up your leftovers. The bonus is that you have lunch (or dinner) for the next day already prepared.

Finish your meals with refreshing green or herbal teas. Ginger tea can help with digestion and green tea is good for your overall health. Many restaurants are now serving a variety of exotic teas, so help yourself to some! Some teas are so fruity that they're a perfect replacement for dessert.

2. Know What You're Up Against: The Restaurant Guidelines

Here are some tried-and-tested tips for ordering at specific types of restaurants. These suggestions will help you keep your food life right on track. One type of restaurant we haven't included is a French restaurant. Despite their popularity, most French restaurant food is not conducive to a Real Food Life. What makes most French restaurant food so delicious is the liberal use of fat in cooking. That being said, consider French restaurant meals as a well-earned splurge and indulgence.

British/American

Starter Recommendations
▶ Steamed asparagus or artichoke
▶ Mixed salad (with vinegar or lemon juice and olive oil dressing on the side)
▶ Vegetable-based soups
▶ Grilled vegetables (light on oil or without it)

Top Foods to Keep in Your Desk or Locker

When you get an attack of the midday munchies, feast on one of the foods listed below. It will keep you humming along through the afternoon.

• Nuts and seeds – particularly soya nuts
• Dried fruit
• Any fresh fruit
• Wholewheat crackers or rice cakes and all-natural peanut butter
• Pop-top tinned tuna packed in water
• Ginger tea and green tea
• A small bag of low-fat, oven-baked crisps
• Carrots

▶ Steamed mussels in a light broth
▶ Melon
▶ Fruit salad

Main Course Recommendations

▶ Grilled fish or chicken with a small sweet potato or rice
▶ Grilled chicken breast with a large salad (sauce and dressing on the side)
▶ Grilled or roasted chicken or turkey breast sandwich
▶ Grilled prawns with rice
▶ Roast chicken
▶ Roast beef
▶ Barbecued chicken breast with a baked potato (try eating half the portion)

▶ Steamed vegetables and rice dressed with lemon juice or vinegar and olive oil
▶ Grilled tuna or swordfish steak with a small portion of rice and lightly steamed vegetables
▶ Grilled whole fish with herbs (no oil or butter)
▶ Grilled fillet steak with grilled vegetables
▶ Vegetarian chilli with a small bowl of brown rice
▶ Large salad (with beans, sprinkle of cheese and 1 hard-boiled egg, and dressed with lemon or vinegar and olive oil)

Chinese

▶ Try to get your own small bowl of steamed brown rice.

- Eat small amounts of food with the rice.
- Ask for no MSG in your food.
- Use only low-sodium soy sauce.
- Drink water before, during and after the meal.

Starter Recommendations

- Steamed prawn, chicken or vegetable dumplings
- Steamed spring roll with rice paper
- Grilled vegetable sticks (satay or skewers)
- Grilled chicken sticks (chicken satay or chicken skewers)
- Small bowl of hot and sour or wonton soup (if you're sensitive to salt, you might want to avoid this)

Main Course Recommendations

- Grilled prawns
- Steamed fish in ginger sauce (try to have very little sauce)
- Peking-style chicken (remove excess fat and skin)
- Steamed prawns or chicken with vegetables (sauce on the side)
- Dry-sautéed string beans (take from the beans at the top of the pile when served to avoid all the sauce)
- Steamed Chinese broccoli with oyster sauce on the side
- Steamed scallops with sauce on the side
- Steamed mixed vegetables and tofu with sauce on the side

- Stir-fried pak choi, spinach, broccoli or other green leaf with garlic

Indian

- Avoid curries at all costs – they're made with coconut milk and butter (ghee) and are loaded with saturated fat.
- Do not order samosas, puri or paratha. These are loaded with oil.

Starter and Main Course Recommendations

- Small portion of raita (yogurt and cucumber)
- Mixed salad
- Chicken and vegetable kebab
- Pilau rice (small portion)
- Dal (lentils)
- Tandoori chicken, fish or vegetables
- Chicken or fish tikka
- Naan bread (a small portion)

Italian

- When you sit down, don't eat bread; in fact, get the waiter to remove it from the table.
- Drink water before and during the meal.
- Order a starter-portion for your main course.

Starter Recommendations

- Mussels in a light tomato broth
- Mixed salad (with balsamic vinegar or lemon juice and olive oil on the side)

▶ Grilled mixed vegetables (light on oil)

▶ Seafood salad (light on oil)

▶ A small portion of pasta with tomato sauce (eat only half a main course portion)

▶ Caponata (have only a small amount if it is very oily)

▶ Grilled portobello mushrooms

▶ Steamed artichoke or asparagus with dressing on the side

▶ Minestrone soup

▶ Pasta e fagioli (pasta and bean soup)

Main Course Recommendations

▶ Pasta with prawns or chicken in tomato sauce

▶ Pasta with clams in tomato sauce

▶ Pasta with mushrooms, peas and beans in tomato sauce

▶ Grilled salmon or red snapper (no oil)

▶ Grilled chicken breast with salad or cooked vegetables (no oil)

▶ Gnocchi in a light tomato sauce

▶ Half a vegetable pizza with a very small amount of cheese

▶ Prawn marinara

Japanese

▶ Ask for low-sodium soy sauce.

▶ If the restaurant offers brown rice order that instead of the white rice.

▶ Fresh lemon juice or rice wine vinegar are tasty, low-sodium alternatives to soy sauce for dressing sushi, sashimi or salad.

▶ The avocado in sushi rolls is a great way to get some good fat.

Starter Recommendations

▶ Steamed vegetable, chicken or prawn dumplings

▶ Japanese salad with seaweed (dressing on the side)

▶ Yakitori (grilled chicken skewers)

▶ Edamame (cooked fresh soyabeans)

▶ Oshitashi (cold boiled spinach salad)

▶ Tofu with soy dressing

Main Course Recommendations

▶ Soba noodles (made from buckwheat) with sauce on the side

▶ Sushi and sashimi (all kinds)

▶ Grilled fish or chicken (no soy sauce)

▶ Steamed vegetables with chicken or seafood

▶ Beef negimaki (grilled beef slices stuffed with green onion)

Mexican

▶ Avoid sour cream and cheese.

▶ Don't have nachos, chimichangas and taco salads since all of these are loaded with saturated fats.

▶ Eating some guacamole is fine – but limit your chips to dip to about 10.

▶ Avoid dishes made with minced beef or pork.

▶ Avoid refried beans unless they're low-fat (they are often made with beef or pork fat).

Banish a Bad Mood

When you're in a foul mood, do yourself – and those around you – a favour by following the tips below.

• Start exercising! Working out releases endorphins, brain chemicals that help lift moods.

• Carbohydrates release serotonin, a mood-enhancing brain chemical. So try some brown rice, quinoa, fruit or vegetables.

• If you're on a high-protein diet, get off it now. The lack of carbs – as well as the general lack of variety in food choices these diets entail – will throw off your energy level and put you in a bad mood.

• Make sure you're getting enough calories. Eating fewer than 1,500 calories a day will decrease your energy level and put you in a bad mood.

• Essential fatty acids – especially omega-3s – protect the nervous system and may lift your mood. To take advantage of these beneficial fats, top your next salad with a handful of nuts or seeds and some extra-virgin olive oil.

• Caffeine can make you irritable and moody if you drink too much, so cut back on caffeinated beverages or cut them out of your diet completely. Reduce your intake gradually, though, to avoid headaches and fatigue, two common withdrawal symptoms.

• Cut back on sugary foods. They can jumble up blood sugar levels and create mood swings.

• The B vitamins play a role in your moods. Take a B-complex vitamin or eat foods containing the Bs, such as bananas, avocados, fish, beans, eggs and dark green, leafy vegetables.

▶ Many Mexican restaurants use beef or pork fat even in vegetarian dishes, so be sure to ask and order accordingly.

Starter and Main Course Recommendations

▶ Soft taco stuffed with grilled chicken, with salsa, lettuce and tomato (with a sprinkle of cheese but no sour cream)

▶ Soft taco with bean or vegetable filling (make sure the filling is low-fat)

▶ Vegetable or chicken burrito with rice and beans (with a sprinkle of cheese but no sour cream)

▶ Vegetarian chilli (lard-free)

▶ Chicken or beef fajita (with only a little fried onions and peppers)

▶ Chicken or vegetable quesadilla (with a sprinkle of cheese)

▶ Grilled chicken with lemon and rice

▶ Grilled chicken salad with dressing on the side

▶ Grilled prawns with rice

▶ Sliced roast pork (a small portion with sauce on the side and the fat cut off) with rice and beans

Middle Eastern

▶ Avoid falafel or limit yourself to only one fritter (they're delicious, but they're deep-fried).

▶ Order wholemeal pitta bread (if available).

▶ Limit pitta bread to one.

Starter and Main Course Recommendations

▶ Bean salads

▶ Stuffed grape leaves (avoid if they're extremely oily)

▶ Stuffed tomatoes

▶ Tabbouleh (bulgar wheat and herb salad)

▶ Hummus (chickpea dip)

▶ Baba ghanoush (aubergine dip)

▶ Mixed vegetable salad (with lemon and a sprinkle of olive oil)

▶ Grilled chicken or fish and rice

▶ Fish, chicken, lamb or vegetable kebabs

▶ Couscous (small portion)

3. Devise a 'Junk Food' Strategy

It lurks. In vending machines, at petrol stations, at supermarket checkouts, at almost every cafe and even on your work colleague's desk – everywhere, surrounding us at all hours of the day, is junk food.

Of course, junk food may be in the eye of the beholder. What I consider to be junk food may not be what you consider to be junk food. Since I'm the nutritionist, I'll define it my way – by reading the label. Simply put, if you feel you'd need a chemistry degree to identify more than five of the ingredients that are listed on the label, the item is probably junk food.

Choosing 'Good Junk'

We can't ignore processed foods – we do live in the real world, after all. In fact, I actually like some of them. They're convenient and often taste really good. Throughout this book, I recommend certain processed foods. But the ones I approve of are generally less harmful to your health than others.

In general, stay as close to nature as possible. Many packaged foods are very processed, so be careful and read the labels; see what's in them and then decide if you want to eat them. Can they boast any fibre or soya?

People often turn to junk foods because they crave a flavour or a texture and they think nothing else will satisfy. Instead of the usual junk, try one of these more healthy options.

▶ If you crave sweet and creamy, try a low-fat yogurt or a serving of sorbet.

▶ If you crave sweet and chewy, try some dried fruit – it's nature's sweets.

▶ If you crave crunchy, try baby carrots or celery.

▶ If you crave salty and crunchy, try all-natural pretzels, pistachios or lightly salted roasted pumpkin seeds.

▶ If you crave burgers or hot dogs, try vegetarian soya alternatives. Many people don't notice a big difference in taste.

Where you can, try to find healthy alternatives to what you crave. If you miss the crisps on the side, try thinly slicing pears or apples for that crispy crunch that goes well with a sandwich. All foods do fit into a Real Food Life, so if you have a craving, just be sensible. If it's a food you wouldn't typically regard as healthy, go easy on it – you'll feel better later.

4. Add a Food You've Been Afraid Of

I see it all the time with my clients – people are very 'afraid' of certain food groups and go out of their way to avoid eating from that group. A huge part of having a Real Food Life

is feeling confident to eat from any food group (unless, of course, you are a vegetarian and don't eat meat or if you're allergic to a food group).

Carbohydrates for Protein Lovers

Attention, protein lovers: carbs aren't evil. Carbohydrates are the body's major source of energy and the only source of fuel for the brain and muscles. Foods with carbs can also be great sources of fibre, which is necessary for optimal functioning of the digestive system.

To get more carbohydrates in your diet, start adding 1 slice of wholemeal bread, 2 wholewheat crackers or a bowl of wholegrain cereal to your meal plan each day for a week. Gradually add an additional serving of complex carbohydrates each day for a week until you feel comfortable both physically and emotionally. When you find the amount that feels good to you, stick with it. Everyone, even the protein lover, needs a bare minimum of 2 servings of complex carbohydrates every day.

Proteins for Carbohydrate Lovers

Carb crunchers often forget that protein is the basic building material for the brain, heart, muscles, blood, skin, hair and nails and is essential for growth and development.

Start with a few small servings of protein each day. For example, have beans plus a small piece of chicken or lean beef each day for a week. Or have an egg and a slice or two of low-fat cheese every day for several days (try to limit the eggs to no more than seven each week or four if you have diabetes or high cholesterol or are overweight).

Even carb lovers should have a minimum of 110 grams (4 oz) of protein-rich food each day. Eating this amount of protein will mean that you'll be less sore after exercise and you'll feel satisfied longer after a meal. Adding a small handful of nuts and/or seeds each day will also help you get some protein with the added bonus of essential fatty acids.

Big Meals for Grazers

Grazers are often pleasantly surprised to find that when their bodies are well nourished, they can process and digest larger meals without any problems. Don't be afraid to try eating a large meal once in a while. You may even discover that a larger meal actually suits you when you are so busy you don't have the time or access for your regular mini-meals.

Quality Protein from Plant Sources

I often see that vegetarians get a majority of their daily calories from fruit, vegetables and grains, unconsciously avoiding protein. Because grains are quick, easily available and contain some protein, vegetarians often rely on them, not realising that they might not be getting as much high-quality protein as they need.

Try to have a daily 110-gram (4-oz) serving of tofu – flavoured, plain, cooked or not. This satisfying, quality vegetable protein source is nutritionally equivalent to meat – without the saturated fat. Another way to get quality plant-based protein is to have a meal of whole grains and legumes, such as low-fat beans with brown rice (see recipe on page 286). You should also try a protein- and calcium-filled low-fat regular or soya yogurt as part of a meal or a snack a few times a week.

Don't Fear Fat

Fat has got a bad reputation. Fat helps stave off hunger, makes food more appetising and – oh, yes – allows the body to function.

While saturated animal fats such as those found in full-fat dairy products and fatty cuts of meat, trans fats and hydrogenated fats can all promote chronic health problems, most vegetable fats actually promote good health. Eat a little daily fat, even if you're watching your weight. Just make sure it's the right fat.

You'll find that it's easy to incorporate health-boosting omega-3s into your diet each day with the following tips.

▶ Try some all-natural nut butters such as walnut, almond or peanut butter.

▶ Eat fish three or four times a week.

▶ If you prefer, get your omega-3s from tinned fish such as sardines, salmon or tuna.

(continued on page 240)

LIVING A REAL FOOD LIFE

Melissa Overcame Her Fear of Protein – and Gained Energy in the Process

Name: Melissa
Real Food Life Issue: Fear of protein

Melissa is in her mid-twenties and works long hours at her job in the fashion design industry. In her field, there is a high priority on being thin and good-looking and she is determined to maintain this standard for herself. Her diet was very poor, however, and as a result, her hair was thinning and falling out, her skin was very dry and she lacked muscle tone even though she worked out several times a week. She felt tired and hungry all the time. Here's where I found her:

18 April

This afternoon, I was in a cubicle in the ladies loos when I heard my boss come in with the shoot director to check their hair before going into a big meeting. My boss started criticising the new receptionist, calling her 'big bum' and cackling about how she'd probably applied her makeup with a trowel. Please God, don't let her be saying the same things about me! I have been so good, following this vegetarian diet I found on the Internet, but I'm getting so frustrated! All I want to do is lose a measly 5 pounds and then I have to look at that plastic-y Carlotta – who you just KNOW had liposuction – while everyone tells her how good she looks! I can barely get through the day as it is – how can I eat even less food? But then I think about my boss and 'big bum' and I'm scared to put a single thing in my mouth . . .

Melissa confessed that she didn't have time to cook for herself. She was also afraid to eat many different types of food because she thought everything, especially fish, chicken and meat, would make her put on weight. I immediately identified two things Melissa would need to do to get a Real Food Life: she had to start eating better foods for her overall health and she needed to realise that high-quality protein wouldn't make her gain weight.

After Melissa kept a food journal for a week, it was easy to see that she ate very little protein and virtually no fat or oil, which is a key source of essential fatty acids. Most of her calories came from carbohydrates such as fruit and vegetables, which she thought would keep her thin since they contained hardly any fat. She was scared that protein and fats would cause her to put on weight and make her 'out of control' with food.

After reviewing her journal, I helped Melissa understand the importance of eating from all food groups. Usually my clients need a push in the fruit and vegetables department, but Melissa was just the opposite. She needed to incorporate a variety of foods into her diet and while vegetables and fruit were certainly a part of that, they wouldn't be able to supply her body with all the essential nutrients it needs. Because many of her meals were eaten out, we focused on foods she could enjoy that were easy to find. Since she loved vegetables, we explored salad bars and I pointed out easy, complete meals that were also nutritious and would help her maintain her energy level and make her feel better. She also stocked up on wholesome snacks to keep at her desk so she could eat throughout the day without having to focus on three main meals.

We gradually added a little protein to her diet in the form of beans, soya foods and low-fat cheese, which she ate in small amounts throughout the day to keep her hunger in check. This also got her used to eating a greater variety of foods. We then added some nuts, seeds and a little olive oil to her daily food plan. Nuts and seeds took some time for her to get used to, so we started with just two walnuts a day and increased the amount until she felt comfortable eating a handful daily. By week 3, we added 75–110 g (3–4 oz) of tinned tuna or poached prawns to her daily eating plan. She had forgotten how much she loved both of these.

Within 4 weeks, Melissa noticed that she had much more energy, which helped her get more out of her workouts. She had more vigour during and after her long working day. Melissa also noticed that she had started craving more balanced meals. Soon she was adding tuna and grilled chicken to her salads. She also soon realised that her balanced diet didn't make her put on weight at all. In fact, by week 8, she became aware that she woke up with more energy than she had had in years and she saw her body finally becoming more toned. She loved the fact that meals now satisfied her for hours after eating. She also noticed that her hair was shinier and her skin was more supple and moist. Most important, she felt more confident about her food life – and better about herself.

▶ Try one of the easy fish recipes from this book each week.

▶ Soyabeans (edamame) or roasted soya nuts, wheat germ, walnuts, flaxseeds (freshly ground) or flaxseed oil, and pumpkin and sesame seeds all have omega-3s.

To incorporate monounsaturated fats into your diet, try the following foods.

▶ Olives and olive oil, almonds and peanuts (and almond and peanut butter) are rich in monounsaturated fat.

▶ Avocados can supply a part of your daily fat. Add some avocado to your salad or mash some on a slice of wholemeal toast with or without low-fat mayonnaise and sliced tomato.

Finally, experiment with different oils.

▶ Try using a few drops of toasted (dark) sesame oil in your cooking or salad dressing. It adds a sweet, typically Chinese taste (this oil is intense, so you don't need a lot).

▶ Dress salads with a little walnut oil.

▶ Use rapeseed or extra-virgin olive oil to lightly sauté vegetables such as baby carrots, broccoli, courgettes and cauliflower.

▶ Dress steamed vegetables with a little high-quality extra-virgin olive oil.

▶ Oils do become rancid after 6 months to a year, so unless you're feeding a lot of people, buy small bottles.

▶ To preserve their flavour, oils should be kept out of the light and away from heat.

Get Real Check-in

Assess your progress by checking off each of the following items you achieved during week 7.

❏ Instant Makeover 7: I replaced my after-noon coffee or sweet treat with an invigor-ating 10-minute walk and a healthy snack.
❏ I achieved my week 7 mini-goals.
❏ I set my week 8 mini-goals.
❏ I read the guidelines for ordering at restau-rants.
❏ I ate out using the Real Food Life strategies.

❏ I learned how to eat junk food.
❏ I added a food I was afraid of – and sur-vived!
❏ I kept my food journal each day.
❏ I exercised for at least 15 minutes on 3 separate days.
❏ I rewarded myself for my intentions and my efforts.

Weekly Words: Write a couple of paragraphs in your journal about what it's like to feel educated in restaurants. Does it limit your options? Does it make the whole experience less of a mystery? Discuss how learning these strategies will help you achieve your ultimate goal.

CHAPTER 14

Week Eight:

EMBRACING YOUR REAL FOOD LIFE

You like fish? I've certainly talked about its benefits enough. Perhaps you know the maxim: 'Give a man a fish and he'll eat for a day. Teach a man to fish and he'll eat for ever.'

Week 8 is all about making sure you have the fish on the hook.

For the first 7 weeks, we've laid the foundation for your Real Food Life: you've learned your carb/protein quotient, your meal style, your favourite eating times, the foods you crave and why. You've examined your Real Food Life from every angle – except the ones that haven't cropped up yet.

That's where week 8 comes in. Together, we'll look at some of the traps that ensnare new Food Lifers and I'll give you strategies to escape from them. We'll develop a Real Food

> **During this week, you will:**
>
> ▶ Accomplish Instant Makeover 8: replace two meat-based meals with bean-based meals
>
> ▶ Follow your week 8 mini-goals
>
> ▶ Keep week 8 of your food journal
>
> ▶ Discover your personal traps and outsmart them
>
> ▶ Exercise for at least 20 minutes on 3 separate days – more if possible!
>
> ▶ Give yourself your ultimate reward
>
> ▶ Establish a Real Life Ritual
>
> ▶ Create a food action plan for the future
>
> ▶ Do your last Get Real Check-in

Instant Makeover 8:

Replace Two Meat-based Meals with Bean-based Meals

If you barged into many homes around the world at meal times, you might be surprised to see that the food dishes in many cultures don't revolve around a pile of burgers or roast chicken or sausages. Instead, you'll see lots of beans, vegetables, grains and the like – with maybe just a bit of meat as a treat or a condiment, not the main course.

Bring good health – and some international flair – to your own table by replacing two meat-based meals with meals that use beans as their main dish. Think South American: a zesty, spicy chilli, full of kidney beans and chunks of tomato. Or Mediterranean: a bowl of hummus, topped with a bit of olive oil and dotted with ripe olives, which you can dip out with pieces of pitta bread. Your options are endless.

By doing this, you'll be cutting out sizable amounts of saturated fat, which is the bad, artery-clogging fat found in meats. You'll also be offering your body plenty of great bean-based fibre, which helps fill you up with fewer calories and keeps your digestive system working well.

Life ritual that will help to reconnect you to your goals and remind you why you set them in the first place. And finally, we'll create an action plan, so you can go forth and conquer what's left of your food demons, confidently and permanently.

But first, take a moment to really savour this accomplishment. You've devoted 2 months of your life to taking responsibility for everything you put into your body. You are probably enjoying the fruits of your labour with more energy, greater mental focus and better control over your emotions. Congratulations!

1. Discover Your Personal Traps and Outsmart Them

As you move ahead in your Real Food Life, you may be faced with new challenges. Since we're getting near to the end of your 8 weeks of coaching, I want to make sure you are well fortified to deal with some challenges you might face now or in the future.

Even though you're nearing the end of your first 8 weeks, your life in the coming months will certainly present some food challenges you haven't thought of yet. I see this with clients all the time – after several months of working with me, they may have difficulty with one or a couple of aspects of their food lives. That's perfectly normal. A Real Food Life isn't rigid; it's adjustable and constantly evolving.

In your journal, right now, write down this sentence: 'All challenges are manageable.' When you come up against a challenge in the future, revisit this rule. Make the challenge concrete by writing about it in your journal. Then focus on just one challenge every week or two.

Keep reminding yourself that it may take time to overcome challenges – you may not even conquer them for good, but you can contain them and find strategies to live with them. Try out some of these strategies for dealing with common food challenges.

Trap 1: You Don't Have Time for a Real Food Life

First of all, you do have time. I don't care how busy or important you are, you always have time to take care of your food life. What you need to do is to work out what's standing in your way and then deal with each issue one by one. Ask yourself these questions:

▶ Do you eat out too often and find you make bad food choices? Reread chapter 13 and think about if your problem occurs before, during or after ordering.

▶ Are there too many temptations in your

daily life? Use your food journal to help you decipher those temptations. Reread pages 35 to 41 for tips to combat emotional eating.

▶ Is it hard to find foods that fit your food life and that your family likes, too? If you feel like you're cooking twice, once for yourself and again for your family, you are probably overwhelmed by the time you're spending in the kitchen. Explain why you have made the changes you have and ask for your family's support, whether it be helping you with the cooking or simply being willing to try new things.

If you have time for a bad food life, you have time for a Real Food Life. It just takes time to form your new habits. Train yourself to acknowledge that every food decision is about taking care of your body and your emotions. Once you do, finding time for your food life will come automatically. Don't give up.

Trap 2: Eating Enough Fish Is Difficult

In the past decade or so, fish has really taken off. A booming 'fish farming' industry has made fresh fish available to local markets and the quality has vastly improved. Here are some great strategies for fitting more fish into your diet.

▶ Even if you don't cook fish at home order it whenever you go out for dinner.

▶ Tinned tuna is just about the easiest

(continued on page 246)

LIVING A REAL FOOD LIFE

David Lost Weight – And His High Cholesterol Plummeted – When He Changed His Way of Eating

Name: David

Real Food Life Issues: Carbohydrate addict, overweight, high cholesterol

David is in his mid-forties and has his own consulting business. He can set his own hours, so he can work out daily. Nevertheless, when we met, he was more than 13.5 kg (2 st) overweight and had suffered from back problems caused by the extra weight. David came to see me very reluctantly. The only reason we met was on the orders of his doctor, who told David that unless he lowered his cholesterol and triglyceride levels, he would need to go on medication. Here's where I found him:

> *19 March*
>
> *Beat Nathan at squash again today. He really needs to work on his serve. I tried to show him how to get a better spin on it, but he just brushed me off. I suppose that made him think he could lecture me about water. The way he gulps down litre after litre, you'd think we were stuck out in the desert somewhere. He said I was going to get ill if I didn't rehydrate. Poor guy - I didn't have the heart to tell him water was going to make him blow up like a balloon.*

When we met, David said this would be the only time he would see me. I convinced him to keep a food journal for a week and come back to me at least once more. When he sent over his journal, I saw that most of his meals were big portions of fat-free refined carbohydrates, such as cereals, baked goods and spaghetti. He wrote in his journal that he always felt hungry. He told me most of his meals were takeaways or ready-meals – even his breakfast of a bagel with jam and a banana, and his dinner of pasta and tomato sauce. His afternoon snacks were often half a box of cereal. Other than his daily banana, he ate no fruit and he ate hardly any vegetables or high-quality protein. He also consumed virtually no fats or oils. Most alarmingly, David drank no water at all because he believed water would bloat him and cause him to put on more weight. The only things he did drink were a cup of coffee in the morning and a diet fizzy drink in the evening.

When he came back to see me, I shared the analysis of his food journal. When I told him that by making changes in his diet, he could really improve his health, he shrugged. With a little more goading, I finally convinced him to change his food life for just 8 weeks. I told him he had nothing to lose, except some of the extra weight and the bad cholesterol levels. So, with that, he complied hesitantly.

First, I asked him to take a daily multivitamin and a B-complex supplement to help protect against high homocysteine levels. My next suggestion was to increase his water intake dramatically. Since he wasn't used to drinking water, we had to do this gradually. During the first week, he had just 1 glass a day; for the second week, he drank 2 glasses a day and so on. It wasn't until week 6 that he finally came to understand why water was important to his overall health and energy. At first he rang twice a week to make sure the water wouldn't cause him to gain weight; he now drinks at least 10 glasses a day and recognises that drinking a lot of water gives him more energy and makes his workouts more productive.

Next, I got him to show me all his takeaway menus. We went through each of them and I showed him how to order sensible dishes and how to eat realistic portions. I got him to cut back on refined carbohydrates and replace them where he could with whole grains. We also added protein to each meal. For example, instead of the bagel, jam and banana breakfast, I now got him to eat a hard-boiled egg, wholemeal toast and a fruit salad. Instead of dinners of pasta and tomato sauce, I got him to eat grilled chicken breast topped with rocket, tomatoes and lemon juice.

Instead of half a box of cereal for a snack, David began to eat wholegrain crackers with hummus or even a single bowl of cereal with fresh fruit cut into it. He also started eating a salad every day dressed with olive oil and lemon and he ordered grilled fish dinners. And always, David would try to leave about half of what was on his plate.

By week 8, David had lost 7 kg (just over a stone) and his back pains had subsided almost completely. Furthermore, when his cholesterol and triglyceride levels were checked a month later, they had come down enough for his doctor to hold off on the medication. David realised that his new food life made him much less hungry and his fears of protein and water were almost gone. He also realised that the changes in his diet he had been so loath to try really improved his health and sense of well-being. Now, 20 months later, David has happily stuck with his new way with food.

fish there is. Open a tin, drain it, chop up some green onions or celery, add a tablespoon of low-fat mayo and voilà! A fish lunch or dinner.

▶ If you really cannot abide seafood at all, be sure to eat other sources of omega-3 fatty acids and monounsaturated fats. Soyabeans, nuts and seeds and their oils all have some form of these necessary and 'good' fats.

Trap 3: Vegetables Are Too Much Work

Is breathing too much work? Vegetables are as essential for a Real Food Life as oxygen. They are crammed full of nutrients that you need for good living. You should strive for at least 5 servings daily. Here are some tips to help you work more vegetables into your Real Food Life.

▶ Use frozen vegetables! They're already cleaned, cut and ready to use. Steam, microwave or lightly sauté them in olive oil with a little garlic.

▶ Chop up a ripe tomato and cucumber, dress with 2 teaspoons of olive oil and balsamic vinegar and there you have it: a vegetable salad (which counts as at least one or two servings).

▶ Buy bags of prewashed, preprepared salad leaves. Open up the bag, pour in a tablespoon of olive oil, a healthy dash of lemon juice or vinegar and as many herbs

and spices as you want. Shake. You have an instant, perfectly coated salad. Toss in some sliced peppers and you'll have a few servings of vegetables!

▶ Buy prewashed and peeled baby carrots, cherry tomatoes and chopped cauliflower and broccoli from the salad bar. If time or expense are your stumbling blocks, work out a way to get over that – veggies are worth every second and all the money you spend on them.

Trap 4: There's No Time for Breakfast

You know you need to give your metabolism a kick start in the morning with breakfast. If you feel too taxed by your morning routine to eat, try these quick and easy ways to fit breakfast into your Real Food Life.

▶ Take a piece of fruit, a yogurt or a muffin with you to eat in your car or on the train.

▶ Toast a piece of wholemeal bread and top it with a slice of low-fat cheese. Toasting bread takes 3 minutes.

▶ Pour a serving of dry cereal into a bowl. Add skimmed milk. This is the definition of fast food.

▶ If you really can't stomach food in the morning, try drinking breakfast. Smoothies or soya shakes are the perfect way to get wholesome nutritious food without ingesting anything too heavy.

Top Foods to Eat before a Big Exam

Bone up on the following superfoods, which may help you to think more clearly and focus more intently for that big exam.

• Fish: grilled, sautéed, poached or tinned

• Brown rice

• Nuts and seeds

• Sweet potatoes

• A variety of mixed vegetables, either in a soup or salad

• Avocados

❚ Reheat and eat leftovers from last night's dinner. It may sound odd, but it's a quick and tasty way to get a morning meal.

Trap 5: You Still Feel Hungry All Day

If you still feel hungry by week 8, you need to find foods that will satisfy you. Consult your journal and see what types of foods you're eating and how long they sustain you before you're hungry again. Focus on the foods that keep hunger at bay for the longest amount of time and experiment with eating those types of foods. Also, try these tips.

❚ Make sure it's not dehydration that you're feeling. Always drink at least eight 225-ml (8-fl oz) glasses of water each day.

❚ Your diet may be too low in fat, so

check your intake. If you're hovering at the lower level, this may be making you hungrier faster. (Nut butter on an apple or wholemeal bread is a quick way to get some good fat.)

❚ You may not be getting enough protein. Protein lingers in your stomach longer than carbohydrates alone, so be sure to eat a little protein with your carbohydrates to keep yourself feeling fuller, longer.

❚ Add more high-water and high-fibre snacks to your eating plan. Try a bowl of soup, melon, berries, yogurt, tomatoes, cucumbers, asparagus, broccoli, carrots or high-fibre cereal with milk.

Trap 6: Regular Exercise Is Hard

Many people find exercise to be their Real Food Life Achilles' heel. If they work long hours or have many commitments, exercise will often take a back seat in their lives.

▶ If you feel too busy, make an appointment in your diary to exercise and don't break it. Then you'll stop trying to 'fit it in', because it will be there, in your diary.

▶ Set exercise as one of your mini-goals every week. Start by setting a goal of exercising just once a week. Then – here's the critical part – just do it. Put one foot in front of the other until you walk around the park. Next week do it twice. And so on.

▶ Take classes at the gym that will keep you interested in exercise. You might discover you really enjoy yoga, Pilates, spinning or weight-lifting classes. Make friends – just knowing people at the gym will help keep you exercising.

▶ Walking, running and many other solitary exercises are great for clearing your head. If your exercise time doubles as your private mind-clearing alone time, that's OK. We're all under pressure and free time must often serve double duty.

▶ Hobbies can be exercise, too. Gardening, cycling, running around the garden with your children, walking in the park, even walking around the shops is exercise. Just keep your body moving.

▶ An exercise partner – a spouse, pet or friend – can make time pass more quickly while you are exercising and will keep you motivated to stick with it.

2. Give Yourself Your Ultimate Reward

You have worked hard and have probably achieved your ultimate goal – maybe even several of them – by now. No matter how often you reach and surpass your goals, take the moment to give yourself the reward you promised yourself when the goal was set.

It's easy to brush it away and pretend it doesn't matter, but what you've done is nothing short of revolutionary. Seize this revolutionary spirit and forever burn it in your brain with the reinforcement of the reward you promised yourself at the outset.

Many of my clients are tempted to forego this part – don't! Get out there and buy yourself that new dress or CD player. You earned it, you deserve it.

3. Establish a Real (Food) Life Ritual

Many of my clients really become attached to their weekly check-ins. They like the idea of a quiet oasis of time in their otherwise hectic week, time to think just about themselves, their growth and their goals.

I'll encourage you as I encourage them – please continue. Pick a place in your house where you will try to sit every week at the same time to revisit your goals and set new ones for the coming week. If you feel that

Solve Your Energy Crisis

When you're so tired you feel like you need someone to pick you off the sofa, try one of these natural pick-me-ups instead. You'll be surprised by the extra energy you gain.

- If you're feeling lethargic, drink lots of water. It hydrates your cells, prevents dehydration and provides instant energy.

- Avoid sugary foods, including most so-called energy bars. After giving you an initial burst, sugar will stop energy dead in its tracks.

- Carbohydrates provide almost all of the energy for your muscles and brain – so eat a variety of fruit, vegetables and whole grains daily. When you need a pick-me-up, try eating a complex carbohydrate along with protein. Good choices include a sliced apple with a tablespoon of all-natural nut butter or a handful of nuts with a handful of raisins.

- Add foods that are rich in B vitamins to your diet. Good choices include oranges, yogurt, chicken, bananas, soyabeans and cheese.

- Graze. Eating smaller meals more often will provide a constant stream of energy. Your body will be able to use the food more efficiently, so you won't experience extreme highs and lows in your energy levels.

- Exercise. Physical activity helps blood to flow through your muscles and your brain and it releases endorphins (which make you feel good) and hormones that provide sustained energy.

- Eat enough. Eating too few calories will make you feel tired. At the very least, you need 1,500 calories each day.

- Get at least 8 hours of sleep a night. If you're feeling particularly tired during the day, take a 20-minute nap, if possible. (Napping longer than that can leave you feeling groggy and moody.)

- Turn the television off and read before you go to bed. Watching TV can promote active sleep, which can leave you feeling more tired in the morning.

you're getting to grips with your Real Food Life, use the time for yourself in another way.

Not so long ago, a Real Food Life was just one of your hopes and dreams – now it's your reality. Take these same skills and apply them to the rest of your life. By doing your check-in in the same place every week, you'll be physically reconnecting with the person who sat in that chair those many months ago. Use that person's strength to buoy you through the rest of life.

4. Create a Food Action Plan for the Future

All the pieces of your newly acquired food knowledge are really the tools of your Real Food Life. By learning what foods are necessary for the human body, finding out which work best for you, and identifying and avoiding food 'gimmicks', you have all the tools you'll need to continue your Real Food Life into the future.

Just as you learned to set mini-goals, deal assertively with people pushing food on you and manage temptation, you've also come to realise that a Real Food Life is about experimenting with food, knowing your body and using practical strategies to solve food challenges.

You've begun to recultivate your natural instinct with food, eating when you're hungry, feeding your body nourishing foods and avoiding foods that make you feel sluggish, tired and bloated. You are now empowered to be your own nutritionist, armed with the knowledge you need to make good food choices that need only to suit you – nobody else.

You now know that every individual has his or her own food needs and that a one-size-fits-all eating plan doesn't suit anyone. You now know how to take responsibility for your own food life because you have begun to discover what works for you and what doesn't.

To create a plan of action for your future food life, you must recognise that eating plans are dynamic and ongoing. Just as change is part of life, it is also part of your food life. Your own way of dealing with food will change and grow as you continue to listen to your body and learn about its needs. Permanent change takes time and is the result of many small changes.

Any of the tools here – the mini-goals, the ultimate goals, the Instant Makeovers, the checklists, the weekly check-ins – any of these can help you formulate your own action programme. Start at the beginning – where are you now? Where do you want to go?

I'm going to leave you with just a few remaining strategies. You already have everything you need to succeed in the future – consider these the icing on the cake.

Continue with the principle of starting small. Try new foods by sampling. Go to a wholesome salad bar and try small amounts of new foods, including new vegetables and fruit. Take note of what you like. Many supermarkets also have healthy prepared foods.

Don't be afraid of food. There are so many wonderful foods out there that can be part of your food life.

Try a new recipe every week. Review the recipes in this book for dishes that will fit anyone's Real Food Life. Or treat yourself to a new cookbook that is full of healthy recipes that fit in with your new style of eating.

Remember, this eating plan is for the long haul. You need to enjoy every bite you take.

Visit the local farmers' market. I love going to the farmers' market. Walking around admiring the bounty of fresh produce makes me happy and gives me inspiration for eating and cooking well.

Pick up this book often. Often a well-timed paragraph can answer just the challenge you've been encountering. Come back to any week if you need additional reinforcements or fresh ideas for your Real Food Life. And don't forget all the yummy recipes that are sure to keep your food life interesting.

Get Real Check-in

Assess your progress by checking off each of the following items you achieved during week 8.

❏ Instant Makeover 8: I replaced two meat-based meals with bean-based meals.

❏ I achieved my week 8 mini-goals.

❏ I kept my food journal each day.

❏ I exercised for at least 20 minutes on 3 separate days.

❏ I learned about the traps I've been setting for myself – and this time, I didn't bite!

❏ I gave myself my ultimate reward for my intentions, my efforts and my success!

❏ I established my Real Food Life ritual.

❏ I devised an action plan for the future of my Real Food Life.

Weekly Words: Write a couple of paragraphs about what it feels like to finish. Are you proud of yourself? (You should be!) Tentative about the future? Discuss the three most important changes you've made, how they make you feel and how they will keep you focused on what really defines your Real Food Life.

PART 4

THE REAL
FOOD LIFE
RECIPES

CHAPTER 15

THE REAL FOOD LIFE STARTER KIT

One of the most empowering steps you can take towards achieving a new food life is to begin cooking for yourself rather than relying on restaurants, takeaways and packaged foods. Consider the recipes that follow, then, to be your starter kit for achieving and maintaining your Real Food Life: they're nutritious, they're fast and they use *delicious*, healthy ingredients that will delight and satisfy you.

Cooking is one of the most empowering things you can do for yourself. It lets you connect with your food directly because it allows you to choose and prepare the foods you know will make your body happy. When you cook wholesome meals, you are nourishing yourself, both in body and soul. And when you cook for friends and family, you're giving them a gift of nourishment and love. Most of all, cooking should be fun! It's an activity you can share with your friends, family and children.

If you're a novice when it comes to cooking, take a deep breath and relax. Generally speaking, cooking is not an exact science. If you do ruin a meal, it's not the end of the world – it's an education. If you make a mistake and the outcome isn't what you expected, think of it this way: it's only one dish (or one meal) out of thousands you will eat in your life and you shouldn't accept it as a defeat. Just try again (or try another recipe). The likelihood, though, is that you won't make a mistake in the first place.

Like many home cooks, I learned to cook not by taking lessons, but by reading cookbooks, watching my mother cook and watching cooking shows. I've had my share of mistakes along the way. But I truly believe that the more you cook, the more intuitive you become with cooking. Once you gain a little confidence in the kitchen, cooking will come more naturally and you'll be able to look at a recipe and adapt it to your tastes.

I personally use all the recipes that follow, so you know that they're going to taste good! Furthermore, these recipes have been 'tested' in the homes of my clients and friends.

Before you begin, please read through the following pointers. They will make your time in the kitchen more pleasant and help you to work quickly and efficiently through any recipe.

▶ Before you start, read the recipe all the way through. I learned this lesson the hard way, but you don't have to. If you read the whole recipe, you know what steps you have to follow and approximately how long the recipe will take.

▶ Before you cook, get everything ready. In professional kitchens, this is called *mise en place*, which is just a French phrase meaning to be prepared. Do all the washing, rinsing, drying, chopping and measuring before you start, so you can cook efficiently. The pros do it, I do it and so should you.

▶ When you're shopping, always choose the healthiest, most abundant-looking fruit, vegetables and herbs. If an item doesn't look fresh, it's not. The freshest and best ingredients make the best final dishes.

▶ If the selections in the fresh produce aisle look tired and old, use frozen produce (making sure there are no added sugars, salts, syrups or artificial ingredients in the products you choose), substitute with related produce that looks better, go to another shop or do without. If you cook with old ingredients, your dishes won't taste their best.

▶ I love herbs and use them in practically everything. I particularly like fresh herbs – if you're used to only dried herbs, try some fresh varieties. They add a lively flavour and, well, *freshness* to everything they touch.

▶ When a recipe calls for herbs but you don't like the ones listed, feel free to substitute with herbs you do like.

▶ Whenever a recipe calls for fruit or vegetables, it is very important to wash them well under running water for at least a minute. Bacteria and dirt can cling to produce, but a thorough washing gets rid of them. There are a number of produce sprays on the market that really help clean fruit and vegetables well. They're definitely not a requirement, but they do save time and get your fruit and vegetables very clean. Look for them in your supermarket or health food shop.

▶ Before using raw chicken, red meat or fish, rinse them very well. This will help to get rid of bacteria, which could otherwise promote food poisoning. Dry the chicken, meat or fish with paper towels, which you then should throw away immediately.

▶ After handling raw fish or chicken, make sure you wash your work surfaces, knives and hands thoroughly. Raw chicken in particular has a lot of bacteria and you can cross-contaminate other foods if you use the same knife or cutting board without washing it in hot, soapy water first.

▶ I think it's fine to use tinned beans in recipes. However, try to buy low-sodium or sodium-free varieties. They may not be labelled as such, but if you read the label, you can determine the brand lowest in sodium. Regardless of sodium content, beans should always be rinsed well – under running water for 3 to 5 minutes, or soaked in a bowl of cold water for 5 minutes – and drained before using.

▶ Many of the following recipes call for liquid aminos. This is a chemical-free seasoning liquid protein concentrate made from soya beans. It is similar to soy sauce, but is lower in sodium, isn't fermented and doesn't taste nearly as salty. I use it because it really does give a nice flavour to food, adding a depth of flavour to dishes without extra salt. It's sold simply as 'Bragg Liquid Aminos', and it's available in health food shops. For more information, visit the company's Web site www.bragg.com.

▶ If you can't find liquid aminos or don't want to use them, you have the option of using salt instead. When I use salt, which is rare, I use kosher salt or sea salt.

▶ Many recipes call for extra-virgin olive oil. I love the flavour, but if you find it too assertive, choose the mildest olive oil available. Many cooks use regular olive oil to cook with and extra-virgin in dressings. I use extra-virgin for everything.

▶ Many recipes call for tinned tomatoes or passata (sieved tomatoes). I use these ingredients a lot because they are convenient and adds lots of body, flavour and moisture to dishes. Try to get brands without added sugars, salt or additives.

▶ Some recipes call for vegetable or chicken stock. For ready prepared stock, I'll buy almost any type that's labelled low-sodium. For dried bouillon, I prefer Vogue or Marigold brands (available at health food shops and some supermarkets) because they're lower in sodium than most other brands. If you can't find them, try to get the lowest-sodium variety available.

▶ Many recipes call for a food processor or blender. These are great time-saving devices. If a food processor isn't in your budget, alternatives are a mini-food processor or a hand-held blender. I love my hand-held blender – it makes extremely quick work of soups, shakes, smoothies, sauces and dressings.

▶ Recipes are meant to be adjusted to suit the cook and the eaters. Tweak each recipe to suit your tastes. Do you love onions? Add more. You don't like peppers? Don't use them or replace them with more of an ingredient you do like.

▶ Most of the recipes make 2, 4 or 8 servings. You can double the small recipes to serve more people or cut the bigger ones in half to serve fewer. But remember, leftovers make quick meals for the next day!

▶ Finally, don't switch between metric and imperial measurements within a recipe, otherwise the small differences in equivalent weights could affect the proportions of your ingredients.

Lemony Carrot Salad

6 large, thick carrots
Juice of 1 lemon
2 teaspoons white vinegar
1 tablespoon olive oil
2 teaspoons sugar
¼ teaspoon salt
Ground black pepper

Makes 4 servings

Per serving: *Energy* 90 cals/378 kJ; *Protein* 1 g; *Carbohydrate* 15 g (of which 14 g sugars); *Fat* 3 g (of which 0.5 g saturates); *Sodium* 178 mg.

1. Grate the carrots on the wide-holes side of a box grater.

2. In a medium bowl, combine the carrots, lemon juice, vinegar, oil, sugar, salt and pepper to taste. Toss well and serve.

Asian Sesame Slaw

1 medium head green or red cabbage
3 large carrots (or 4 medium)
2 tablespoons sesame seeds
110 ml (4 fl oz) rice wine vinegar
2 teaspoons toasted (dark) sesame oil
2 tablespoons honey
2 tablespoons reduced-sodium soy sauce

Makes 8 servings

Per serving: *Energy* 72 cals/302 kJ; *Protein* 2 g; *Carbohydrate* 11 g (of which 9 g sugars); *Fat* 3 g (of which 0.5 g saturates); *Sodium* 174 mg.

1. Shred the cabbage and carrots using a box grater or the grater attachment in a food processor.

2. Toast the sesame seeds in a small nonstick frying pan over medium heat, stirring often, about 3 minutes, or until the seeds start to turn brown and become fragrant.

3. In a large bowl, combine the cabbage, carrots, sesame seeds, vinegar, sesame oil, 1 tablespoon of the honey and 1 tablespoon of the soy sauce. Toss well.

4. Add the remaining 1 tablespoon each of honey and soy sauce to taste, if desired. Refrigerate for at least 1 hour or up to 1 day before serving to allow flavours to develop.

Herby Tomato Salad

Salad

6 ripe plum tomatoes
1 spring onion
1 small bunch fresh basil
1 small bunch fresh dill

Dressing

1 clove garlic
¼ teaspoon salt
Juice of ½ lemon
1½ tablespoons extra-virgin olive oil
1 tablespoon water
1 teaspoon Dijon mustard
2 teaspoons fresh basil or ½ teaspoon dried
2 teaspoons fresh oregano or ½ teaspoon
  dried
Ground black pepper

Makes 2 servings

Per serving: *Energy* 120 cals/504 kJ; *Protein* 2 g;
Carbohydrate 8 g (of which 8 g sugars); *Fat* 6 g (of which
1.5 g saturates); *Sodium* 120 mg.

1. *To make the salad:* Chop the tomatoes. Slice the onion into 0.5cm (¼ in) pieces. Cut the stems off the basil and dill and discard. Roughly chop the herb leaves. In a large bowl, combine the tomatoes, onion, basil and dill.

2. *To make the dressing:* Peel the garlic and chop finely. In a small bowl, stir the salt and lemon juice until the salt dissolves. Add the garlic, oil, water, mustard, basil, oregano and pepper to taste. Mix well. Pour 2 to 3 tablespoons of the prepared dressing on to the salad. Toss well and serve. Store leftover dressing in a covered glass jar in the refrigerator for up to 5 days.

Chunky Potato and Spring Onion Salad

3 medium red potatoes (450 g/1 lb)
2 spring onions
50 g (2 oz) low-fat mayonnaise
1 tablespoon fat-free natural yogurt
¼ teaspoon salt
Ground black pepper

Makes 4 servings

Per serving: *Energy* 134 cals/562 kJ; *Protein* 3 g;
Carbohydrate 20 g (of which 2 g sugars); *Fat* 5 g (of which
0.5 g saturates); *Sodium* 142 mg.

1. Cut the potatoes into small chunks. Place in a large saucepan and cover with water. Boil for 15 to 20 minutes, or until the potatoes can be easily pierced with a knife point or fork. Drain and set aside to cool.

2. Slice the onions thinly.

3. In a small bowl, combine the mayonnaise, yogurt, salt and pepper to taste. Whisk well.

4. In a large bowl, combine the cooled potatoes, onions and mayonnaise mixture. Toss well. Refrigerate until ready to serve or serve immediately.

This salad is easy to prepare and it boasts delicious homemade flavour. Best of all, the fat content is reduced by using low-fat mayonnaise and fat-free yogurt instead of the traditional full-fat mayonnaise.

Caesar Salad

Dressing

2 tablespoons extra-virgin olive oil
65 ml (2½ fl oz) white wine vinegar
3 tablespoons balsamic vinegar
2 tablespoons fat-free natural yogurt
1–2 small cloves garlic
2 teaspoons Dijon mustard
2 anchovy fillets (optional)
2 teaspoons Worcestershire sauce
½ teaspoon salt or liquid aminos
Ground black pepper
2 tablespoons grated Parmesan cheese

Salad

1 cos lettuce
175 g (6 oz) cherry tomatoes

Makes 4 servings

Per serving: *Energy* 124 cals/520 kJ; *Protein* 6 g;
Carbohydrate 5 g (of which 4.5 g sugars); *Fat* 9 g (of
which 2.5 g saturates); *Sodium* 677 mg.

1. *To make the dressing:* In a blender or food processor fitted with the chopping blade, combine the oil, white wine vinegar, balsamic vinegar, yogurt, garlic, mustard, anchovies (if using), Worcestershire sauce, salt or aminos and pepper to taste. Blend or process until smooth. Stir in the cheese.

2. *To make the salad:* Remove and discard the outer leaves of the lettuce. Wash and thoroughly dry the lettuce. Tear or cut the lettuce into bite-size pieces. In a large bowl, combine the lettuce and tomatoes. Top with the dressing. Toss well and serve.

Fresh Vegetables and Blue Cheese Dressing

Dressing

225 ml (8 fl oz) low-fat natural yogurt
110 g (4 oz) low-fat mayonnaise
50 ml (2 fl oz) white wine vinegar
2 cloves garlic
½ teaspoon ground white or black pepper
75 g (3 oz) crumbled blue cheese

Salad

6 large carrots or 50 baby carrots
6 sticks celery
225–450 g (½–1 lb) green beans
2 red or yellow peppers
150 g (5 oz) broccoli florets
300 g (10½ oz) cherry tomatoes

Makes 8 servings

Per serving: *Energy* 165 cals/693 kJ; *Protein* 6 g;
Carbohydrate 14 g (of which 13 g sugars); *Fat* 10 g (of
which 3 g saturates); *Sodium* 250 mg.

1. *To make the dressing:* In a blender or food processor fitted with the chopping blade, combine the yogurt, mayonnaise, vinegar, garlic, pepper and 50 g (2 oz) of the blue cheese. Blend or process for about 1 minute or until smooth. Pour into a medium bowl. Stir in the remaining 25 g (1 oz) blue cheese. Cover with clingfilm and refrigerate.

2. *To prepare the vegetables:* If using large carrots, peel and cut into 1 x 7 cm (½ x 3 in) pieces. Discard celery leaves and cut sticks into 1 x 7 cm (½ x 3 in) pieces. Cut off ends of green beans. Remove seeds from the pepper and cut into strips 0.5 cm (¼ in) thick.

3. Arrange the vegetables on a serving dish and serve with the dressing as a dip.

> *You can use any fresh or gently cooked vegetable you like. Asparagus spears, mange-tout, sugar snap peas and endive are great, too.*

Greek-Indian Cucumber Salad

2 medium cucumbers
2 cloves garlic
225 ml (8 fl oz) low-fat natural yogurt
50 g (2 oz) low-fat crème fraîche
1 teaspoon lemon juice
½ teaspoon salt
Pinch of dried red-pepper flakes
Ground black pepper

Makes 4 servings

Per serving: *Energy* 88 cals/370 kJ; *Protein* 6 g; *Carbohydrate* 10 g (of which 9 g sugars); *Fat* 2.5 g (of which 2 g saturates); *Sodium* 354 mg.

1. Peel the cucumbers. Halve them lengthwise and scoop out the seeds with a spoon. Cut the cucumber halves into thin slices and place in a medium bowl. Peel the garlic and chop finely.

2. In a medium bowl, combine the garlic, yogurt, crème fraîche, lemon juice, salt, red-pepper flakes and black pepper to taste. Mix well. Add the cucumbers and mix well.

3. Let sit for 15 minutes and serve or refrigerate for up to 8 hours and serve.

This salad is sort of a hybrid between the Indian raita (made with cucumbers and yogurt) and the Greek tzatziki (also made with cucumbers and yogurt). It's a great dish for a hot summer night.

Incredibly Tasty Mediterranean Roasted Peppers

2 tablespoons olive oil
4 red peppers
2 cloves garlic
16 cherry tomatoes
Ground black pepper
Large handful fresh basil leaves

Makes 4 servings

Per serving: *Energy* 112 cals/470 kJ; *Protein* 2 g; *Carbohydrate* 12 g (of which 11 g sugars); *Fat* 6 g (of which 1 g saturates); *Sodium* 12 mg.

1. Preheat the oven to 180°C/350°F/gas mark 4. Coat a large roasting pan with 1 to 2 teaspoons of the oil. Set aside.

2. Carefully halve the red peppers, keeping the stems intact. Cut out the seeds and ribs without piercing the pepper. Peel the garlic and chop finely.

3. Arrange the pepper halves, skin side down, in the pan.

4. Place two tomatoes in each pepper half, along with a little garlic, a sprinkle of the remaining oil and black pepper to taste.

5. Roast for 30 minutes. Remove from the oven. Add 3 or 4 torn basil leaves to each pepper half. Return to the oven and continue to roast for 15 to 30 minutes longer or until the edges are charred and the peppers are soft but remain intact. Remove from the oven and let cool. Serve at room temperature or cold.

Roasted Baba Ghanoush

1 large aubergine
1 clove garlic
2 tablespoons low-fat mayonnaise
1 tablespoon fat-free natural yogurt
½ teaspoon ground cumin
3 tablespoons lemon juice
½ teaspoon salt or 1 teaspoon liquid aminos
Ground black pepper
3 tablespoons chopped parsley

Makes 4 servings

Per serving: *Energy* 70 cals/294 kJ; *Protein* 2 g;
Carbohydrate 3 g (of which 2 g sugars); *Fat* 6 g (of which
1 g saturates); *Sodium* 370 mg.

1. Preheat the oven to 260°C/500°F/gas mark 9. Pierce the aubergine in several places with a fork or sharp knife. Place the aubergine on a baking sheet lined with foil. Roast for about 35 to 40 minutes, or until the skin starts to blacken and the flesh softens. Remove from the oven and let cool. When the aubergine is cool enough to handle, either scoop the flesh from the skin (it's fine if some skin is left on), or chop roughly and place in a medium bowl.

2. Peel the garlic and chop finely. Stir into the aubergine. Add the mayonnaise, yogurt, cumin, lemon juice, salt or aminos and pepper to taste. Stir to combine, making the mixture as smooth or chunky as you like. Sprinkle with the parsley.

This recipe requires you to roast the aubergine in a 260°C/500°F/gas mark 9 oven. Do not be alarmed. Yes, the oven is hot and you might smell a little burning, but you need this hot an oven to get the rich, smoky flavour from the aubergine.

You can serve this dish as a side dish or a sandwich spread or use it as a dip with crackers or pittas.

Roasted Vegetables

1 butternut squash
3 medium courgettes
2 large beetroot, peeled
4 large carrots
1 medium aubergine
4 tablespoons fresh herbs (such as thyme, rosemary, basil, parsley, tarragon or any combination of these) or 1½ tablespoons dried
½ teaspoon salt or dash of liquid aminos
2 tablespoons olive oil
300g (10½ oz) cherry tomatoes

Makes 8 servings

Per serving: *Energy* 76 cals/319 kJ; *Protein* 2 g; *Carbohydrate* 10 g (of which 9 g sugars); *Fat* 3.5 g (of which 0.5 g saturates); *Sodium* 190 mg.

1. Preheat the oven to 230°C/450°F/gas mark 8. Coat a large baking sheet or dish with cooking spray.

2. Cut the squash, courgettes, beetroot, carrots and aubergine into 2.5 to 5 cm (1 to 2 in) pieces and spread over the prepared baking sheet or dish. If using fresh herbs, cut off the stems and roughly chop the leaves. Sprinkle the vegetables with the herbs and salt or aminos. Drizzle with the oil.

3. Roast for 30 minutes. Then stir the vegetables and add the tomatoes. Cook for 30 minutes longer or until the vegetables are browned.

4. Serve immediately or let cool for about 30 minutes. Transfer cooled leftovers into covered containers and refrigerate for up to 4 days.

You can include any seasonal vegetable you like. Mushrooms, broccoli, cauliflower, yellow and red peppers and fennel bulbs are all nice options.

Layered Potato and Courgette Pie

4 medium waxy potatoes
4 medium-large courgettes
2 large onions
3 tablespoons fresh basil or 4 teaspoons dried
50 g (2 oz) grated Parmesan cheese
25 g (1 oz) plain flour
2 tins (400 g/14 oz each) light condensed milk
½ teaspoon salt
Ground black pepper

Makes 8 servings

Per serving: *Energy* 253 cals/1062 kJ; *Protein* 11 g; *Carbohydrate* 34 g (of which 3 g sugars); *Fat* 9 g (of which 7 g saturates); *Sodium* 313 mg.

1. Preheat the oven to 180°C/350°F/gas mark 4. Coat a 32.5 x 23 cm (13 x 9 in) baking dish or roasting pan with cooking spray. Set aside.

2. Slice the potatoes into 0.5 cm (¼ in) pieces. Slice the courgettes into 0.5 to 1 cm (¼ to ½ in) pieces. Peel the onions and cut into 0.5m (¼ in) pieces. Set the vegetables aside. If using fresh basil, cut off the stems and roughly chop the leaves. Set aside.

3. Layer a third of the potatoes in an overlapping manner in the bottom of the pan. Layer a third of the courgettes on top of the potatoes. Then layer a third of the onions on top of the courgettes. Sprinkle with 2 to 3 tablespoons of the cheese, 2 tablespoons of flour and 1½ tablespoons of fresh basil or 2 teaspoons dried. Then make a second layer of each vegetable, using half of the remaining amount and sprinkle with 2 to 3 tablespoons of the cheese, 2 tablespoons of flour and 1½ tablespoons of fresh basil or 2 teaspoons dried. Finally, make a third layer with each of the remaining vegetables. Top the pie with the remaining cheese and pour the light condensed milk over all. Sprinkle the salt and pepper to taste over the top.

4. Cover with aluminium foil and bake for 1 hour or until the vegetables are tender. Remove the foil and cook for 20 minutes longer or until browned.

5. Cool for at least 20 minutes, then cut into portions and serve. (If you don't let the pie cool first, it is difficult to serve in slices.) Transfer cooled leftovers into covered containers and refrigerate immediately.

Veggie Trio

2 medium carrots, peeled
½ red pepper
900 g (2 lb) fresh asparagus
1 tablespoon mustard
3 tablespoons balsamic vinegar
1 teaspoon lemon juice
1 teaspoon dried basil
1 tablespoon extra-virgin olive oil
¼ teaspoon salt

Makes 4 servings

Per serving: *Energy* 111 cals/466 kJ; *Protein* 7 g;
Carbohydrate 10 g (of which 9 g sugars); *Fat* 5 g (of which
0.5 g saturates); *Sodium* 226 mg.

1. Finely grate the carrots using a box grater or food processor. Remove seeds from the pepper and cut into strips 0.5 cm (¼ in) thick.

2. Cut off and discard the woody ends of the asparagus. Wrap the asparagus loosely in grease proof paper or place on a microwaveable dish covered with microwaveable clingfilm. Microwave on high power for about 2 minutes, or until the asparagus turns bright green and softens slightly. Remove, let cool and cut into 2.5 cm (1 in) pieces.

3. In a small bowl, combine the mustard, vinegar, lemon juice, basil, oil and salt. Whisk well.

4. In a large bowl, combine the carrots, pepper and asparagus. Add the dressing. Toss and serve.

Aubergine Caponata

1 clove garlic
1 medium onion
1 tablespoon olive oil
1 large aubergine
1 stick celery
75 g (3 oz) tomato purée
1 tin (400 g /14 oz) chopped tomatoes
2 tablespoons red wine vinegar
1 tablespoon capers
1 teaspoon dried oregano
1 teaspoon dried basil
½ teaspoon salt or 2 teaspoons liquid aminos
10–12 black olives, pitted and chopped
    (optional)
Ground black pepper

Makes 8 servings

Per serving: *Energy* 35 cals/147 kJ; *Protein* 1 g;
Carbohydrate 4 g (of which 3 g sugars); *Fat* 2 g (of which
0.5 g saturates); *Sodium* 500 mg.

1. Peel the garlic and chop finely. Peel the onion and cut into 0.5 to 1 cm (¼ to ½ in) pieces. Coat a large pan with the oil. Add the garlic and onion and cook over medium heat, stirring often, until the onion starts to brown. Add water, 1 tablespoon at a time, as necessary to prevent burning.

2. Peel the aubergine and cut into 2.5 cm (1 in) chunks. Add the aubergine to the garlic-onion mixture. Cook together for about 15 minutes, or until the aubergine starts to soften.

3. Cut the celery into 0.5 to 1 cm (¼ to ½ in) pieces. Add the celery, tomato purée, tinned tomatoes, vinegar, capers, oregano, basil and salt or aminos to the pan. Reduce the heat to low. Add the olives (if using). Cover and cook for 35 minutes, or until tender. Add the pepper to taste. Serve warm or at room temperature. Refrigerate cooled leftovers.

Puréed Sweet Potatoes

4 medium sweet potatoes
2 teaspoons cinnamon + additional to taste
2 tablespoons honey
2–4 tablespoons skimmed milk

Makes 4 servings

Per serving: *Energy* 177 cals/743 kJ; *Protein* 2 g;
Carbohydrate 44 g (of which 20 g sugars); *Fat* 0.5 g (of
which 0.2 g saturates); *Sodium* 68 mg.

1. Peel the sweet potatoes and cut into 2.5 to 5 cm (1 to 2 in) chunks. Place in a large pan and cover with water. Boil for about 20 minutes, or until soft.

2. Drain well. In a food processor fitted with the chopping blade, add the sweet potatoes, 2 teaspoons cinnamon and honey. Process until smooth. If the mixture seems too thick, add 2 tablespoons of milk and process for a few seconds longer. Keep adding milk, by the tablespoonful, until the desired texture is achieved. Sprinkle with additional cinnamon, if desired, and serve immediately.

'Unfried' French Fries

4 large waxy potatoes (about 900 g/
    2 lb)
1 teaspoon dried oregano
1 teaspoon dried basil
½ teaspoon dried rosemary
1–2 tablespoons olive oil
Ground black pepper

Makes 4 servings

Per serving: *Energy* 207 cals/869 kJ; *Protein* 5 g;
Carbohydrate 39 g (of which 1.5 g sugars); *Fat* 5 g (of
which 0.5 g saturates); *Sodium* 16 mg.

1. Preheat the oven to 230°C/450°F/gas mark 8. Coat a nonstick baking tray with cooking spray. Set aside. Fill a large pan with water and bring to the boil.

2. Scrub the potatoes well (do not peel). Cut the potatoes into wedges 1 cm (½ in) thick. Boil in the water for 7 minutes. Drain the potatoes and rinse under very cold water to stop the cooking process.

3. Arrange the potatoes in a single layer on the baking tray. Sprinkle with the oregano, basil, rosemary and oil. Coat them with the cooking spray.

4. Bake for 45 to 55 minutes, turning the potato wedges every 15 minutes, or until evenly browned on all sides. Add the pepper to taste. Serve immediately or let cool.

Roasted Rosemary Potatoes

4 medium red potatoes (about 450 g/1 lb)
2 tablespoons olive oil
5 cloves garlic, finely chopped
1 tablespoon dried rosemary
¼ teaspoon salt or 1 teaspoon liquid aminos
Ground black pepper

Makes 4 servings

Per serving: *Energy* 137 cals/575 kJ; *Protein* 3 g; *Carbohydrate* 20 g (of which 1 g sugars); *Fat* 6 g (of which 1 g saturates); *Sodium* 105 mg.

1. Preheat the oven to 200°C/400°F/gas mark 6. Scrub the potatoes well. Cut the potatoes into 1 to 2.5 cm (½ to 1 in) squares (irregular chunks are fine, too, as long as they're more or less the same size).

2. Coat a nonstick baking tray with the oil. Add the potatoes and garlic. Sprinkle with the rosemary and salt or aminos. Toss well.

3. Bake for 20 minutes. Stir well and bake for 30 minutes longer or until browned.

4. Add the pepper to taste. Serve hot.

Sautéed Broccoli and Garlic

1 clove garlic
1 large head broccoli
2 tablespoons olive oil
¼ teaspoon salt or 1 teaspoon liquid aminos
1 tablespoon white wine or squeeze of fresh lemon juice

Makes 4 servings

Per serving: *Energy* 96 cals/403 kJ; *Protein* 6 g; *Carbohydrate* 3 g (of which 2 g sugars); *Fat* 7 g (of which 1 g saturates); *Sodium* 150 mg.

1. Peel the garlic and chop finely. Cut off and discard the thick broccoli stalks, leaving about 2.5 cm (1 in) of stalk attached to the florets.

2. Coat a large nonstick frying pan with the oil and place over medium heat. Add the garlic and cook for about 1 minute or until the garlic becomes fragrant. Add the broccoli and cook for 3 to 4 minutes, stirring occasionally or until the broccoli turns bright green and the stems soften slightly. Add the salt or aminos and the wine or lemon juice.

3. Serve immediately or when cooled. Transfer cooled leftovers into covered containers and refrigerate immediately.

Asian Red Lentil Soup

2 large onions
1 clove garlic
2 tablespoons olive oil
2.5 cm (1 in) piece fresh ginger
2 teaspoons coriander seeds or 1 medium
    bunch fresh coriander
1 teaspoon ground cumin
250 g (9 oz) red lentils
225 ml (8 fl oz) passata (sieved tomatoes)
½ teaspoon salt or 2 tablespoons liquid
    aminos
1 teaspoon dried basil
1 teaspoon dried oregano
1.4 litres (2½ pints) water

Makes 8 servings

Per serving: *Energy* 127 cals/617 kJ; *Protein* 7 g;
Carbohydrate 21 g (of which 4.5 g sugars); *Fat* 3 g (of
which 0.5 g saturates); *Sodium* 200 mg.

1. Peel the onions and garlic. Chop the onions into rough 1 to 2.5 cm (½ to 1 in) pieces. Chop the garlic finely. Warm the oil in a large pan over medium heat. Add the onions and garlic and cook, stirring often, for about 10 minutes, or until the onions just start to brown. Add water, 1 tablespoon at a time, as necessary to prevent burning. Meanwhile, peel the ginger and chop finely.

2. Add the ginger, coriander seeds (if using) and cumin. Cook on medium heat for about 1 minute or until the spices get very fragrant.

3. If using fresh coriander, cut off the stems and chop the leaves roughly and set aside.

4. Add the lentils, passata, salt or aminos, basil, oregano, fresh coriander (if using) and water to the pot. Bring to a boil, then reduce the heat to a simmer for 30 minutes.

5. Purée in a blender or food processor fitted with the chopping blade or use a hand-held blender directly in the pan. Serve immediately. Transfer cooled leftovers into covered containers and store in the refrigerator or freezer.

French Onion Soup

2 large Spanish onions
2 medium red onions
2 cloves garlic
2 tablespoons olive oil
225 ml (8 fl oz) white wine
900 ml (1½ pints) low-sodium beef, chicken
    or vegetable stock
850 ml (1½ pints) water
2 teaspoons dried basil
2 teaspoons dried oregano
Parmesan cheese

Makes 8 servings

Per serving: *Energy* 102 cals/428 kJ; *Protein* 4 g;
Carbohydrate 5 g (of which 4 g sugars); *Fat* 5 g (of which
2 g saturates); *Sodium* 275 mg.

1. Peel the Spanish and red onions and the garlic. Cut the onions into 0.5 cm (¼ in) slices. Chop the garlic roughly. Warm the oil in a large pan over medium heat. Add the onions and garlic and cover the pot. Cook over medium-low heat, stirring occasionally, for about 30 minutes, or until the onions start to brown. Add water, 1 tablespoon at a time, as necessary to prevent burning.

2. Stir in the wine, scraping up any browned bits from the bottom of the pan. Add the stock, water, basil and oregano. Simmer on low heat for 30 minutes. Serve immediately, sprinkled with Parmesan cheese to taste. Transfer cooled leftovers into covered containers and store in the refrigerator or freezer.

This recipe depends on the browning of the onions for good flavour and colour, so don't rush cooking the onions. Allow them to brown and not burn.

Chicken Soup

4 large carrots
2 medium courgettes
2 sticks celery
Small bunch fresh dill
Small bunch fresh parsley
350 g (12 oz) boneless, skinless chicken
    breasts
1 large onion
2 cloves garlic
2 tablespoons olive oil
2 bay leaves
1 teaspoon dried basil
1 teaspoon dried oregano
2 tablespoons low-sodium chicken bouillon
    granules
850 ml (1½ pints) low-sodium chicken stock
850 ml (1½ pints) water
Ground black pepper

Makes 8 servings

Per serving: *Energy* 108 cals/454 kJ; *Protein* 11 g;
Carbohydrate 6 g (of which 5 g sugars); *Fat* 4 g (of which
1 g saturates); *Sodium* 290 mg.

1. Peel the carrots and cut them into 1 cm
(½ in) pieces. Cut the courgettes and celery
into 1 cm (½ in) pieces. Cut off the dill and
parsley stems and roughly chop the dill
fronds and parsley leaves. Set aside.

2. Rinse the chicken and blot dry with
paper towels. Cut the chicken into 2.5 cm
(1 in) pieces and set aside.

3. Peel the onion and garlic. Chop the
onion into rough 1 to 2.5 cm (½ to 1 in)
pieces. Chop the garlic finely. Warm the oil
in a large pan over medium heat. Add the
onions and garlic and cook, stirring often,
for about 10 minutes, or until the onions
just start to brown. Add water, 1 tablespoon
at a time, as necessary to prevent burning.

4. Add the carrots, celery, dill, parsley,
chicken, bay leaves, basil, oregano,
bouillon, chicken stock and water. Cook
over medium-low heat for 45 minutes.
Then add the courgettes and pepper to
taste and cook for 15 minutes longer or
until the chicken is cooked through.
Remove and discard the bay leaves. Serve
immediately or transfer cooled leftovers
into covered containers and store in the
refrigerator or freezer.

Smokin' Fish Chowder

1 large onion
1 clove garlic
2 tablespoons olive oil
450 g (1 lb) carrots
1 medium courgette
1 yellow squash
2 sticks celery
Handful chopped fresh dill
1 medium potato, peeled and cubed
75 g (3 oz) sweetcorn
1 bay leaf
Ground black pepper
50 ml (2 fl oz) dry white wine
¼ teaspoon salt or 1 tablespoon liquid aminos
1.4 litres (2½ pints) water
110 g (4 oz) smoked trout or mackerel
225 g (8 oz) cod, sole, halibut or salmon fillet,
    small bones removed

Makes 8 servings

Per serving: *Energy* 159 cals/667 kJ; *Protein* 9 g;
Carbohydrate 13 g (of which 7 g sugars); *Fat* 8 g (of which
1.5 g saturates); *Sodium* 220 mg.

1. Peel the onion and cut into 0.5 cm (¼ in) slices. Peel the garlic and chop finely. Warm the oil in a large pan over medium heat. Add the onion and garlic and cook, stirring often, for about 10 minutes, or until the onion just starts to brown. Add water, 1 tablespoon at a time, as necessary to prevent burning.

2. Meanwhile, peel the carrots and chop into 0.5 to 1 cm (¼ to ½ in) pieces. Chop the courgette, squash and celery into 0.5 to 1 cm (¼ to ½ in) pieces.

3. Add the carrots, courgettes, squash, celery, dill, cubed potato, sweetcorn, bay leaf, pepper to taste, wine, salt or aminos and water. Simmer over low heat for 30 minutes. Meanwhile, cut the smoked and fresh fish into 2.5 cm (1 in) pieces.

4. Add the fish. Cook for 5 to 10 minutes longer over low heat or until the fresh fish is cooked through. Remove and discard the bay leaf. Serve immediately. Transfer cooled leftovers into covered containers and store in the refrigerator or freezer.

Creamy Carrot Soup

6 large carrots
5 cm (2 in) piece fresh ginger
Large bunch fresh parsley
Small bunch fresh coriander
3 large onions
2 cloves garlic
2 tablespoons olive oil
1.8 litres (3 pints) water
3 tablespoons low-sodium soy sauce or liquid
    aminos
2 tablespoons low-sodium chicken or
    vegetable bouillon granules
Peel of 1 orange, with no white pith
Ground black pepper

Makes 8 servings

Per serving: *Energy* 76 cals/319 kJ; *Protein* 2 g;
Carbohydrate 11 g (of which 9 g sugars); *Fat* 3 g (of which
0.5 g saturates); *Sodium* 325 mg.

1. Peel the carrots and chop into 5 to 7.5 cm (2 to 3 in) pieces. Set aside. Peel the ginger and chop finely. Cut off the parsley and coriander stems. Cut the leaves roughly. Set aside.

2. Peel the onions and garlic. Chop the onions into 1 to 2.5 cm ($\frac{1}{2}$ to 1 in) pieces. Chop the garlic roughly. Warm the oil in a large pan over medium heat. Add the onions and garlic and cook, stirring often, for about 10 minutes, or until the onions just start to brown. Add water, 1 tablespoon at a time, as necessary to prevent burning.

3. Add the carrots, ginger, water, soy sauce or aminos and bouillon. Cook over low heat for 25 minutes. Add the parsley and coriander, orange peel and pepper to taste. Continue cooking for 15 minutes longer. Remove the orange peel.

4. Purée in a blender or food processor fitted with the chopping blade or use a hand-held blender directly in the pan. Blend until creamy and medium-thick. If the soup is too thick, add more water. Serve hot, warm or cool.

Roasted Tomato and Basil Soup

1.4 kg (3 lb) whole ripe plum tomatoes, halved
2 cloves garlic
1 large onion
1 tablespoon olive oil
Handful loosely packed chopped fresh basil
    leaves
455 ml (16 fl oz) passata (sieved tomatoes)
½ teaspoon salt or 2 tablespoons liquid
    aminos
1 teaspoon dried oregano
1.4 litres (2½ pints) low-sodium chicken or
    vegetable stock or water

Makes 8 servings

Per serving: *Energy* 69 cals/290 kJ; *Protein* 3 g;
Carbohydrate 11 g (of which 10 g sugars); *Fat* 2 g (of
which 0.5 g saturates); *Sodium* 300 mg.

If you want a creamy version of this soup, add some semi-skimmed milk to taste at the end.

---

1. Preheat the oven to 230°C/450°F/gas mark 8. Coat a large baking tray with cooking spray. Place the tomatoes, cut side down, in the baking tray. Peel the garlic and chop finely. Sprinkle the tomatoes with half of the garlic.

2. Coat the tops of the tomatoes with cooking spray and roast in the oven for about 1 hour or until the edges of the tomatoes are well roasted and start to blacken. If the tomatoes start drying out while cooking, add a little bit of water to the bottom of the tray. Remove from the oven and set aside. When the tomatoes are cool enough to handle, slip off the skins. Coarsely chop the tomatoes.

3. Meanwhile, peel the onion and cut into rough 1 x 2.5 cm (½ x 1 in) pieces. Warm the oil in a large pan over medium heat. Add the onions and remaining half of the garlic. Cook, stirring often, for about 15 minutes, or until the onion turns light brown. Add water, 1 tablespoon at a time, as necessary to prevent burning.

4. Add the roasted tomatoes, basil, passata, salt or aminos, oregano and stock or water. Cook over medium heat for 30 minutes, stirring often to break up the tomatoes. Serve hot or warm. Transfer cooled leftovers into covered containers and store in the refrigerator for up to 5 days or in the freezer for up to 2 months.

Texas Black Bean Soup

900 g (2 lb) tinned black beans
2 large carrots
2 cloves garlic
1 large onion
2 tablespoons olive oil
200 ml (7 fl oz) passata (sieved tomatoes)
1 tablespoon low-sodium chicken bouillon
    granules
2 tablespoons dry sherry
1.4 litres (2½ pints) water
1 teaspoon chilli powder
¼–½ teaspoon cayenne pepper
1 teaspoon dried oregano
1 teaspoon liquid smoke (hickory seasoning)

Makes 8 servings

Per serving: *Energy* 188 cals/790 kJ; *Protein* 11 g;
Carbohydrate 27 g (of which 6 g sugars); *Fat* 4 g (of which
0.5 g saturates); *Sodium* 400 mg.

1. Drain the beans. Rinse well and drain again. Set aside.

2. Peel the carrots and cut into 0.5 to 1 cm (¼ to ½ in) pieces. Set aside.

3. Peel the garlic and chop finely. Peel the onion and cut into rough 1 to 2.5 cm (½ to 1 in) pieces. Warm the oil in a large pan over medium heat. Add the garlic and onion and cook, stirring often, for about 15 minutes, or until the onion turns light brown. Add water, 1 tablespoon at a time, as necessary to prevent burning.

4. Add the beans, carrots, passata, bouillon, sherry, water, chilli powder, cayenne pepper and oregano. Cook over medium heat for 50 to 55 minutes, or until the soup is medium-thick. Stir in the liquid smoke. Add more spices to taste. Add more water if you prefer a thinner soup. Serve hot or warm.

Roasted Acorn Squash Soup

1 large acorn squash
3 large carrots
1 large onion
1 clove garlic
1 tablespoon olive oil
1 bay leaf
½ teaspoon salt or 1 tablespoon liquid aminos
2 teaspoons dried rosemary
1 teaspoon dried sage
2 tablespoons chicken bouillon granules
2 litres (3½ pints) water

Makes 8 servings

Per serving: *Energy* 44 cals/185 kJ; *Protein* 1 g; *Carbohydrate* 6 g (of which 5 g sugars); *Fat* 2 g (of which 0.5 g saturates); *Sodium* 337 mg.

1. Preheat the oven to 200°C/400°F/gas mark 6. Cut the squash in half and remove the seeds. Place the squash on a baking sheet, cut side up. Bake for 45 minutes to 1 hour or until soft. Set aside to cool. When cool enough to handle, scoop out the insides and set aside in a bowl.

2. Meanwhile, peel the carrots and chop into 2.5 to 5 cm (1 to 2 in) chunks. Set aside.

3. Peel the onion and garlic. Cut the onion into rough 1 to 2.5 cm (½ to 1 in) pieces. Chop the garlic finely. Warm the oil in a large pan over medium heat. Add the onion and garlic and cook, stirring often, for about 15 minutes, or until the onion turns light brown. Add water, 1 tablespoon at a time, as necessary to prevent burning.

4. Add the carrots, bay leaf, salt or aminos, rosemary, sage, bouillon and water. Cook over low heat for 30 minutes, or until the carrots have softened. Remove and discard the bay leaf. Stir in the cooked squash.

5. Purée in a blender or food processor fitted with the chopping blade or use a hand-held blender directly in the pan. Blend or process until creamy and medium-thick. Return to the pan and simmer for 15 minutes longer. Serve hot or warm. Transfer cooled leftovers into covered containers and store in the refrigerator or freezer.

Chunky Mixed Vegetable Soup

1 large courgette
2 sticks celery
1 medium red pepper
1 medium turnip
1 medium parsnip
1 medium waxy potato
2 cloves garlic
1 large onion
1 tablespoon olive oil
450 g (1 lb) baby carrots
1 tin (400 g/14 oz) chopped or whole
    tomatoes
½ teaspoon salt or 2 tablespoons liquid
    aminos
2 litres (3½ pints) water or vegetable stock
Large handful fresh basil leaves, chopped
Ground black pepper

Makes 8 servings

Per serving: *Energy* 80 cals/336 kJ; *Protein* 2 g;
Carbohydrate 14 g (of which 9 g sugars); *Fat* 2 g (of which
0.5 g saturates); *Sodium* 187 mg.

1. Chop the courgette and celery into 2.5 cm (1 in) pieces. Remove seeds from the pepper and cut into 2.5 cm (1 in) pieces. Set aside.

2. Peel the turnip, parsnip and potato. Chop each into 1 to 2.5 cm (½ to 1 in) pieces. Set aside.

3. Peel the garlic and onion. Chop the garlic roughly. Cut the onion into 0.5 cm (¼ in) pieces. Warm the oil in a large pan over medium heat. Add the onion and garlic and cook, stirring often, for about 10 minutes, or until the onion just starts to brown. Add water, 1 tablespoon at a time, as necessary to prevent burning.

4. Add the courgette, celery, pepper, turnip, parsnip, potato, baby carrots, tomatoes (with juice), salt or aminos, water or stock, basil and black pepper to taste. Simmer over low heat for 45 to 60 minutes, stirring occasionally to break up the whole tomatoes (if using). Add more water if the soup seems too thick. Serve hot or warm. Transfer cooled leftovers into covered containers and store in the refrigerator or freezer.

This is a filling and yummy soup. Feel free to use any vegetables you like.

Wild Mushroom Soup

2 cloves garlic
1 large onion
1 tablespoon olive oil
350 g (12 oz) white mushrooms
225 g (8 oz) shiitake mushrooms (and/or other mushrooms such as oyster or maitake)
½ teaspoon salt or 2 tablespoons liquid aminos
1 bay leaf
½ teaspoon dried oregano
½ teaspoon dried basil
1.4 litres (2½ pints) water

Makes 8 servings

Per serving: *Energy* 29 cals/122 kJ; *Protein* 2 g; *Carbohydrate* 2 g (of which 1 g sugars); *Fat* 2 g (of which 0.5 g saturates); *Sodium* 150 mg.

1. Peel the garlic and onion. Chop the garlic roughly. Cut the onion into 0.5 cm (¼ in) pieces. Warm the oil in a large pan over medium heat. Add the garlic and onion and cook, stirring often, until the onion is soft, about 10 minutes. Add water, 1 tablespoon at a time, as necessary to prevent burning.

2. Gently wash the mushrooms. Slice the mushrooms. Add to the pan and cook over medium-low heat for 20 minutes, or until the mushrooms are golden brown.

3. Add the salt or aminos, bay leaf, oregano, basil and water. Simmer over low heat for 25 minutes.

4. Remove and discard the bay leaf. Purée half of the soup in a blender or food processor fitted with the chopping blade or use a hand-held blender until the mixture is medium-thick. Return to the pan. Serve hot or warm. Transfer cooled leftovers into covered containers and store in the refrigerator.

> *If you want a creamy version of this soup, add semi-skimmed milk to taste.*

Roasted Garlic and White Bean Spread

1 bulb garlic (whole head)
1 tin (420 g/15 oz) cannellini beans, rinsed
    and drained
110 g (4 oz) low-fat mayonnaise
½ teaspoon ground cumin
¼ teaspoon salt or ½ teaspoon liquid aminos
2–3 tablespoons lemon juice
Ground black pepper
3 tablespoons chopped parsley

Serves 8 as a dip

Per 2 tablespoons: *Energy* 89 cals/374 kJ; *Protein* 3 g;
Carbohydrate 7 g (of which 1 g sugars); *Fat* 5 g (of which
1 g saturates); *Sodium* 290 mg.

1. Preheat the oven to 180°C/350°F/gas mark 4. Place the unpeeled whole garlic bulb in a shallow baking dish or on a baking sheet and bake for about 1 hour or until soft. (It is acceptable for the skin to char.) Remove from the oven and let cool.

2. Squeeze out at least 2 or 3 cloves of roasted garlic, removing the peel, or as many as you like. Place in the bowl of a food processor fitted with the chopping blade. Add the beans, mayonnaise and cumin. Process for about 20 seconds or until light and creamy. Transfer to a medium bowl and mix in the salt or aminos, lemon juice and pepper to taste. Stir in the parsley.

3. Serve as a dip with raw vegetables or in lightly toasted wholemeal pittas or on wholewheat crackers.

Lemony Hummus

1 clove garlic
1 tin (400 g/14 oz) chickpeas
Grated zest and juice of 1 lemon
3 tablespoons olive oil
2 teaspoons tahini sauce (optional)
¼ teaspoon salt or ½ tablespoon liquid
	aminos
¼ teaspoon ground black pepper
2 tablespoons chopped parsley

Serves 8 as a dip

Per serving: *Energy* 107 cals/449 kJ; *Protein* 4 g;
Carbohydrate 8 g (of which 0.5 g sugars); *Fat* 6 g (of
which 1 g saturates); *Sodium* 159 mg.

1. Peel the garlic and place in the bowl of a
food processor fitted with the chopping
blade. Process for 5 seconds or until the
garlic is chopped. Drain the chickpeas well,
rinse and drain again. Add to the food
processor, along with the lemon zest,
lemon juice, oil, tahini (if using), salt or
aminos, pepper and parsley. Process for
about 20 seconds or until smooth.

2. Serve as a dip with raw vegetables or in
lightly toasted wholemeal pittas or on
wholewheat crackers.

Lentil Salad with Lemon and Feta

350 g (12 oz) dried green or puy lentils
1 large beefsteak tomato or 3 or 4 plum
	tomatoes
1 spring onion
Large handful fresh coriander leaves
110 g (4 oz) feta cheese
2 tablespoons extra-virgin olive oil
Grated zest of 1 lemon
Juice of 2 lemons
¼ teaspoon ground black pepper

Makes 8 servings

Per serving: *Energy* 194 cals/815 kJ; *Protein* 13 g;
Carbohydrate 22 g (of which 2 g sugars); *Fat* 6 g (of which
2.5 g saturates); *Sodium* 206 mg.

1. In a medium saucepan, bring 700 ml
(1¼ pints) of water to the boil. Add the
lentils and return the heat to boiling.
Simmer over medium-low heat for about
25 minutes, or until the lentils are tender.
Drain the lentils and rinse under cold
water. Drain again and set aside.

2. Chop the tomato(es) into 0.5 cm (¼ in)
pieces and place in a medium bowl. Chop
the spring onion and coriander finely and
add to the bowl. Crumble the cheese into
the bowl and add the lentils.

3. In a small bowl, whisk the oil, lemon
zest, lemon juice and pepper. Add to the
lentil mixture and toss well. Refrigerate for
at least 1 hour or overnight and serve.

Bean and Barley Salad

Dressing

Juice of ½ lemon
¼ teaspoon salt or ½ tablespoon liquid
   aminos
1 clove garlic
2½ tablespoons extra-virgin olive oil
2 tablespoons water
2 teaspoons Dijon mustard
2 teaspoons fresh basil or ¾ teaspoon dried
2 teaspoons fresh oregano or ¾ teaspoon
   dried
Ground black pepper

Salad

455 ml (16 fl oz) water or low-sodium chicken
   stock
225 g (8 oz) pearl barley
1 small courgette
1 small carrot
1 tablespoon olive oil
75 g (3 oz) broccoli florets
75 g (3 oz) cauliflower florets
175 g (6 oz) tinned black beans, rinsed and
   drained

Makes 8 servings

Per serving: *Energy* 189 cals/794 kJ; *Protein* 5 g;
Carbohydrate 28 g (of which 2 g sugars); *Fat* 6 g (of which
1 g saturates); *Sodium* 190 mg.

1. *To prepare the dressing:* In a small bowl, combine the lemon juice and salt or aminos, stirring until the salt dissolves. Peel the garlic and chop finely. Add the garlic, oil, water, mustard, basil, oregano and pepper to taste. Mix well with a fork.

2. *To prepare the salad:* Bring water and barley to a boil in a medium heavy-based saucepan, then reduce heat and simmer, covered, until barley is tender, about 45 minutes. Remove from heat and let stand, covered, 5 minutes. Drain barley in a colander, then rinse under cold water and let cool to room temperature.

3. Meanwhile, cut the courgette and carrot into 0.5 cm (¼ in) slices. Warm the oil in a large nonstick frying pan over medium heat. Add the carrot and cook for about 4 minutes. Add the broccoli and cauliflower and cook for 3 minutes longer or until they just start to cook. Add the courgette and cook for 1 or 2 minutes longer or until the vegetables are just cooked but still a little crisp.

4. In a large bowl, combine the barley, vegetable mixture and beans. Add the dressing and toss well. Serve the salad immediately or refrigerate until ready to serve. (The salad can be made up to 4 days in advance.)

Mexican Rice and Beans

150 g (5 oz) brown rice
525 ml (18 fl oz) water
2 tins (420 g/15 oz each) low-sodium red
    kidney beans
1 clove garlic
1 medium onion
1 tablespoon olive oil
1 spring onion, roughly chopped
2 tablespoons chopped fresh coriander
1 teaspoon ground cumin
¼ teaspoon salt or 1 teaspoon liquid aminos
Ground black pepper

Makes 4 servings

Per serving: *Energy* 339 cals/1554 kJ; *Protein* 15 g;
Carbohydrate 63 g (of which 9 g sugars); *Fat* 5 g (of which
1 g saturates); *Sodium* 160 mg.

1. In a medium saucepan, combine the brown rice and water. Cook, covered, over medium heat for 45 minutes or until the water is absorbed and the rice is tender. Drain the beans, rinse well and drain again. Set aside.

2. Meanwhile, peel the garlic and chop roughly. Peel the onion, halve it and slice. Warm the oil in a medium saucepan over medium heat. Add the garlic and onion and cook, stirring often, for about 7 minutes, or until the onion starts to brown. Add the beans and cook for 4 minutes, or until the beans are heated through.

3. In a large bowl, combine the bean mixture with the rice, spring onion, coriander, cumin, salt or aminos and pepper to taste. Serve immediately.

> *While I've suggested using red kidney beans, you may use any beans you like. By using tinned beans, you'll save a lot of time. You can also use rice left over from another meal, which will turn this into a super-fast dish. If using precooked rice, place it in a dish covered with micro-waveable clingfilm and microwave on high power for 2 minutes.*

Brown Rice Pilaf

600 ml (1 pint) water
175 g (6 oz) brown rice
1 medium onion
1 clove garlic
1 tablespoon olive oil
¼ teaspoon salt or 2 teaspoons liquid aminos
2 tablespoons pine nuts (optional)

Makes 4 servings

Per serving: *Energy* 230 cals/966 kJ; *Protein* 4 g;
Carbohydrate 39 g (of which 3 g sugars); *Fat* 7 g (of which
1 g saturates); *Sodium* 140 mg.

1. In a medium saucepan, combine the water and rice and cook over medium heat for 45 minutes or until the water is absorbed and the rice is tender. Do not overcook. Rice grains should separate easily. Set aside to cool.

2. Peel the onion and cut into 3 mm (⅛ in) slices. Peel the garlic and chop finely.

3. Warm the oil in a large nonstick frying pan over medium heat. Add the onion, garlic and salt or aminos. Cook, stirring often, for about 7 minutes, or until the onion starts to brown. Add water, 1 tablespoon at a time, as necessary to prevent burning. Cool.

4. Combine the cooled rice with the onion mixture. If using pine nuts, toast them in a nonstick frying pan over medium heat for about 3 minutes, or until they start to brown. Then toss the toasted nuts with the rice mixture. Serve immediately or refrigerate.

Because it's made with brown rice, this dish is an excellent way to incorporate more fibre into your diet. It's delicious without the pine nuts, but adding them takes the flavour to the next level.

Italian Risotto with Wild Mushrooms

850 ml (1½ pints) low-sodium vegetable stock
25 g (1 oz) dried porcini mushrooms
110 ml (4 fl oz) boiling water
1 large onion
2 tablespoons olive oil
175 g (6 oz) Arborio rice
110 ml (4 fl oz) dry white wine
50 g (2 oz) sliced shiitake mushrooms
¼ teaspoon salt
1 tablespoon chopped parsley
25 g (1 oz) grated Parmesan cheese

Makes 4 servings

Per serving: *Energy* 283 cals/1188 kJ; *Protein* 7 g; *Carbohydrate* 41 g (of which 2 g sugars); *Fat* 9 g (of which 2.5 g saturates); *Sodium* 500 mg.

1. Pour the stock into a medium saucepan and warm over low heat. Soak the porcini mushrooms in the water for about 10 minutes, or until soft. Strain the soaking liquid and set both the mushrooms and liquid aside.

2. Meanwhile, peel the onion and chop into 3 mm (⅛ in) pieces. Warm the oil in a medium pan over medium heat. Add the onion and cook over medium-low heat for 7 to 10 minutes, or until the onion is soft and transparent. Add stock, 1 tablespoon at a time, as necessary to prevent the onion from browning.

3. Add the rice to the pan and continue cooking over low heat for 3 to 5 minutes, or until the rice turns opaque. Add the wine and cook until it is absorbed. Then add 225 ml (8 fl oz) of the stock. Cook, stirring frequently, until the rice has absorbed the stock, about 15 minutes.

4. Add the reserved mushroom soaking liquid and 110 ml (4 fl oz) of stock. Continue to simmer, stirring frequently, until all the liquid has been absorbed. Add the reserved porcini mushrooms, shiitake mushrooms and 110 ml (4 fl oz) of stock. Stir frequently until the rice has absorbed all the stock.

5. If the rice is still too firm, continue adding the remaining stock, 110 ml (4 fl oz) at a time and stir until the stock is absorbed and the rice becomes tender. The rice should be a little chewy and creamy. Stir in the salt, parsley and cheese. Serve immediately as a side dish.

Jasmine Rice Pilaf

175 g (6 oz) jasmine rice
350 ml (12 fl oz) water
1 small leek
1 medium onion
1 stick celery
1 tablespoon olive oil
Ground black pepper

Makes 4 servings

Per serving: *Energy* 207 cals/869 kJ; *Protein* 4 g;
Carbohydrate 40 g (of which 2 g sugars); *Fat* 4 g (of which
1 g saturates); *Sodium* 20 mg.

1. Rinse the rice under running water until the water turns clear. In a medium saucepan, combine the rice and water. Bring to a boil and cover. Reduce the heat to very low and cook for 20 minutes. Turn off the heat and leave undisturbed for 10 minutes. Let cool.

2. Cut off the green leafy part of the leek and discard. Halve the white part lengthwise and rinse thoroughly. Cut into 0.5 cm ($\frac{1}{4}$ in) slices. Peel the onion and cut into similar size slices. Cut the celery into 0.5 cm ($\frac{1}{4}$ in) slices. Warm the oil in a large nonstick frying pan over medium-low heat. Add the leek, onion and celery. Cook for about 10 minutes, or until the onion turns soft and lightly brown. Add water, 1 tablespoon at a time, as necessary to prevent burning. Let cool.

3. Combine the onion mixture, cooled rice and pepper to taste.

Quinoa with Fried Onions

75 g (3 oz) quinoa
225 ml (8 fl oz) water
2 medium onions
2 tablespoons olive oil
2 tablespoons chopped parsley
25 g (1 oz) grated Parmesan cheese
Ground black pepper

Makes 4 servings

Per serving: *Energy* 191 cals/802 kJ; *Protein* 6 g;
Carbohydrate 24 g (of which 3 g sugars); *Fat* 8 g (of which
2 g saturates); *Sodium* 126 mg.

1. Rinse the quinoa under cold running water until the water turns clear.

2. In a medium saucepan, combine the quinoa and water. Simmer over medium-low heat for about 15 minutes, or until the quinoa begins to soften. Remove from the heat and drain.

3. Meanwhile, peel the onions and cut into 0.5 cm (¼ in) slices. Warm the oil in a large frying pan over medium-low heat. Add the onions and cook for about 10 minutes, or until they soften and brown. Add water, 1 tablespoon at a time, as necessary to prevent burning.

4. In a medium bowl, combine the quinoa, onions, parsley, cheese and pepper to taste. Toss well. Serve as a side dish.

Pronounced 'keen-wah', this grain, native to South America, has been cultivated for more than 5,000 years. In fact, it is not a true grain at all, but a relative of spinach and Swiss chard. Over the past 20 years, it has enjoyed a resurgence. This might have to do with its nutty flavour or maybe the fact that it has more iron than any other grain around and is a great source of vitamins, minerals and protein.

Middle Eastern Tabbouleh Salad

Juice of 1 lemon
110 g (4 oz) bulgar
2 large ripe plum tomatoes
2 medium cucumbers
2 tablespoons extra-virgin olive oil
¼ teaspoon salt or 2 teaspoons liquid aminos
Ground black pepper
2 tablespoons chopped parsley
2 tablespoons chopped fresh mint

Makes 4 servings

Per serving: *Energy* 180 cals/756 kJ; *Protein* 5 g;
Carbohydrate 26 g (of which 6 g sugars); *Fat* 6 g (of which
1 g saturates); *Sodium* 140 mg.

1. Place the lemon juice in a measuring jug and add enough cold water to make 225 ml (8 fl oz). Place the bulgar in a small bowl and add the lemon-water mixture. Stir, then allow to sit for 30 minutes, or until soft.

2. Chop the tomatoes into 0.5 cm (¼ in) pieces and place in a medium bowl. Peel and seed the cucumbers. (To seed a cucumber, halve it lengthwise and scoop out the seeds with a spoon.) Slice the cucumber halves into 0.5 cm (¼ in) pieces and add to the bowl.

3. Add the bulgar, olive oil, salt or aminos, pepper to taste, parsley and mint. Mix well. Stir in additional parsley and mint to taste. Serve the salad immediately or refrigerate until ready to serve (can be made up to 2 days in advance).

> *Bulgar – also known as cracked wheat – has a slightly nutty flavour and comes from wheat berries. The best thing about this refreshing salad? No cooking. Simply soaking the grains for about half an hour 'cooks' them.*

Roasted Vegetable Lasagne

1 large onion
1 clove garlic
2 tablespoons olive oil
1½ tins (400 g/14 oz each) chopped
    tomatoes
1 tablespoon tomato purée
1 teaspoon dried oregano
1 teaspoon dried basil
⅓ x Roasted Vegetables (page 267), with
    beetroot omitted
6 oven-ready lasagne sheets or 6 semicooked
    regular lasagne sheets
110 g (4 oz) grated reduced-fat mozzarella
    cheese
10 g (½ oz) grated Parmesan cheese

Makes 6 servings

Per serving: *Energy* 327 cals/1373 kJ; *Protein* 11 g; *Carbohydrate* 47 g (of which 9 g sugars); *Fat* 12 g (of which 3 g saturates); *Sodium* 471 mg.

1. Preheat the oven to 180°C/350°F/gas mark 4.

2. Peel the onion and chop into 0.5 cm (¼ in) pieces. Peel the garlic and chop finely. Warm the oil in a medium saucepan over medium heat. Add the onion and garlic and cook, stirring often, for about 10 minutes, or until the onion just starts to brown. Add water, 1 tablespoon at a time, as necessary to prevent burning. Add the tomatoes, tomato purée, oregano and basil, and cook for about 20 minutes, or until the sauce thickens.

3. While the sauce is cooking, cut the roasted vegetables into 1 to 2.5 cm (½ to 1 in) pieces.

4. Coat a 30 x 18 cm (12 x 7 in) baking dish with cooking spray. Spread about four tablespoons of the tomato sauce on the bottom of the dish.

5. Place 2 lasagne sheets, overlapping, on top of the sauce. Spread about one-third of the roasted vegetables over the sheets, then sprinkle with about 3 tablespoons mozzarella. Top with about four tablespoons of tomato sauce, then place another layer of lasagne on top.

6. Keep layering – vegetables, mozzarella, sauce, lasagne sheets – until all the sheets are used and the roasted vegetables with cheese are on top. There should be 3 layers.

7. Top with the remaining sauce. Sprinkle the Parmesan and remaining mozzarella on top and cover the dish with aluminium foil. Bake for about 45 minutes to 1 hour or until bubbling and heated completely through.

8. Remove from the oven and let rest for 10 minutes before serving.

Sesame Noodles

225 g (8 oz) linguine
1 large carrot
2 spring onions
2 cloves garlic
2 tablespoons all-natural peanut butter
2 teaspoons sesame oil
2 tablespoons low-sodium soy sauce
1 tablespoon clear honey
½ teaspoon chilli powder
4 teaspoons rice wine or cider vinegar

Makes 4 servings

Per serving: *Energy* 355 cals/1491 kJ; *Protein* 10 g;
Carbohydrate 52 g (of which 10 g sugars); *Fat* 13 g (of
which 2 g saturates); *Sodium* 369 mg.

1. Cook the pasta according to package directions. Drain and set aside.

2. While the pasta cooks, peel the carrot and grate on the wide-holes side of a box grater. Chop the spring onions roughly. Peel the garlic and crush with the side of a knife.

3. In a blender or food processor fitted with the chopping blade, combine the carrot, spring onions, garlic, peanut butter, oil, soy sauce, honey, chilli powder and vinegar. Blend or process for 15 to 30 seconds or until smooth.

4. In a bowl, combine the pasta and sauce and mix well. Serve immediately or refrigerate for up to 3 days.

Macaroni Cheese

350 g (12 oz) macaroni
600 ml (1 pint) skimmed milk
3 tablespoons unbleached plain flour
3 teaspoons mustard powder
Ground black pepper
400 g (14 oz) grated reduced-fat Cheddar
    cheese

Makes 8 servings

Per serving: *Energy* 340 cals/1428 kJ; *Protein* 24 g;
Carbohydrate 43 g (of which 5 g sugars); *Fat* 9 g (of which
5 g saturates); *Sodium* 446 mg.

1. Preheat the oven to 180°C/350°F/gas
mark 4. Coat a 2-litre (3½-pint) baking
dish with cooking spray. Set aside.

2. Prepare the macaroni according to
package directions. Drain.

3. In a large bowl, combine 225 ml (8 fl oz)
of milk with the flour, mustard and pepper,
to taste. Whisk until smooth.

4. Pour the remaining milk into a medium
pan and bring to a simmer over medium
heat, stirring constantly. Add the milk-and-
flour mixture and keep stirring for 3 to 5
minutes, or until thick and bubbling.
Reduce the heat. Add the cheese. Mix until
the cheese melts.

5. Remove the pan from the heat and add
the macaroni. Transfer the macaroni
mixture to the prepared baking dish. Bake
for 35 to 40 minutes, or until hot and
bubbling around the edges. Serve hot.

Pasta Primavera

175 g (6 oz) fusilli pasta
1 medium courgette
1 red pepper
1 large or 2 medium cloves garlic
1 large onion
2 tablespoons extra-virgin olive oil
75 g (3 oz) broccoli florets
1 tin (400 g/14 oz) chopped tomatoes
1 tablespoon tomato purée
½ teaspoon salt or 2 teaspoons liquid aminos
Ground black pepper
1 teaspoon dried oregano
1 teaspoon dried basil
3 tablespoons chopped fresh basil
110 g (4 oz) fresh or frozen peas

Makes 8 servings

Per serving: *Energy* 138 cals/580 kJ; *Protein* 5 g;
Carbohydrate 23 g (of which 5 g sugars); *Fat* 4 g (of which
0.5 g saturates); *Sodium* 185 mg.

1. Cook the pasta according to package directions. Drain and set aside.

2. Cut the courgette into 0.5 x 7.5 cm (¼ x 3 in) strips and set aside. Remove the ribs and seeds from the pepper and cut into strips 0.5 cm (¼ in) wide and set aside. Peel the garlic and chop roughly. Peel the onion and cut into 0.5 cm (¼ in) slices.

3. Heat 1 tablespoon of the oil in a large frying pan over medium heat. Add the garlic and onion and cook, stirring often, for about 10 minutes, or until the onion starts to brown. Add water, 1 tablespoon at a time, as necessary to prevent burning.

4. Add the courgette, pepper, broccoli, tomatoes, tomato purée, salt or aminos, black pepper to taste, oregano, dried basil and the remaining 1 tablespoon oil. Cook for 10 minutes on medium-low heat. Add the fresh basil and fresh peas (if using) and cook for 15 minutes longer. If using frozen peas, stir them in in the last 2 minutes.

5. In a large bowl, combine the pasta and sauce and toss well. Serve immediately or refrigerate for up to 3 days.

Salmon or Tuna Burgers

2 small onions
1 tablespoon olive oil
400 g (14 oz) tinned salmon or water-packed
    tuna, drained and flaked with a fork
1 egg white
3 tablespoons dried bread crumbs
1 teaspoon dried basil
1 teaspoon dried oregano
1 tablespoon toasted wheat germ
¼ teaspoon salt or 1 tablespoon liquid aminos
Ground black pepper

Makes 6

Per serving: *Energy* 128 cals/538 kJ; *Protein* 18 g;
Carbohydrate 9 g (of which 2 g sugars); *Fat* 3 g (of which
0.5 g saturates); *Sodium* 407 mg.

1. Preheat the oven to 190°C/375°F/gas mark 5. Coat a baking tray with nonstick spray. Set aside.

2. Peel the onions and cut into 0.5 cm (¼ in) pieces. Warm the oil in a large frying pan over medium heat. Add the onions and cook, stirring often, for about 10 minutes, or until they start to brown. Remove from the heat, transfer to a large bowl and let cool for 10 minutes.

3. To the same bowl, add the salmon or tuna, egg white, bread crumbs, basil, oregano, wheat germ, salt or aminos and pepper to taste. Mix well. Shape the mixture into 6 burgers and place on the baking tray.

4. Bake for 15 minutes. Turn each burger. Bake for 10 to 20 minutes longer or until heated all the way through and browned. Serve immediately.

Turkey Burgers

3 medium onions
1 clove garlic
2 tablespoons olive oil
600 g (1⅓ lb) minced turkey breast
3 tablespoons dried bread crumbs
2 tablespoons barbecue sauce
3 tablespoons quick-cooking oats (not instant)
1 teaspoon dried basil
1 teaspoon dried oregano
1 tablespoon toasted wheat germ
¼ teaspoon salt or 1 tablespoon liquid aminos
Ground black pepper

Makes 9

Per serving: *Energy* 154 cals/647 kJ; *Protein* 17 g;
Carbohydrate 12 g (of which 2.5 g sugars); *Fat* 4 g (of
which 1 g saturates); *Sodium* 163 mg.

1. Peel the onions and cut into 0.5 cm (¼ in) pieces. Peel the garlic and chop finely.

Warm the oil in a large frying pan over medium heat. Add the onions and garlic and cook over medium heat, stirring often, for about 10 minutes, or until the onions start to brown. Add water, 1 tablespoon at a time, as necessary to prevent burning. Remove from the heat, transfer to a large bowl and let cool for 10 minutes.

2. To the same bowl, add the turkey, bread crumbs, barbecue sauce, oats, basil, oregano, wheat germ, salt or aminos and pepper to taste. Mix well. Shape the mixture into 9 burgers.

3. Coat a large nonstick frying pan with cooking spray. Cook the burgers over medium heat for about 5 minutes, or until browned and crispy. Flip the burgers carefully and cook for 5 minutes longer or until golden brown and a thermometer inserted in the centre registers 72.5°C/165°F and the meat is no longer pink. Serve the burgers hot.

Deli Sandwiches with Russian Yogurt Dressing

Russian Yogurt Dressing

75 ml (3 fl oz) fat-free natural yogurt
1 tablespoon low-fat mayonnaise
2 teaspoons tomato ketchup
¼ teaspoon dried oregano
¼ teaspoon dried basil
Ground black pepper

Sandwiches

4 leaves cos lettuce
8 slices wholegrain or wholemeal bread or
    4 wholemeal pittas (halved and split to
    form a pocket)
450 g (1 lb) thinly sliced roast beef or turkey
    breast
2 ripe tomatoes, sliced thinly

Makes 4

Per serving: *Energy* 328 cals/1377 kJ; *Protein* 36 g;
Carbohydrate 33 g (of which 4 g sugars); *Fat* 6 g (of which
1.5 g saturates); *Sodium* 503 mg.

1. T*o make the dressing:* In a small bowl, combine the yogurt, mayonnaise, ketchup, oregano, basil and pepper to taste. Whisk until well blended.

2. *To make the sandwiches:* Cut or tear the lettuce into 2.5 cm (1 in) strips.

3. For each sandwich, spread 2 tablespoons of the dressing on 2 slices of bread, or inside 2 pitta halves. Place ¼ each of the meat, lettuce and tomatoes on or in the prepared breads.

> *Whether you make it at home or get it from the deli counter, roast beef is surprisingly lean. Add some vegetables and a low-fat Russian dressing and you've got a sandwich to crow about. Feel free to use sliced turkey breast instead of the roast beef, if you prefer.*

Vegetarian Asian Tofu Sandwiches

Dressing
110 g (4 oz) soft tofu, drained
1 teaspoon peanut butter or tahini
1 tablespoon low-fat mayonnaise
1 teaspoon miso (fermented soya paste)
1 tablespoon lemon juice
Ground black pepper

Sandwiches
4 leaves cos, red leaf or green leaf lettuce, or
    50 g (2 oz) mixed baby salad leaves
2 ripe tomatoes
1 cucumber
1 ripe avocado
4 wholemeal pittas (halved and split to form a
    pocket) or 8 slices wholegrain or
    wholemeal bread

Makes 4

Per serving: *Energy* 314 cals/1319 kJ; *Protein* 12 g; *Carbohydrate* 35 g (of which 5 g sugars); *Fat* 14 g (of which 3 g saturates); *Sodium* 497 mg.

1. *To make the dressing:* In a blender or food processor fitted with the chopping blade, combine the tofu, peanut butter or tahini, mayonnaise, miso, lemon juice and pepper to taste. Blend or process for 15 seconds or until well mixed.

2. *To make the sandwiches:* If using large lettuce, cut or tear into bite-size pieces. Slice the tomatoes. Peel the cucumber, halve and scoop out the seeds. Cut into 0.5 cm (¼ in) slices. Peel the avocado, remove the stone, and cut into similar size slices. In a large bowl, combine the lettuce, tomatoes, cucumber and avocado.

3. Add the dressing and toss lightly until coated. Divide among the pittas or bread. Serve immediately.

Mexican Fajitas

450 g (1 lb) boneless, skinless chicken breast
2 cloves garlic
3–4 tablespoons lime juice
2 teaspoons ground cumin
¼ teaspoon red-pepper flakes
¼ teaspoon salt or 1 tablespoon liquid aminos
1 red pepper
1 yellow pepper
2 medium red onions
3 tablespoons olive oil
50 g (2 oz) chopped fresh coriander
8 wheat tortillas (25 cm/10 in diameter)
110 g (4 oz) low-fat crème fraîche
225 g (8 oz) chunky salsa

Makes 8

Per serving: *Energy* 311 cals/1306 kJ; *Protein* 19 g;
Carbohydrate 31 g (of which 10 g sugars); *Fat* 11 g (of
which 4 g saturates); *Sodium* 514 mg.

1. Rinse the chicken and blot dry with paper towels. Slice the meat across the grain into strips 0.5 cm (¼ in) wide. Peel the garlic and chop finely. In a large bowl or sealable plastic bag, place the chicken, garlic, lime juice, cumin, red-pepper flakes and salt or aminos. Stir. Cover the bowl if using. Refrigerate for 1 to 24 hours.

2. Remove and discard the seeds and ribs from the peppers and slice into strips 0.5 cm (¼ in) wide. Set aside. Peel the onions and cut into 0.5 cm (¼ in) slices. Set aside.

3. Heat 1½ tablespoons oil in a large frying pan over medium-high heat. Add the peppers and cook for about 5 minutes, or until the peppers begin to soften slightly. Add the onions and continue cooking until the onions are browned. Remove from the heat. Transfer the cooked vegetables to a medium bowl and set aside. Drain the chicken from the marinade. Discard the marinade.

4. In the same frying pan, add the remaining 1½ tablespoons oil and chicken. Cook on medium heat, stirring occasionally, for about 10 minutes, or until the chicken is no longer pink when tested with a knife. Add the reserved cooked vegetables and coriander and cook for about 1 minute longer.

5. Divide the chicken and vegetable mixture evenly among the tortillas and place 2 tablespoons of crème fraîche in each fajita. Roll up or fold in half. Serve the fajitas with the salsa on the side.

Bean Enchiladas

1 green pepper
2 medium carrots
1 medium-large courgette
1 clove garlic
1½ tablespoons olive oil
600 g (1⅓ lb) tinned black beans, red kidney
    beans or pinto beans
1 tin (400 g/14 oz) chopped tomatoes
1 teaspoon cayenne pepper
¼ teaspoon salt or 1 tablespoon liquid aminos
3 teaspoons chilli powder
Ground black pepper
6 corn or wheat tortillas (25 cm/10 in
    diameter)
2 spring onions
1 lime

Makes 6

Per serving: Energy 283 cals/1189 kJ; *Protein* 12 g;
Carbohydrate 45 g (of which 10 g sugars); *Fat* 6 g (of
which 2 g saturates); *Sodium* 891 mg.

1. Preheat the oven to 150°C/300°F/gas
mark 2. Remove and discard the seeds and
ribs from the pepper and cut into strips
0.5 cm (¼ in) wide. Peel the carrots and cut
into 0.5 cm (¼ in) pieces. Cut the courgette
into 0.5 cm (¼ in) pieces. Peel the garlic
and chop roughly.

2. Warm the oil in a large nonstick frying
pan over medium-high heat. When the pan
is hot, add the garlic and cook for 30
seconds. Then add the pepper, carrots and
courgette and cook, stirring frequently, for

12 minutes, or until the vegetables are
cooked through. Remove from the heat and
set aside.

3. Drain the tinned beans and rinse well.
Drain again. In a large bowl, combine the
cooked vegetables, beans, 350 g (12 oz)
tinned tomatoes, cayenne pepper, salt or
aminos, chilli powder and black pepper to
taste. Mix well.

4. Wrap each tortilla in a damp paper towel
and microwave on high power for 15
seconds or until warm and soft.

5. Coat a large baking tray with cooking
spray. Spoon 50 g (2 oz) tinned tomatoes
into the bottom of the pan (blend into a
smoother paste if overly chunky) and set
aside.

6. Lay 1 tortilla on a plate or work surface
and place a scoop of bean-vegetable
mixture on the lower third of the tortilla
and roll up. Place the rolled tortilla in the
baking tray. Repeat the procedure until all
the tortillas are filled and placed in the
baking tray.

7. Top with the remaining bean mixture.
Cover the pan with aluminium foil and
bake for 10 minutes. Remove the foil and
bake for 10 minutes longer. Meanwhile, cut
the spring onions into 0.5 cm (¼ in) pieces.
Cut the lime into slices.

8. Remove the tray from the oven and let
cool for a few minutes. Place 1 tortilla on
each plate and garnish with a lime slice and
a sprinkle of chopped spring onions.

Grilled Chicken-Veggie Wrap

Sauce
¼–½ red pepper
2 tablespoons low-fat mayonnaise
2 tablespoons low-fat natural yogurt
1 clove garlic, peeled

Wrap
1 medium onion (optional)
1 tablespoon olive oil (optional)
1 grilled chicken breast half (about 175 g/6 oz)
4 wholewheat tortillas (25 cm/10 in diameter)
    or 4 flatbreads (25 cm/10 in)
⅛ Roasted Vegetables (see page 267), cut
    into bite-size pieces

Makes 4

Per serving: *Energy* 286 cals/1201 kJ; *Protein* 17 g;
Carbohydrate 28 g (of which 7 g sugars); *Fat* 11 g (of
which 3 g saturates); *Sodium* 566 mg.

1. *To make the sauce:* Preheat the grill. Place the pepper on the grill pan and grill about 5 cm (2 in) from the heat. Cook, turning with the tongs, for 15 to 20 minutes, or until the skin is evenly blackened.

2. Transfer the pepper to a small bowl. Cover and let sit for about 10 minutes. Peel, seed and cut the pepper into chunks. In a blender or food processor fitted with the chopping blade, combine the pepper, mayonnaise, yogurt and garlic. Blend for about 30 seconds or until smooth and well blended. Refrigerate the sauce until ready to use (it will last for 5 days, covered).

3. *To make the wrap:* If using the onion, peel it and cut into 0.5 cm (¼ in) slices. Warm the oil in a medium nonstick frying pan over medium heat. Add the onion and cook, stirring often, for about 8 minutes, or until the onion starts to brown. Add water, 1 tablespoon at a time, as necessary to prevent burning. Set aside to cool.

4. Slice the chicken into strips 0.5 cm (¼ in) thick. Spread each tortilla or flatbread with 2 tablespoons of the sauce. Lay ¼ of the chicken, ¼ of the onions (if using) and ¼ of the Roasted Vegetables on the bottom third of the tortilla or flatbread. Roll up and serve.

These sandwiches are a terrific use for leftover chicken and Roasted Vegetables. You can also customise them to your tastes or whatever you happen to have to hand. For instance, you can exclude the chicken and use grilled portobello mushrooms or just use leftover roasted vegetables.

Aubergine Parmesan

3 medium aubergines
2 cloves garlic
1 large onion
2 tablespoons olive oil
1¾ tins (400 g/14 oz each) chopped
    tomatoes
75 g (3 oz) tomato purée
2 teaspoons dried oregano
2 teaspoons dried basil
225 g (8 oz) grated reduced-fat mozzarella
    cheese
25 g (1 oz) grated Parmesan cheese

Makes 6 servings

Per serving: *Energy* 190 cals/798 kJ; *Protein* 10 g;
Carbohydrate 12 g (of which 11 g sugars); *Fat* 12 g (of
which 5 g saturates); *Sodium* 554 mg.

1. Preheat the oven to 180°C/350°F/gas
mark 4. Peel the aubergines and cut into
thick rounds of 1 cm (½ in). (You should
have about 30 slices.) Coat a large nonstick
frying pan with cooking spray. Warm the
pan over medium heat and add 3 or 4 slices
of aubergine. Fry the aubergine for about
10 minutes, or until each side is brown and
soft in the middle. Remove the aubergine
to a plate. Coat the frying pan again and
continue frying the aubergine in batches
until it is all cooked.

2. Peel the garlic and chop roughly. Peel the
onion and chop it into 0.5 cm (¼ in)
pieces. Warm the oil in a medium pan over
medium heat. Add the garlic and onion
and cook, stirring often, for about 10
minutes, or until the onion starts to
become transparent. Add the tomatoes,
tomato purée, oregano and basil. Cook on
medium heat for 15 to 20 minutes, or until
the sauce thickens slightly.

3. Coat a 32.5 x 23 cm (13 x 9 in) baking
tin with cooking spray. Spread a layer of the
tomato sauce over the bottom. Place a layer
of cooked aubergine slices on top of the
sauce to cover the bottom of the tin. On
top of the aubergine, spread 3 to 4
tablespoons of tomato sauce and a thin
layer (about 3 tablespoons) of mozzarella.

4. Repeat the layers until all the aubergine
and mozzarella are used and the sauce
finishes on top. Sprinkle the Parmesan over
the top. Cover the pan with aluminium foil
and bake for 30 minutes.

5. Remove the foil and continue baking for
10 minutes longer or until the top is lightly
browned.

Spaghetti Squash Marinara

1 medium spaghetti squash
1 large onion
1 clove garlic
1 small courgette
1 small yellow squash
1 medium red pepper
2 tablespoons olive oil
1 tin (400 g/14 oz) chopped tomatoes
Large handful fresh basil leaves
½ teaspoon salt
Ground black pepper

Makes 8 servings

Per serving: *Energy* 60 cals/252 kJ; *Protein* 2 g; *Carbohydrate* 7 g (of which 6 g sugars); *Fat* 3 g (of which 0.5 g saturates); *Sodium* 168 mg.

1. Prick the spaghetti squash all over with a fork. Place the squash in a microwave-safe dish and microwave on high power for 15 to 20 minutes, or until the squash gets soft. Remove from the microwave and let cool. (Be careful because it gets very hot.)

2. When the squash is cool enough to handle, halve it lengthwise and scrape out the seeds and some fibrous strings. Set aside.

3. Meanwhile, peel the onion and halve it. Cut each half into long, thin strips and set aside. Peel the garlic and chop very finely. Cut the courgette and yellow squash into 0.5 x 10 cm (¼ x 4 in) strips. Set aside.

Remove the seeds from the pepper and cut into 0.5 x 10 cm (¼ x 4 in) strips. Set aside.

4. Warm 1 tablespoon oil in a large pan over medium heat. Add the onion and garlic and cook, stirring often, for about 10 minutes, or until the onion starts to brown. Add water, 1 tablespoon at a time, as necessary to prevent burning. Add the remaining 1 tablespoon oil, courgette, yellow squash and pepper to the frying pan and cook for about 10 minutes, or until the vegetables soften slightly.

5. Add the tomatoes and basil and simmer over low heat for about 15 minutes.

6. While the sauce is simmering, gently remove the squash strands with 2 forks and place in a medium bowl. Stir in the salt and black pepper to taste. Add the spaghetti squash to the sauce and cook for 1 or 2 minutes longer or until the squash is heated through. Serve.

Spaghetti squash is a very interesting vegetable. Although it is a squash, when cooked, the flesh turns stringy like strands of spaghetti. This is a filling and lower-calorie version of traditional spaghetti with tomato sauce. If you can't find spaghetti squash, you could use a medium marrow instead. Cook bite-size chunks of peeled and deseeded marrow for 20–30 minutes until tender, then follow recipe as for spaghetti squash.

Spinach and Cheese Pie

2 packs (300 g/10½ oz each) frozen chopped
   spinach, thawed
2 spring onions
1 tablespoon olive oil
2 tablespoons chopped parsley
2 tablespoons chopped fresh dill
Ground black pepper
1 egg, lightly beaten
Grated zest of 1 lemon
110 g (4 oz) grated reduced-fat mozzarella
   cheese
50 g (2 oz) crumbled feta cheese
12 sheets filo pastry
Oil cooking spray
10 g (½ oz) grated Parmesan cheese

Makes 4 servings

Per serving: *Energy* 287 cals/1117 kJ; *Protein* 14 g;
Carbohydrate 24 g (of which 4 g sugars); *Fat* 16 g (of
which 6 g saturates); *Sodium* 531 mg.

1. Preheat the oven to 180°C/350°F/gas mark 4. Squeeze out as much moisture as you can from the thawed spinach. Chop the spinach roughly and place in a medium bowl. Set aside. Slice the spring onions thinly.

2. Warm the oil in a large frying pan over medium heat. Add the spring onions and cook for 2 minutes. Add the spinach, parsley, dill and pepper to taste. Cook for 2 minutes longer. Transfer to a medium bowl and set aside to cool.

3. When the spinach mixture is cooled, add the egg, lemon zest, mozzarella and feta. Mix well. Set aside.

4. Coat a 25 x 20 cm (10 x 8 in) baking tray with cooking spray. Place 1 sheet of filo pastry in the bottom of the tray and trim the sides to fit. Coat with cooking spray. Repeat this procedure until there are 6 sheets of filo pastry in the bottom of the pan. Spread the spinach mixture evenly over the pastry.

5. Top the spinach with the remaining 6 sheets of filo pastry, coating each sheet with cooking spray. Top the pie with the Parmesan.

6. Bake for 40 to 50 minutes, or until brown. Let sit for about 10 minutes before cutting. Serve hot or at room temperature. Refrigerate leftovers for up to 1 day.

Salmon, Chicken or Tofu Teriyaki

2 spring onions
1 clove garlic
4 teaspoons grated fresh ginger
110 ml (4 fl oz) low-sodium soy sauce
3 tablespoons sweet rice wine (mirin) or apple
    juice
3 tablespoons clear honey
5 tablespoons lemon juice
4 salmon fillets or chicken cutlets (150 g/
    5 oz each) or 450 g (1 lb) firm or extra-
    firm tofu, drained

Makes 4 servings

Per serving for salmon teriyaki: *Energy* 317 cals/1331 kJ; *Protein* 28 g; *Carbohydrate* 11 g (of which 9 g sugars); *Fat* 18 g (of which 3 g saturates); *Sodium* 735 mg.

Per serving for chicken teriyaki: *Energy* 218 cals/916 kJ; *Protein* 34 g; *Carbohydrate* 11 g (of which 10 g sugars); *Fat* 4 g (of which 1 g saturates); *Sodium* 696 mg.

Per serving for tofu teriyaki: *Energy* 145 cals/609 kJ; *Protein* 12 g; *Carbohydrate* 11 g (of which 10 g sugars); *Fat* 6 g (of which 1 g saturates); *Sodium* 594 mg.

1. Cut the spring onions into 0.5 cm (¼ in) pieces. Peel and crush the garlic. In a large, sealable plastic bag, combine the spring onions, garlic, ginger, soy sauce, rice wine or apple juice, honey and lemon juice.

2. If using salmon or chicken, rinse under running water and blot dry with paper towels. If using tofu, drain and then cut the block into 4 equal pieces. Add the salmon, chicken or tofu to the plastic bag and seal. Shake the bag well and refrigerate for 1 to 24 hours, turning occasionally.

3. Coat a grill pan with cooking spray. Preheat the grill. Transfer the salmon, chicken or tofu to the grill pan and place in the oven about 10 cm (4 in) from the heat. Discard the leftover marinade. Grill the salmon for 10 to 12 minutes, or until the fish is opaque. Grill the chicken for 10 to 15 minutes, turning after 8 minutes. The chicken is done when a thermometer inserted in the thickest portion registers 70°C/160°F and the juices run clear. Grill the tofu for 6 to 8 minutes, turning after 4 minutes. The tofu is cooked when heated through and browned on both sides.

Whether you prefer to use salmon, chicken or tofu, this teriyaki marinade works beautifully. When you serve this with steamed vegetables, such as broccoli and carrots, and brown rice, you've got a delicious, wholesome and filling dinner.

Simple Poached Salmon

2 salmon steaks (175 g/6 oz each)
1 large lemon

Makes 2 servings

Per serving: *Energy* 323 cals/1357 kJ; *Protein* 32 g;
Carbohydrate 1 g (of which 1 g sugars); *Fat* 21 g (of which
4 g saturates); *Sodium* 173 mg.

1. Rinse the salmon steaks and blot dry with paper towels. Place the salmon in a microwaveable dish. Squeeze the lemon over the salmon, using as much as you like. Cover the dish with a microwaveable cover or use microwaveable clingfilm.

2. Microwave the salmon on high power for 3 to 4 minutes (longer if the salmon is thick). Remove the salmon and let it rest for 5 minutes so that it can continue to cook. The salmon should be opaque and light pink. If you prefer it cooked more, microwave it for 30 seconds to 1 minute longer.

Oven-Baked Crispy Sole

50 g (2 oz) dried bread crumbs
4 sole fillets (200 g/7 oz each)
Olive oil cooking spray
1 lemon, quartered

Makes 4 servings

Per serving: *Energy* 206 cals/865 kJ; *Protein* 36 g;
Carbohydrate 8 g (of which 0.5 g sugars); *Fat* 3 g (of
which 0.5 g saturates); *Sodium* 302 mg.

1. Preheat the oven to 200°C/400°F/gas mark 6. Coat a baking tray with olive oil cooking spray. Place the bread crumbs on a plate or in a shallow bowl.

2. Rinse the sole. While it's still damp, place 1 fillet in the bread crumbs to cover both sides well. Place the sole on the baking sheet. Repeat with each piece of fish.

3. Coat the top of each fillet with cooking spray. Bake for about 10 minutes, then check to see that it's not overcooking. If it is underdone, bake for 2 minutes longer or until the fish flakes easily. Serve hot with lemon wedges for garnish.

> *This recipe couldn't be easier. If you like, you can add your favourite dried herbs or spices to the bread crumbs for a flavour boost.*

Tuna with Green-Herb Pesto

Bunch fresh parsley (about 75 g/3 oz)
Bunch fresh basil and/or coriander (about
    75 g/3 oz)
2 medium cloves garlic, peeled
2 teaspoons pine nuts
Grated zest and juice of 1 lemon
2 tablespoons extra-virgin olive oil
¼ teaspoon salt
Ground black pepper
4 tuna steaks (110–150 g/4–5 oz each)

Makes 4 servings

Per serving: *Energy* 238 cals/999 kJ; *Protein* 24 g;
Carbohydrate 1 g (of which 0.5 g sugars); *Fat* 15 g (of
which 2.5 g saturates); *Sodium* 212 mg.

1. Cut off most of the stems of the parsley, basil and/or coriander. Place the leaves in the bowl of a food processor fitted with the chopping blade. Add the garlic and process for about 15 seconds or until the herbs and garlic are well cut up. Add the pine nuts, lemon zest, half of the lemon juice, 1 tablespoon oil, salt and pepper to taste. Process for 30 seconds or until the mixture comes together to form a sauce. Place in a bowl and cover with clingfilm.

2. Rinse the tuna and blot dry with paper towels. Sprinkle each side with salt and pepper to taste.

3. Warm the remaining 1 tablespoon of oil in a large nonstick frying pan over medium-high heat. Add the fish and cook for 5 minutes. Turn the tuna over and cook for 3 to 5 minutes longer or until the fish is just opaque.

4. Serve with 1 tablespoon of the pesto spooned on top of each tuna steak and drizzle with remaining lemon juice.

> *Brown rice, jasmine rice or boiled baby new potatoes go very well with this dish.*

Mama's Meat Loaf

1 medium carrot
½ medium onion
450 g (1 lb) minced turkey breast
2 tablespoons bread crumbs
2 tablespoons toasted wheat germ
110 ml (4 fl oz) passata (sieved tomatoes)
2 egg whites
1 teaspoon garlic powder
1 teaspoon dried basil
1 teaspoon dried oregano
8 tablespoons tomato ketchup
1 tablespoon clear honey

Makes 6 servings

Per serving: *Energy* 155 cals/651 kJ; *Protein* 21 g; *Carbohydrate* 15 g (of which 10 g sugars); *Fat* 2 g (of which 0.5 g saturates); *Sodium* 370 mg.

1. Preheat the oven to 180°C/350°F/gas mark 4. Grate the carrot finely using the small holes on a box grater. Peel the onion and grate finely.

2. In a large bowl, combine the carrot, onion, turkey, bread crumbs, wheat germ, passata, egg whites, garlic powder, basil, oregano and 6 tablespoons ketchup. Mix well. Transfer the mixture into a 23 x 13 cm (9 x 5 in) loaf tin. Bake for about 55 minutes, or until the meat loaf is firm and browned. A thermometer inserted in the centre should register 72.5°C/165°F.

3. Spread the remaining 2 tablespoons of ketchup and the honey on top of the loaf and bake for 5 minutes longer. Remove from the oven, let sit for 5 minutes and serve.

Shepherd's Pie

Topping
3 medium red potatoes (450 g/1 lb)
175 g (6 oz) low-fat crème fraîche
¼ teaspoon salt or 2 teaspoons liquid aminos

Pie
3 medium onions
2 tablespoons olive oil
450 g (1 lb) minced turkey breast
225 ml (8 fl oz) passata (sieved tomatoes)
3 teaspoons dried oregano
2 teaspoons chilli powder
1 pack (350 g/12 oz) frozen mixed vegetables,
    thawed
25 g (1 oz) grated Parmesan cheese

Makes 8 servings

Per serving: *Energy* 221 cals/928 kJ; *Protein* 19 g;
Carbohydrate 18 g (of which 6 g sugars); *Fat* 8 g (of which
4 g saturates); *Sodium* 270 mg.

1. *To make the topping:* Quarter the potatoes, then cut each quarter in half. Place the potatoes in a medium pan filled with water. Boil for about 12 minutes, or until the potatoes are soft and can be pierced easily with a fork or knife. Drain the potatoes and let cool slightly.

2. Place the potatoes in a medium bowl. Add the crème fraîche and salt or aminos. Mash with a fork until smooth. Add more crème fraîche if the mixture is too stiff. Set aside.

3. *To make the pie:* Preheat the oven to 180°C/350°F/gas mark 4. Coat a 23 x 13 cm (9 x 5 in) loaf tin with cooking spray. Set aside.

4. Peel the onions and cut very finely. Warm the oil in a large frying pan over medium heat. Add the onions and cook, stirring often, for about 10 minutes, or until the onions start to brown. Add water, 1 tablespoon at a time, as necessary to prevent burning. Transfer to a bowl to cool slightly.

5. Cook the turkey over medium heat in the same frying pan used for the onions. Stir to crumble the meat. Cook until the meat is no longer pink. Add the passata, oregano, chilli powder and onions. Cook until the mixture is heated through.

6. Spoon the turkey mixture into the prepared pan. Arrange the mixed vegetables in a layer over the top. Then spread the mashed potatoes over the vegetables and top with the Parmesan.

7. Bake, uncovered, for about 35 minutes, or until the top is light brown. Cool for 10 minutes before serving.

Unfried Chicken Breasts

4 boneless, skinless chicken breasts (about
    175 g/6 oz each)
75 g (3 oz) bread crumbs
1 clove garlic
½ teaspoon ground black pepper

Makes 4 servings

Per serving: *Energy* 257 cals/1079 kJ; *Protein* 40 g;
Carbohydrate 11 g (of which 8 g sugars); *Fat* 6 g (of which
2 g saturates); *Sodium* 246 mg.

1. Preheat the oven to 230°C/450°F/gas mark 8. Rinse the chicken and blot dry with paper towels.

2. Place the bread crumbs in a pie dish. Peel the garlic and chop very finely. Add to the bread crumbs along with the pepper. Toss the bread crumb mixture with a fork.

3. Coat each chicken breast with cooking spray and coat each side well with the bread crumbs.

4. Place the chicken breasts on an ungreased baking tray and bake for 15 minutes. Turn the chicken over and cook for about 10 minutes longer on the other side or until a thermometer inserted in the thickest portion registers 70°C/160°F and the juices run clear. Serve hot.

If you want a variation on this easy, crunchy chicken dish, add a teaspoon or two of your favourite spices and/or dried herbs to the bread crumbs. I personally like to add paprika, cayenne pepper or even Cajun spice mix.

Tender Chicken Salad

4 small boneless, skinless chicken breasts
(about 110 g/4 oz each)
1 stick celery
1 large carrot
1 small apple
½ small red onion
75 g (3 oz) raisins
110 g (4 oz) low-fat mayonnaise
2 tablespoons chopped coriander or parsley
(optional)
Ground black pepper
4 large lettuce leaves

Makes 4 servings

Per serving: *Energy* 303 cals/1273 kJ; *Protein* 25 g;
Carbohydrate 20 g (of which 19 g sugars); *Fat* 14 g (of
which 3 g saturates); *Sodium* 165 mg.

1. Preheat the oven to 180°C/350°F/gas mark 4. Rinse the chicken breasts and blot dry with paper towels. Place the chicken on a baking tray coated with cooking spray. Bake for 25 to 35 minutes (depending on the thickness) or until a thermometer inserted in the thickest portion registers 70°C/160°F. Let cool.

2. Remove and discard the celery leaves and cut the celery stick into 0.5 cm (¼ in) pieces. Peel the carrot, apple and onion. Cut each into 0.5 cm (¼ in) pieces. Place in a large bowl.

3. With your fingers, shred the cooked chicken into small pieces and add to the bowl. Add the raisins, mayonnaise, coriander or parsley (if using) and pepper to taste. Mix well.

4. Line each of 4 plates with a lettuce leaf. Scoop the salad on to each leaf and serve.

> *If you like, adding a teaspoon or two of curry powder to this chicken salad brings it to a whole new level.*

Chicken and Root Vegetable Stew

4 large carrots
1 medium turnip
1 large parsnip
1 large onion
1 clove garlic
2 boneless, skinless chicken breasts (about
    150 g/5 oz each)
75 g (3 oz) cauliflower florets
Large handful chopped fresh coriander
1 teaspoon dried oregano
1 teaspoon dried basil
1 teaspoon dried rosemary
110 ml (4 fl oz) white wine
1 tin (400 g/14 oz) chopped tomatoes
2 tablespoons tomato purée

Makes 2 servings

Per serving: *Energy* 411 cals/1726 kJ; *Protein* 40 g;
Carbohydrate 40 g (of which 33 g sugars); *Fat* 7 g (of
which 2 g saturates); *Sodium* 274 mg.

1. Preheat the oven to 180°C/350°F/gas mark 4. Peel the carrots, turnip and parsnip and cut into 2.5 to 5 cm (1 to 2 in) pieces. Peel the onion and garlic. Cut the onion into 2.5 cm (1 in) pieces. Chop the garlic finely. Wash the chicken and blot dry with paper towels. Cut the chicken into 2.5 cm (1 in) pieces.

2. In a large casserole dish, combine the carrots, turnip, parsnip, onion, garlic, chicken, cauliflower, coriander, oregano, basil, rosemary, wine, tomatoes and tomato purée. Mix well.

3. Cover the casserole dish and bake for 45 minutes to 1 hour or until the vegetables are soft and the chicken is no longer pink and the juices run clear. Serve hot.

Stir-Fried Chicken and Vegetables

1 large onion
2 cloves garlic
1 large red or yellow pepper
1 large courgette
1 large carrot
2 spring onions
2 boneless, skinless chicken breasts (about
    150 g/5 oz each)
2 tablespoons rapeseed oil
2 tablespoons toasted (dark) sesame oil
2 tablespoons low-sodium soy sauce
1 tablespoon finely chopped fresh ginger
75 g (3 oz) broccoli florets
75 g (3 oz) cauliflower florets
75 g (3 oz) mange-tout or sugar snap peas

Makes 4 servings

Per serving: *Energy* 249 cals/1046 kJ; *Protein* 21 g; *Carbohydrate* 11 g (of which 8 g sugars); *Fat* 14 g (of which 2.5 g saturates); *Sodium* 382 mg.

1. Peel the onion and garlic. Cut the onion into 0.5 cm (¼ in) pieces. Set aside. Chop the garlic very finely and set aside.

2. Remove the seeds and ribs from the pepper. Cut the pepper into thin strips and set aside. Cut the courgette into thin strips and set aside. Grate the carrot on the wide-holes side of a box grater and set aside. Slice the spring onions thinly and set aside.

3. Wash the chicken and blot dry with paper towels. Cut the chicken into 2.5 cm (1 in) pieces. Set aside.

4. Warm 1 tablespoon each of the rapeseed and sesame oils in a large nonstick frying pan over medium heat. Add 1 tablespoon soy sauce, ½ tablespoon ginger and half of the chopped garlic. Cook for 30 seconds to 1 minute. Add the onion, pepper, courgette, carrot, broccoli, cauliflower and mange-tout or sugar snap peas. Cook over medium-high heat for about 10 to 15 minutes, or until the vegetables soften slightly but are cooked through. Transfer to a large bowl.

5. In the same frying pan, heat the remaining 1 tablespoon each of the rapeseed and sesame oils. Add the remaining 1 tablespoon soy sauce, the remaining half of the garlic and the remaining ½ tablespoon ginger. Add the chicken and cook on medium-high heat for 8 minutes, or until the chicken is no longer pink and the juices run clear. Add the spring onions and cook for 30 seconds longer.

6. Combine the chicken with the cooked vegetables. Toss together and serve. Refrigerate leftovers for up to 3 days.

Serve this dish with a helping of brown rice and you've got a tasty and complete meal.

Chicken Spring Rolls

Spring Rolls

2 large carrots
1 spring onion
¼ head chinese cabbage
1 tablespoon olive oil
1 tablespoon low-sodium soy sauce
1 tablespoon finely chopped fresh coriander
¼ teaspoon ground black pepper
75 g (3 oz) dried bean thread noodles
450 g (1 lb) grilled boneless, skinless chicken
    breasts
16 20 cm (8 in) rice-paper spring-roll
    wrappers
2 teaspoons slivered fresh basil

Dipping Sauce

50 ml (2 fl oz) low-sodium soy sauce
1 tablespoon clear honey
1½ teaspoons toasted (dark) sesame oil
½ clove garlic, finely chopped
1 teaspoon finely chopped fresh ginger
1 tablespoon finely chopped fresh coriander

Makes 16

Per spring roll: *Energy* 100 cals/420 kJ; *Protein* 7 g;
Carbohydrate 10 g (of which 2.5 g sugars); *Fat* 3 g (of
which 0.5 g saturates); *Sodium* 300 mg.

1. *To make the spring rolls:* Peel the carrots and cut into 0.5 cm to 7 cm (¼ in to 3 in) strips. Cut the spring onion into 0.5 cm (¼ in) slices. Thinly slice the cabbage.

2. In a large bowl, combine the carrots, spring onion, cabbage, olive oil, soy sauce, coriander and pepper. Mix well. Let sit at room temperature for 10 minutes, stirring occasionally.

3. Meanwhile, place the noodles in a medium bowl. Cover with boiling water and soak for about 30 minutes, or until softened. Drain well and chop into 5 cm (2 in) pieces. Set aside. Slice the chicken breasts thinly.

4. Pour hot water into a large bowl. Using tongs, dip 1 rice-paper wrapper into the water for 5 seconds. Remove from the water and place on a wet towel. Let stand for 30 seconds. (It should be soft and pliable. If still stiff, sprinkle with more water.) Be careful not to oversoak the wrapper or it will fall apart. Repeat until all the wrappers are moistened.

5. Place a scant 2 tablespoons of the noodles, a scant 2 tablespoons of the vegetable mixture and 25 g (1 oz) of chicken breast 2.5 cm (1 in) from the lower edge of each wrapper. Sprinkle each portion with the basil. Fold the bottom edge over the filling, fold in both sides and roll up tightly. Press to seal.

6. *To make the dipping sauce:* In a small bowl, combine the soy sauce, honey, sesame oil, garlic, ginger and coriander. Mix well. Serve with the spring rolls.

Fillet Steak with Mushrooms

2 fillet steaks (110–150 g/4–5 oz each)
¼ teaspoon salt
Ground black pepper
1 clove garlic
2 large or 3 medium shallots
225 g (8 oz) mushrooms
6 teaspoons olive oil
50 ml (2 fl oz) dry red or white wine
3 tablespoons chopped parsley

Makes 2 servings

Per serving: *Energy* 381 cals/1600 kJ; *Protein* 39 g;
Carbohydrate 5 g (of which 3 g sugars); *Fat* 21 g (of which
6 g saturates); *Sodium* 279 mg.

1. Season the steaks well with the salt and pepper to taste. Set aside for 15 minutes to 1 hour or until the steaks reach room temperature.

2. Peel the garlic and shallots. Chop the garlic finely and the shallots roughly. Set aside.

3. Wash or brush the mushrooms well and dry. Cut off the bottoms of the mushroom stems. Cut the mushrooms and trimmed stems into rough 1 cm (½ in) chunks and set aside. Preheat the oven to 110°C/200°F/gas mark 1.

4. Warm a cast-iron frying pan or griddle over high heat until very hot. Swirl 2 teaspoons oil around the frying pan for about 30 seconds. Add the steaks and let

cook, undisturbed, for 5 minutes. Turn the steaks over with tongs and cook for 4 minutes longer. Transfer the steaks to an ovenproof plate and place in the oven to keep warm.

5. Reduce the heat on the hob to medium-low. Add the remaining 4 teaspoons oil to the frying pan. Add the shallots and cook for about 2 minutes, or until they start to soften. Add the mushrooms. Cook, stirring occasionally, for about 5 minutes. Add the garlic and continue cooking for 5 minutes longer. Add the wine and continue cooking, stirring and scraping the bottom of the frying pan with a wooden spoon, until the wine is evaporated. Stir in the parsley and add salt and pepper to taste. Serve the mushrooms on top of the steaks.

This is a special-occasion dish because fillet steak is expensive and, while it is meltingly tender and leaner than most cuts of beef, it (especially with a nice mushroom sauce) is not exactly low-fat. To bring out the most flavour, it's best to cook fillet steak to no more than medium-rare. The main secret of cooking a great steak at home is to use a well-heated cast-iron frying pan or griddle and to turn the steak only once (or twice at most) during the cooking process. A variety of wild mushrooms, including shiitake and oyster, make the sauce a little more complex, but ordinary button mushrooms work very well, too.

Oatmeal Raisin Cookies

75 g (3 oz) light butter or margarine
110 g (4 oz) light brown sugar
2 tablespoons egg whites mixed with 1
    tablespoon fat-free natural yogurt
1½ teaspoons vanilla extract
110 g (4 oz) unbleached plain flour
75 g (3 oz) quick-cooking oats (not instant)
½ teaspoon bicarbonate of soda
75 g (3 oz) raisins
1 teaspoon ground cinnamon

Makes 42

Per biscuit: *Energy* 45 cals/189 kJ; *Protein* 1 g;
Carbohydrate 7 g (of which 4 g sugars); *Fat* 1.5 g (of
which 0.5 g saturates); *Sodium* 31 mg.

1. Preheat the oven to 160°C/325°F/gas mark 3. Line two baking trays with greaseproof paper. Set aside.

2. In the bowl of a food processor or with an electric mixer, combine the margarine, brown sugar, egg white mixture and vanilla extract. Process or mix until smooth. In a large bowl, combine the flour, oats and bicarbonate of soda. Add the flour mixture to the margarine mixture and process or mix well. Stir in the raisins and cinnamon.

3. Drop rounded teaspoonfuls of dough on to the lined baking trays, spacing them 4 cm (1½ in) apart. Flatten each biscuit slightly with the tip of a spoon or fingers dampened with water.

4. Bake for 15 to 18 minutes, or until lightly browned and crisp. Cool on the sheets on racks for 1 minute. Remove to the racks and cool completely.

Scones

225 g (8 oz) unbleached plain flour
40 g (1½ oz) quick-cooking oats (not instant)
2 tablespoons sugar
2 teaspoons baking powder
½ teaspoon bicarbonate of soda
1 teaspoon ground cinnamon (optional)
50 g (2 oz) light butter or margarine, cold, cut
    into small pieces
1 egg white
150–200 ml (5–7 fl oz) fat-free natural yogurt
75 g (3 oz) raisins
2 tablespoons skimmed milk or 1 lightly
    beaten egg white

Makes 12

Per scone: *Energy* 143 cals/600 kJ; *Protein* 3 g;
Carbohydrate 25 g (of which 9 g sugars); *Fat* 4 g (of which
1 g saturates); *Sodium* 156 mg.

1. Preheat the oven to 190°C/375°F/gas mark 5. Combine the flour, oats, sugar, baking powder, bicarbonate of soda and cinnamon (if using). Using 2 knives or a pastry cutter or fork, blend the margarine into the flour mixture until it looks like fine crumbs. Add the egg white and enough of the yogurt to form a stiff dough (start with 150 ml (5 fl oz) of yogurt and then add more if needed). Mix well. Stir in the raisins.

2. Form the dough into a ball and place on a lightly floured surface. With floured hands, pat the dough into a 18 cm (7 in) circle (about 2.5 cm/1 in thick).

3. Using a 2.5 cm (1 in) round biscuit cutter, cut out 12 circles. (As needed, form the scraps into a new ball and flatten.) Place the cut dough on a nonstick baking tray and brush the tops with the milk or lightly beaten egg white.

4. Bake for 10 to 15 minutes, or until light brown. Remove from the oven and let cool at least 10 minutes before eating.

Muffins Galore

75 g (3 oz) quick-cooking oats (not instant)
1 tablespoon baking powder
100 g (3½ oz) sugar
250 g (9 oz) unbleached plain flour
2 egg whites
225 ml (8 fl oz) skimmed milk
75 g (3 oz) light butter or margarine, melted
50 ml (2 fl oz) fat-free natural yogurt
1 teaspoon vanilla extract

Makes 12

Per muffin: *Energy* 200 cals/840 kJ; *Protein* 4 g;
Carbohydrate 34 g (of which 10 g sugars); *Fat* 6 g (of
which 1 g saturates); *Sodium* 193 mg.

1. Preheat the oven to 180°C/350°F/gas mark 4. Coat a 12-cup nonstick muffin tray with cooking spray or line with paper cake cases.

2. In a medium bowl, combine the oats, baking powder, sugar and flour. Mix well. In a large bowl, combine the egg whites, milk, margarine, yogurt and vanilla extract. Mix well. Add the dry ingredients to the wet ingredients, carefully mixing them all. Do not overmix. It is acceptable if the batter is lumpy.

3. Use any of the following flavour boosters mixed inside the individual muffin cups or cases. Bake for about 20 to 25 minutes, or until the muffins turn light brown on top and a skewer inserted in the centre comes out clean.

Variations:

Cranberry-Orange Muffin: 2 heaped tablespoons muffin base, 10 fresh or dried cranberries and ¼ teaspoon orange juice concentrate. Or add 110 g (4 oz) cranberries and 1 tablespoon orange juice concentrate to the whole recipe.

Banana-Raspberry Muffin: 2 heaped tablespoons muffin base, 2 tablespoons chopped bananas and 5 fresh or frozen (unthawed) raspberries. Or add 1 chopped banana and 75 g (3 oz) fresh or frozen raspberries to the whole recipe.

Apple-Cinnamon Muffin: 2 heaped tablespoons muffin base, 1 tablespoon stewed apples (or 2 tablespoons peeled and chopped fresh apple) and ⅛ teaspoon ground cinnamon. Or add 1 medium apple, peeled and chopped and ½ tablespoon ground cinnamon to the whole recipe.

Blueberry Muffin: 2 heaped tablespoons muffin base and 10 fresh or frozen (unthawed) blueberries. Or add 110 g (4 oz) fresh or frozen blueberries to the whole recipe.

As you can see, this is a very adaptable muffin recipe. Mix up the muffin base, then add your choice of flavouring to the muffin cups or cases before baking. By adding the flavouring to the individual muffin cups instead of the whole batter, you can make a batch of 12 muffins in 12 different flavours (not that you'd want to go that mad, but you could).

Apple-Berry-Raisin Crumble

6–8 medium Granny Smith apples, peeled and
    thinly sliced
1 tablespoon cornflour
225 g (8 oz) any variety of mixed fresh or
    frozen berries
75 g (3 oz) raisins
110 ml (4 fl oz) apple juice
2 tablespoons clear honey
4 tablespoons wheat germ
250 g (9 oz) quick-cooking oats (not instant)
40 g (1½ oz) light brown sugar
1 teaspoon ground cinnamon

Makes 10 servings

Per serving: *Energy* 227 cals/953 kJ; *Protein* 6 g;
Carbohydrate 48 g (of which 27 g sugars); *Fat* 3 g (of
which 0.5 g saturates); *Sodium* 12 mg.

1. Preheat the oven to 190°C/375°F/gas mark 5. In a large bowl, toss the apples with the cornflour. Add the berries, raisins, 65 ml (2½ fl oz) juice and honey and toss to mix. Place the mixture in a 23 cm (9 in) deep pie tin or use an 20 x 20 cm (8 x 8 in) baking tin. Combine the wheat germ, oats, brown sugar, cinnamon and the remaining apple juice. Mix until moist and crumbly. Sprinkle the topping over the fruit.

2. Bake for 45 minutes, or until the filling is bubbly and the topping is golden brown. Serve warm.

A nice addition to this crumble is ginger. For Apple-Ginger Crumble, add 1 teaspoon ground ginger to the filling.

Baked Apples

2 large Bramley or other baking apples
2 tablespoons raisins
2 tablespoons clear honey
2 teaspoons vanilla extract
1 teaspoon ground cinnamon
2 tablespoons maple syrup

Makes 2 servings

Per serving: *Energy* 251 cals/1054 kJ; *Protein* 1 g;
Carbohydrate 65 g (of which 65 g sugars); *Fat* 0.5 g (of
which 0 g saturates); *Sodium* 77 mg.

1. Preheat the oven to 180°C/350°F/gas
mark 4. Core the apples to within 1 cm (½
in) of the bottom. Alternatively, core the
apples with an apple corer. Cut 1 cm (½ in)
off the bottom of the core and 'plug' the
bottoms of the apples. Peel a 2.5 cm (1 in)
strip of skin around the middle of each
apple or peel the upper half of the apples to
prevent splitting.

2. Coat a 23 cm (9 in) pie dish with
cooking spray and add 0.5 cm (¼ in) of
water to the bottom. Place the apples in the
dish. Put 1 tablespoon of raisins, 1
teaspoon of honey and 1 teaspoon of
vanilla extract in each apple. Sprinkle the
apples with the cinnamon. Add the
remaining honey and the maple syrup to
the water in the dish.

3. Cover with foil and bake for 40 minutes,
basting (spooning the liquids over the
apples) every 20 minutes. Remove the foil
and bake uncovered for 10 minutes longer.
Let cool for at least 10 minutes before
serving. (These get very hot, so be careful.)

Blueberry Angel Food Cake

175 g (6 oz) plain cake flour
300 g (10½ oz) sugar
150 g (5 oz) fresh or frozen and unthawed
    blueberries
10 egg whites, at room temperature
2 teaspoons vanilla extract
¼ teaspoon almond extract (optional)

Makes 12 servings

Per serving: *Energy* 153 cals/643 kJ; *Protein* 4 g;
Carbohydrate 36 g (of which 26 g sugars); *Fat* 0.5 g (of
which 0 g saturates); *Sodium* 51 mg.

1. Preheat the oven to 180°C/350°F/gas mark 4. Sift the flour and 110 g (4 oz) of the sugar 3 times and set aside. Toss the blueberries with 2 tablespoons of the flour-sugar mixture. Set aside.

2. Using the whisk attachment of an electric hand mixer, beat the egg whites until foamy. Gradually add the remaining sugar, 2 tablespoons at a time, while beating the egg whites. Add the vanilla extract and almond extract (if using) with the last addition of sugar. Continue to beat the egg whites until soft peaks form. Do not overbeat.

3. With a spatula, gently fold the flour-sugar mixture into the beaten egg whites, being careful not to deflate the egg whites. Very gently fold in the blueberries. Gently spoon the batter into an ungreased 25 cm (10 in) diameter deep ring tin.

4. Bake for 40 to 45 minutes, or until the cake is golden brown and springs back to the touch. Remove from the oven and immediately invert the cake on to a funnel or bottle to cool. Serve at room temperature.

> *Angel food cake hangs upside down to cool so that its delicate structure won't collapse in on itself. In most ring tins, either the rim has feet on it or the funnel in the centre is slightly higher than the rim, so the pan can balance itself as it cools. Otherwise, you can hang your pan on a heatproof funnel or bottle to cool.*

Banana-Date Cake

300 g (10½ oz) wholemeal flour
2¼ teaspoons bicarbonate of soda
1 teaspoon cream of tartar
1 teaspoon ground cinnamon
¼ teaspoon ground nutmeg
250 g (9 oz) clear honey
75 g (3 oz) maple syrup
2 teaspoons vanilla extract
2 egg whites
2 very ripe bananas, puréed
1 large ripe banana, chopped
110 ml (4 fl oz) boiled water
110 g (4 oz) chopped dates
2 egg whites, lightly beaten

Makes 12 servings

Per serving: *Energy* 218 cals/916 kJ; *Protein* 5 g;
Carbohydrate 51 g (of which 34 g sugars); *Fat* 1 g (of
which 0.5 g saturates); *Sodium* 140 mg.

1. Preheat the oven to 160°C/325°F/gas mark 3. Coat a 23 cm (9 in) Bundt tin (a deep fluted cake tin) with cooking spray. Set aside.

2. In a large bowl, combine the flour, ¾ teaspoon of the bicarbonate of soda, cream of tartar, cinnamon and nutmeg.

3. In a medium bowl, combine the honey, maple syrup, vanilla extract, 2 egg whites and the puréed and chopped bananas. Stir in the flour mixture until just blended.

4. In a blender or food processor, combine the water, dates and the remaining 1½ teaspoons bicarbonate of soda. Blend or process on high speed until the dates are puréed. Stir into the flour-banana mixture. Gently stir the lightly beaten egg whites into the batter. Do not overmix. Spoon the batter into the Bundt tin. Bake for 1 hour or until a skewer inserted in the centre comes out clean. Let cool.

Cinnamon Apple Crumb Cake

Cake

75 g (3 oz) unbleached plain flour
75 g (3 oz) wholemeal flour
110 g (4 oz) sugar
1½ teaspoons baking powder
¼ teaspoon ground nutmeg
110 ml (4 fl oz) skimmed milk
110 g (4 oz) unsweetened apple sauce or
    stewed apple
1 egg white
3–4 peeled and sliced Granny Smith apples

Crumb Topping

60 g (2¼ oz) quick-cooking oats (not instant)
1 tablespoon brown sugar
1 tablespoon maple syrup
1½ teaspoons ground cinnamon
1½ teaspoons toasted wheat germ

Makes 9 servings

Per serving: *Energy* 175 cals/735 kJ; *Protein* 4 g;
Carbohydrate 40 g (of which 24 g sugars); *Fat* 1 g (of
which 0.5 g saturates); *Sodium* 101 mg.

1. Preheat the oven to 180°C/350°F/gas mark 4. Coat a 23 x 23 cm (9 x 9 in) baking tin with cooking spray. Set aside.

2. To make the cake: In a large bowl, combine the flour, wholemeal flour, sugar, baking powder and nutmeg. Add the milk, apple sauce or stewed apple and egg white. Mix well. Pour the batter into the baking pan and arrange the apples on top.

3. To make the topping: In a medium bowl, combine the oats, brown sugar, maple syrup, cinnamon and wheat germ. Sprinkle the topping over the apples.

4. Bake for about 40 minutes, or until a toothpick inserted into the centre comes out clean. Cool and serve.

Very Creamy Cheesecake

5–6 digestive biscuits, crushed
1 tablespoon + 110 g (4 oz) sugar
450 g (1 lb) reduced-fat cream cheese
400 g (14 oz) ricotta cheese
2 eggs
2 egg whites
50 g (2 oz) + 2 tablespoons unbleached plain
   flour
2 teaspoons vanilla extract

Makes 12 servings

Per serving: *Energy* 213 cals/895 kJ; *Protein* 8 g;
Carbohydrate 24 g (of which 15 g sugars); *Fat* 9 g (of
which 5 g saturates); *Sodium* 270 mg.

1. Preheat the oven to 160°C/325°F/gas mark 3. Coat a 23 cm (9 in) springform tin with cooking spray.

2. Combine the digestive crumbs and 1 tablespoon sugar. Press into the tin.

3. In a blender or food processor fitted with the chopping blade, combine the reduced-fat cream cheese, ricotta cheese, eggs, egg whites, flour, the remaining 110 g (4 oz) sugar and vanilla extract. Blend or process until smooth. Spread over the crust. Bake for 1 hour or until the centre is set.

4. Let cool in the oven with the door ajar for 45 minutes. Chill for 8 hours or overnight.

INDEX

C

G

USEFUL INFORMATON

Herbal Resources

For expert advice, you should always consult a qualified herbal practitioner.

The College of Practitioners of Phytotherapy
Rutherford Park
Marley Lane
Battle
East Sussex
BN33 0TY
Tel: 01424 776780
www.collegeofphytotherapy.com

One of the major professional organisations for herbal medicine in the UK. Provides a list of qualified phytotherapists.

National Institute of Medical Herbalists
56 Longbrook Street
Exeter
Devon EX4 6AH
Tel: 01392 426022
www.nimh.org.uk

The main professional body for medical herbalists in the UK. They can provide details of training courses in herbal medicine and a directory of qualified practitioners.

Register of Chinese Herbal Medicine (RCHM)
P.O. Box 400
Wembley
Middlesex HA9 9NZ
www.rchm.co.uk

For information on qualified practitioners of Chinese herbal medicine.

Australia
National Herbalists Association of Australia (NHAA)
Postal address for Sydney office:
33 Reserve Street
Annandale
NSW 2038
Australia
Tel: (02) 9560 7077
www.nhaa.org.au

Provides details of qualified herbalists in Australia.

Nutritional Products, Supplements and Books

The Nutri Centre
7 Park Crescent
London W1B 1PF
Tel: 020 7436 5122
www.nutricentre.com

Stocks a wide range of nutritional products including Beano, natural medicines, supplements and books. Products can be ordered online.

Organic Foods

Planet Organic Supermarkets
42 Westbourne Grove
London W2 5SH
Tel: 020 7221 7171

22 Torrington Place
London WC1E 7HJ
Tel: 020 7436 1929

Specialists in organic food products and supplements.

OTHER RODALE BOOKS
AVAILABLE FROM PAN MACMILLAN

1-4050-0666-8	Banish Your Belly, Butt and Thighs Forever!	*The Editors of* Prevention *Health Books for Women*	£10.99
1-4050-0667-6	The Green Pharmacy	*Dr James A. Duke*	£14.99
1-4050-0671-4	Laying Down the Law	*Dr Ruth Peters*	£8.99
1-4050-0669-2	The Testosterone Advantage Plan™	*Lou Schuler*	£12.99
1-4050-0668-4	Whole Body Meditations	*Lorin Roche*	£10.99
1-4050-0670-6	Win the Fat War	*Anne Alexander*	£5.99

All Pan Macmillan titles can be ordered from our website, *www.panmacmillan.com,* or from your local bookshop and are also available by post from:

Bookpost, PO Box 29, Douglas, Isle of Man IM99 1BQ
Credit cards accepted. For details:
Telephone: 01624 836000
Fax: 01624 670923
E-mail: bookshop@enterprise.net
www.bookpost.co.uk

Free postage and packing in the United Kingdom

Prices shown above were correct at time of going to press.
Pan Macmillan reserve the right to show new retail prices on covers which may differ from those previously advertised in the text or elsewhere.